LIMPING ON WATER

LIMPING ON WATER

Published by:
Smart Business Network
835 Sharon Dr., Suite 200
Westlake, OH 44145

Printed in the United States of America
Cover illustration and jacket design by Sheridon Wright
Second Printing, 2016

ISBN: 978-0-9964080-2-8
Library of Congress Control Number: 2015955548

LIMPING
ON
WATER

by

Phil Beuth

with K.C. Schulberg

My 40-year adventure with one of
America's outstanding communications companies.

~ CONTENTS ~

This book is dedicated to

my mother,
to Betty,
to Jane,
to Mary,

... and to the rest of the family.

PREFACE

OK! What's up with the title of this book?

First, I have always walked with a slight limp, which is essential to the explanation. Next, I worked for 40 years for one company and for a man who selected me to be the company's first employee. That man was Tom Murphy, who along with an abundance of other qualities, liked to compliment his staff publicly. Deserved or not, I received more than my share of his *"attaboys"* over the years.

On one such occasion, while Tom addressed a gathering of ABC executives shortly after our company had purchased theirs, he apparently went overboard assigning me multiple, new responsibilities. Later, over drinks among his peers, John "Sev" Severino, the mischievous, popular boss at ABC Los Angeles, broke up the gang when he commented, *"For Chrissakes, if you listen to Murphy, you'd think Philly Beuth limped on water!"*

Everyone's pal, Mark Mandela, was on the phone to me in minutes, and as if Twitter existed, the wisecrack got around the building like lightning. For days, I was asked if I knew where the rocks were! So, if you ever read this, Sev, thanks. Thanks also go out to a dozen or so friends and associates who repeatedly asked, *"When is that book ever coming out?"*

Well, if it were not for three specific people, it might still be strewn in parts across my den. First, there is a man whose family name was front page in the 1950s and 1960s in Hollywood and New York. The Schulbergs entertained millions — writing producing and directing television and motion pictures across a wide landscape, highlighted by Budd Schulberg's Oscar-winning "On the Waterfront." In this case, I am grateful that I met K.C. Schulberg a few years ago in Naples, where he was preparing for the production of a feature film. He has been invaluable as an expediter, polisher, detailer, and confidante over the 18 months we have collaborated on this book, and I am privileged to share credits with him.

Keith Raygor likely never felt the need to assemble a book, because as a professional magician for years in Southwest Florida, he could simply conjure one out of thin air! He also performs magic with computer assemblage and has a proclivity for making chocolates disappear. Keeping him in Oreos was easy, and he has been a "can do" guy ever since he had the misfortune to ask, *"What is that you're writing, Phil ...?"*

Thirdly, another creator came along to help. His name is Jim Wagner, and he runs a graphic arts business in Manhattan called Certainly Studios. Years ago, I dragged him from a TV station in Milwaukee to join us at GMA, and he has remained as good a friend as one could hope for ever since.

While all three might have had different tasks, the collaboration was such that each had a part of everything creative in the process of putting the book together. And I can't thank them enough.

In addition, I appreciate having been blessed by my wife, Mary, who handles the caretaker role she inherited elegantly, while filling our marriage with joy.

CHAPTER ONE

A 23-Year-Old's Lucky Day

Wednesday, Oct. 4, 1955, began like many other breezy, autumn days for most New Yorkers. But for *"the faithful,"* as stalwarts of America's favorite pastime in the borough of Brooklyn were known, this day found *"Dem Bums"* fans perched on the edge of their bleacher seats, hoping against hope the day might hold that special, oh so long-awaited promise of snatching the World Series crown from their indomitable foes — *who happened to be my favorite team —* just a short subway ride north in the Bronx.

The seventh and final game of the 1955 World Series, pitting the Brooklyn Dodgers against my *"Damn"* Yankees, was about to get underway in baseball's fabled Yankee Stadium. The "Boys of Summer" had their work cut out for them. They'd never won the classic Series from anyone in 49 tries!! And though they'd taken the pennant a tantalizing seven times, they'd been summarily whipped in every one of the ensuing Series matchups — and the last five times by the very same pin-striped Bronx Bombers I was rooting for on today's field.

As an avid fan of the sport and the Yanks since I was swaddled, I hardly ever missed a game — and certainly not one as critical as this. In fact, if I hadn't been born with an obscure strain of cerebral palsy, known as spastic paresis, I might have allowed myself, like most boys, to dream of a career on the diamond. The condition, though less grave than other forms of CP, nonetheless gave me a signature, pigeon-toed, minor limp that I've carried all my life.

So, on this day I was perched on a stool, nursing a Ballantine beer, my attention fixed to the TV screen behind the bar at Hurley's Saloon — not today's bland retread on 48th Street, but the long-gone sacred watering hole for Big Apple sports enthusiasts and TV professionals — on the corner of 6th Avenue and 49th Street.

Pitching for Brooklyn that day was a young southpaw from the Adirondack Mountains with a changeup so tricky it was known as *"pulling down the lampshade."* Young Johnny Podres had thrown brilliantly and clinched the critical third game of the Series, reviving Brooklyn's hopes after bitter defeats in games one and two. Heading into game seven, the stakes couldn't have been higher with the Series tied three games all. Warming up in the bullpen to the din of the stadium's pipe organ, peddlers hawking hot dogs and 62,000 roaring fans, Podres called to the team's lynchpin captain and shortstop, Pee Wee Reese, *"Just get me one run to win it all."* Embattled Bums fans, whose mantra year after year after year had been a doleful *"Wait till next year,"* were about to hold their collective breath and pin their hopes to the plucky left-handed pitching ace who had celebrated his 23rd birthday just four days earlier.

Like Podres, I had a lot on my mind. With a young wife and newborn baby, I needed a job and was looking for an entry-level position in the still nascent industry of television. Through luck and hard work, I'd obtained a tuition scholarship to that select institution of higher learning founded in 1795, Union College in Schenectady. While working toward my degree, I held down a full-time job at the General Electric-owned NBC affiliate, WRGB-TV. I did well at the station, inveigling myself into every nook and cranny of the operation — so much so that upon graduation from Union, station management enrolled me in the highly reputed Master of Science in Radio-Television program at Syracuse University ... on GE's dime, no less!! *"Just get that degree,"* station manager Bob Hanna promised, *"and we can leap-frog you into management."* So, when my year at Syracuse ended, I raced back to the coop like a proud carrier pigeon, with the newly minted Master's Degree folded under my wing only to find our plan flummoxed by a companywide GE hiring freeze. Bob Hanna, abashed and scrambling to protect his protégé, was now trying to find something to tide me over until the freeze thawed. He'd set up interviews with the CBS and NBC affiliates in New York City. Both made offers that were remarkably similar and equally unappealing. Forty-one dollars a week in the mailroom, with the admonition, *"You make good in that post or in six months, it's bye bye."* Though I did not relish leaving my family in Syracuse, bunking with my in-laws in Staten Island, and cinching my belt to a barely living wage, I was up against it. Like the underdog Dodgers on that fateful day, I was hoping for a lucky break.

Midway through the sixth inning, Brooklyn's prospects seemed rosier than mine. Podres looked confident and in control. Campanella and Reese had both scored, putting the Bums up two to zip. Then came the play that would have hot stove leaguers bantering and debating for decades. The Yanks were coming back strong with Billy Martin and Gil McDougald on base and no outs when Yogi Berra, famous for hitting balls outside the strike zone, connected solidly with Podres' low fastball to launch a high fading fly that hooked deep left toward the corner stands. Cuban born leftie Sandy Amoros had just replaced the more seasoned right-hander Jim Gilliam in left field and Sandy's otherwise undistinguished pro career was about to ascend into legend. Seeming to come out of nowhere, Amoros streaked to the 301 marker in the farthest left corner of the field, stretched to his full 5'7" frame and caught the fly ball in the webbing of his outstretched right glove. Not content with the miracle catch, Sandy slammed on the breaks inches before colliding with the chain link fence, pirouetted and fired a perfect line drive to Reese, who spun and shot the ball to Hodges on first to complete the double play.

In the blink of an eye, the Yank's cards, that seemed so stacked in their favor, came tumbling down as the Bombers watched in blurred horror before retreating ignominiously to their sullen dugout. Makes you wonder. What made Sandy surpass all expectations that day? Only a left-hander could have made that catch. Was it providence, luck or the brilliance of manager Walt Alston to move the young Cuban into that position minutes before he was mobilized for the amazing save? Those three outs ripped the guts and drive out of the Yankee roster. They never recovered their mojo. Podres finished off the Yanks and made his day. The Dodgers reversed the tide of the last decade to finally claim the title; Sandy Amoros became a team and crowd hero; and Johnny Podres cemented his place in World Series history. It was indeed a lucky day for that 23-year-old pitcher.

Wound up by all the excitement, but not as tranquil about my own future, I fished a handful of coins out of my trouser pocket, sauntered over to the telephone booth in the corner of the restaurant to congratulate my father-in-law, Stanley Yost, who was a die-hard Dodgers fan. I got along just fine with Stanley who thought his daughter would do well with this keen, spunky, hardworking kid. He was in high spirits, chiding me over the bet I'd lost and the buck I owed him. We joked about the near perfect game Podres had thrown and as we were about to hang up, Stanley added, *"Oh, wait a minute, son ... somebody called for you. An Albany number. A man named Mr. Murphy wants you to call him back."* I had just enough coins in my pocket to make one last call — long distance to Albany. Little did I know it, but my life, the life of another 23-year-older — as I'd celebrated my birthday several months earlier — was about to turn a corner.

On the phone was the calm confident voice of a woman I would get to know and work with for the next four decades, Ruth Bassett ... *"Mr. Murphy's office."*

❧ ⌘ ☙

CHAPTER TWO

A Policeman at the Door

One distinct image from my early childhood remains seared into my memory and revisits me often to this day. It figures as a part of my unusual upbringing in a working class neighborhood of Staten Island, New York, and relates to my father's death when I was 4 years old. Though nearly eight decades have elapsed since the incident, it still seems like yesterday.

My parents, Margaret Long and Philip Beuth, each from everyday working families, met after high school and went through what mom later recalled as a *"couple of years of parties"* before getting married in 1930. Mom worked in five and dime stores and dad did house painting. They were an animated couple who enjoyed dancing. Dad played the "uke" and early pictures show him as handsome and mustached. Shortly before I was born in 1932, my parents rented a small home near Travis on Staten Island, where both families had immigrated in the early 1900s. Mom's family came from England; dad's from Germany. Though they lived in roughly the same neighborhood, the families had little more than a passing acquaintance. The Beuth clan was large. My paternal grandparents, Frank and Anna Beuth, had five children, my father being the fourth. They lived in a small cottage, framed by carefully tended flowers, which seemed to be in perennial bloom. Behind the house was a large garage, home to the modest family boat building business. From rowboats to small pleasure crafts, the vessels were hand built to order for individual buyers. On visits as a child, I was typically handed sandpaper and invited, a la Tom Sawyer, to join a perpetual sanding ritual on the hulls. I loved those visits, as infrequent as they were, especially on the occasions when my grandfather would retire to the house, plunk himself down at the family's old upright piano and start singing and pounding out his favorite ditty, *"Roll out the barrel; we'll have a barrel of fun!!"* He played with great vigor and surprising dexterity given his huge carpenter hands! To this day, I am always ready with a song. Whether through DNA, or early environmental conditioning, I probably owe that proclivity to Grandpa, Frank Beuth.

My maternal grandparents were Grandma Margaret Sykes and her second husband, Clarence Sykes, who was my mother's stepdad, her natural father, John, having long since passed. There again were five children. Clarence Sykes was in his 60s and a less than happy man. He'd been a photographer in the U.S. Army during the Spanish-American War and had suffered an injury that never properly healed. Shot in the groin area, his internal organs had never been correctly trussed back in place. As a result, several times each day, he would bend over and make some kind of manual adjustment, invariably accompanied by a loud expletive! I never did learn why he couldn't have that groin problem fixed, but it could well have been a matter of finances. Clarence Sykes coughed and cussed constantly, and got little, if any, medical attention. His government stipend amounted to a pittance, and money was always scarce in that household.

My brother, Eugene Clifford Beuth was born in September 1935 just as the Depression was easing up for some lucky Americans. Mom and dad were working sporadically and had cobbled enough money together to buy a used car that my father favored — a convertible ragtop roadster, probably 10 years old. Hanging across the back seat was a child's canvas chair from which my feet would dangle when we took road trips.

One day my father, who was always full of good humor, chased a fire truck on its way to put out a blaze on the other side of town. Suddenly, one of the fire helmets fell off the back of the truck and my father pulled over to retrieve it. He placed the enormous helmet on my tiny head and beamed at me before catching up to the firemen and returning it. I still remember it being very heavy! In these days of ubiquitous cameras, there would certainly be a picture for the family album. I have only the shred of that memory as a mental snapshot. And unfortunately, I have no other recollections of my father ...

However, I do have total recall of the day when, standing in our kitchen, I peered down the long hall to see the silhouette of a lanky policeman at our front door, speaking with my mother and telling her how my father had been in an accident. My dad had set off to his first day of work as a painter at the Bethlehem Steel shipyard when the roadster had collided with a Drake's bakery delivery truck. The article in the Staten Island Advance showed a picture of the car, off the road, on its side, with a child's seat protruding from the rear window. The report said the canvas-topped car had rolled over several times before coming to rest on its side. By the time my mom reached the hospital, her husband had perished and she found herself a widow with two young boys!

The cause of the accident was never officially established, but family lore holds that when a representative from the Drake's company came by the house, my grandfather threw him out on his ear. No one ever seemed to get the whole story, but I learned from my mom years later that she had received a $500 out-of-court settlement. And that was that.

I naturally wondered, many years later as an adult, how that accident, the loss of a parent and subsequent events, shaped my life and the life of my brother, negatively or otherwise. I believe as far as I was concerned, it likely made me more self reliant, and confident in the long run. How would my father have influenced us? Would my mother ever have been as strong as she became had she not raised two young sons on her own? She certainly had a hard go of it during the early years. Circumstances, however, never deterred her. She worked day after day, paid the bills carefully — a little at a time — making her boys her sole mission in life.

Fortunately for us all, the second half of mom's life proved easier and more enjoyable. She lived to the age of 85, proud of her sons and the travel, lifestyle, and experiences we were able to afford her, including occasional brushes with celebrities whose paths just happened to cross hers ...

CHAPTER THREE

Smitty's Crapshoot

The story goes that one fine spring afternoon in 1954, New York Gov. Tom Dewey walked around his backyard in Pawling, New York, with his famous neighbor, Lowell Thomas, hoping to pick the brain of the worldly broadcaster. The Governor wanted to help a friend, Congressman Dean Taylor, get some advice on an investment the congressman held in WROW-TV, a struggling UHF station in the Tri-Cities market of Albany, Schenectady and Troy. Gov. Dewey thought who better to ask than one of the world's foremost journalists, explorers, raconteurs and the notable nightly radio and movie newsreel commentator, who just happened to be his Hammersley Hill neighbor. Lowell Thomas' trademark address and sign-off, *"Hello everybody"* and *"So long until tomorrow,"* were a staple of radio households across the nation. Surely this venerable newsman, the confidante of Franklin Roosevelt and the Dalai Lama, who had attained near legendary status in the world of radio and who'd "discovered" Lawrence of Arabia, would be able to offer some useful guidance in the related realm of television broadcasting. (In retelling the story years later, "LT," as we came to know him, told us *"I didn't know a damn thing about TV stations!"*) Lowell immediately referred the question to his longtime business manager, Frank "Smitty" Smith and, thus, a most interesting chain of events was set in motion. Frank Smith was a man of diminutive stature but oversized reputation. He had recently teamed up with legendary impresario, Mike Todd to roll out Cinerama, a new wide-screen technology that was taking the country by storm. Smith fielded the inquiry and proceeded to seek counsel from a host of associates he'd gotten to know over years in the radio and motion picture business, including Frank Stanton, then President of the CBS television network. Stanton knew the Tri-City market well. It had been dominated, ever since the early 1930s, by the powerful General Electric-owned VHF station, WRGB. A pioneer in the region, WRGB had built a solid reputation for quality programming, news and public service. It controlled a seemingly unassailable market share, carrying all of NBC, plus a handful of delayed broadcasts from CBS. "The Ed Sullivan Show," for example, CBS' flagship Sunday program, aired on kinescope, delayed till the following Friday night. But one thing intrigued or, more accurately, annoyed Stanton; his prized "CBS Nightly News" was generally not available in the capitol of New York State!

Meanwhile, the underfinanced WROW-TV UHF station held a miniscule market share and could not even be received without installing a rooftop antenna contraption that was anything but reliable. This did not deter Frank Smith, who now had his curiosity trained like a mongoose on this quest. He visited Washington and learned from some crafty engineer friends there might be a *"Hail Mary"* long shot possibility for a VHF "drop in" to the Tri-City market. Their initial review of separation and coverage restrictions for the Albany region had revealed VHF signal coverage for cities like Rochester to the west, and Providence to the east. Those pre-existing saturations seemed to preclude additional VHF drop-ins. However, the engineering beagles also spotted a small region near Great Sacandaga Lake, called Vail Mills, where a drop-in might be possible because it fell between the prior contiguous coverage areas. That's all he needed to hear, and so began Frank Smith's Quixotic *"crapshoot"* — the purchase of WROW-TV along with its sister station, WROW-AM, both of which were teetering on the brink of bankruptcy.

One of Smith's very first decisions was only surprising to those unfamiliar with his panache and style. There were 10 original investors in the fledgling WROW group, each of whom had put up $40,000 to get the operation going. Smith could probably have offered pennies on the dollar, given the sorry state of the station's finances, but he elected to offer each investor a choice between stock in the new company, or a full buyout of their original $40,000! Most took the easy money ... and lived to regret the decision.

During the due diligence and negotiation process, Frank Smith had constant dealings with the station's current owner, a most colorful man named Harry Goldman. Goldman had parlayed his taxi/billboard company into a broadcast license and was known for conducting business with sometimes-unorthodox methodology. For instance, WROW-TV had no official network affiliation, but mysteriously aired "The

Mickey Mouse Show," a staple of ABC's lineup. It turned out that Goldman had a friend at the phone company switching station with a relative fondness for Harry, and an even greater fondness for the premium malt Scotch whisky Harry dropped off with faultless regularity!! Standing 6 feet tall with a flowing, jet black, albeit gray-flecked, pompadour, Harry Goldman, with horn-rimmed glasses and a perennial cigar, cut a colorful profile.

Both Goldman and Frank Smith were known to be immaculate dressers, but their tastes stood at opposite ends of the haberdashery spectrum. Frank Smith's style was all Madison Avenue, buttoned-down conservatism, while Goldman tended toward wildly checked, colorful sport jackets, tasseled loafers, and an ever-present colorful bow tie. Central casting would have pegged him as a carnival barker. Goldman was clever, flamboyant with an always creative, sometimes circuitous game plan. Like a 6-foot tall, bold, gesticulating Wizard of Oz, Goldman was the ever-consummate showman. Meanwhile, the impeccable 5-foot-3-inch Frank "Smitty" Smith, slight of build in dapper business suit and fedora, was Harry's unlikely foil.

They did, however, make the deal. One hundred cents on the dollar was an easy putt. Later, Smith recalled the events, saying, *"I loved Harry's ambition and the fact that he was in a deep crapshoot himself. But when I asked him what he thought the station could earn if properly supported with sufficient capital, his answer was so low that I knew he was not right for us long term."*

Harry signed a consultant deal and stayed on at the station for a few years. He later boasted to friends he would have accepted much less than 100 cents on the dollar, but when Smith's vision came fully online, Goldman realized Smith's offer had been less motivated by naiveté or generosity but rather born of caution and wisdom. The diminutive man from Jellico, Tennessee, effectively trumped any future claim from the original owners who might have complained he had special knowledge about a drop-in VHF channel. Smith had accepted the full risk of going forward. Much later, when referring to the offer, Smitty would say, *"It was a crapshoot. After all, we had no guaranty of the VHF conversion ... and furthermore it was LT's last $400,000!"*

None of these players could possibly have imagined — as they concluded their deal to acquire a flea-bitten TV station in Albany's outskirts — that their actions had laid the groundwork for what would become one of the world's premier media conglomerates, a company heralded for its high business standards, brilliant stewardship, and ethical corporate strategy. Capital Cities Communications would go on to become an introductory case study at the Harvard Business School.

CHAPTER FOUR

Papa Sykes

Mom, a recently widowed mother with limited options, was fortunate enough to find employment on the production line, making light bulbs at the Western Electric plant in Manhattan. The job, while a good one, required a lengthy commute by bus from our Staten Island home to South Ferry, by ferry to Manhattan, and then by subway to the plant. That job and requisite travel caused mom to make a decision that would impact our small family unit for a decade, a generation, maybe all our lives ...

She took an apartment near the ferry station and hired a sitter to look after my little brother, Gene. But how could she care for me? It was a tiny apartment, and then there was my condition to take into account. For, as if mom wasn't faced with enough challenges, she had to deal with the circumstances surrounding my birth with cerebral palsy. My particular strain of CP was (and remains) a less invasive variety known as spastic paresis or, more colloquially, Little's Disease. It's a condition that has perplexed doctors for years, with scant research as the malady has not been historically life threatening. Though many fine neurologists from famous medical centers still debate treatments, diagnoses and prognoses for the disease, what it meant for me in laymen's terms was that my legs from the hips down were permanently compromised, resulting in a minor limp and awkward gait. Over time, it became an acceptable inconvenience that sometimes even went unnoticed. And as recently as 10 years prior to this writing, I was still walking, albeit with a limp and occasional cane. However, over the last few years, my balance and motor control have collapsed so that I now use a small lightweight scooter to get around. Overall, despite the limp, I consider myself fortunate, because for most of my life, I had pretty good mobility.

Even as a newborn, it was clear from my first crawl that something was not right. As a toddler, I did more falling than walking; one foot invariably colliding with the other, causing me to trip and tumble face first. As a young boy, I was badly pigeon-toed, an impairment which tripped me constantly and made running a near impossible challenge. Money was scarce, blue-color clinics were ill equipped and uninformed, so remedial medical attention was never a realistic option. Mom recalled me trying to straighten my gimpy legs by doing sit-ups with my feet pinned under a couch or radiator. In school, a gym teacher suggested that by walking with my hands in my side pockets, thumbs pointed outward, my feet would turn out as well. Really?! Though I might not have been the most coordinated kid in my class, I did my utmost to remain active in the schoolyard, then at stickball and, in later years, playing baseball. But because I ran slowly I was always the last player chosen when picking teams, and always relegated to right field. A problem I later solved ... by picking and forming my own teams!

So, because of financial pressure and the complication of my condition, mom sent me to live with her parents, the Sykes in Travis. That separated me from mom and Gene except for occasional weekend visits on a pretty chaotic schedule — one that nonetheless lasted more than six years.

That's how Clarence Sykes, my mom's stepdad, became "Papa" Sykes, the de facto, unintended (and involuntary) stand-in for my own father. Papa Sykes was an earnest and responsible man, but also frustrated and embittered, believing his army experience, war injury, destitute life, and now, in his twilight years, the burden of caring for his stepdaughter's handicapped boy, all amounted to his having been dealt a bad hand.

Papa Sykes' vocation was collecting and selling junk, though it seemed to my young eyes that there was a heap more collecting than selling going on in our backyard. Papa started amassing his stockpiles of debris shortly after his war years and never stopped to his very last breath. Papa Sykes' house was wood-framed, with a stairway leading to the second floor bedrooms. The ground floor had a porch that practically butted right up to the street, behind which was a living room with lots of chairs, a big rug, and the ever-present, cherished centerpiece — an RCA console radio. Behind the living room was a large open kitchen with a tub-shaped, hand-crank ringer washing machine, and a wood burning stove whose venting flues carried heat to the four corners of the house, upstairs and down. I slept on a makeshift cot in the upstairs hall, directly over one of the second floor heating grates. It also happened to be ground zero for grandma's constant battle against a constant infestation of bedbugs. The whole house smelled of a (probably toxic) spray called Flit. I still remember the popular radio commercial of the era, *"Quick, Henry, the Flit!"* Our cellar had a dirt floor, an icebox, a furnace for winter, a coal bin, and shelves containing more junk, including some decaying photo equipment. Papa prided himself on fashioning his own foul smelling hand-soap that burned my skin and he cooked us cubed watermelon rind to chew on. *"Don't have money for gum, ya know,"* he would say. Papa Sykes would sit for hours on the back steps off the kitchen, puffing on cheap cigars and gazing out over his large backyard. The scene likely pleased him. The yard was long, reaching out to a swamp in the distance. It had a hardpan dirt walkway right down the center. On the left was his "victory garden," planted with an array of edible vegetables: corn, tomatoes, carrots, radishes, green beans, lettuce, and eggplant, all carefully tended by him and my Grandma. At the far end of the dirt path was a giant oak tree with a rope and a rubber tire swing. Papa never ran out of tires because just across from the victory garden, bordering the entire right side of the path, was his expansive junk yard. The debris field included leaning stacks of old tires, a 30 by 30 foot patch of old newspapers, stacked waist-high and sheltered from the rain by tattered oilcloth and canvas tarps. There were oil cans, gas cans, and a few cannibalized hulks of rusted out old cars. There were also — and these seemed to be especially prized by Papa Sykes — boxes and boxes of what he labeled "tools and dies." In the driveway was his trusty "Tin Lizzie" four-door Ford automobile, outfitted with a wooden two-by-four contraption that wrapped around the sides at the roofline and could be folded down to form a makeshift table behind the car. This homemade retractable platform served to display his wares whenever he attended county fairs and exhibitions. During my early childhood, I watched as this vast collection of debris, rubbish, rubble and junk grew and expanded week after week, month after month, year after year. The rusting relics seemed to me like forlorn orphans that gradually, over time, began to lose all hope they might ever be adopted.

When I was 7 or 8, Papa fashioned me a funny Rube Goldberg bicycle fitted with homemade handlebars, mismatched fenders and a threadbare seat. Others might have scoffed at the odd looking vehicle, but to me the bike was a godsend as it afforded me two things I had never ever known: freedom and mobility. After a few bruised elbows and skinned knees, I mastered the bike to the point where I began to charge around the neighborhood at breakneck speed, showing off my riding prowess by crossing my arms over my chest and smiling left and right, while coasting past my neighbors' stoops. That funny looking two-wheeler did wonders to build my self-confidence. A lifetime later, I wonder whether not using those handlebars was a compensating mechanism for me — a way for a young boy to seek and display a bit of much needed normalcy.

CHAPTER FIVE

TSM

Thomas Sawyer Murphy was born in Brooklyn, New York, on May 31, 1925. He grew up in an upper middle class section of Flatbush, a mixed Irish, Italian, and Jewish neighborhood. He was Jesuit-educated, claims he loved the movies and that his family was *"not rich, but better off than many."* His father, Charles Murphy, was an esteemed lawyer who rose to prominence with several judicial appointments, including corporate counsel for the city of New York and a New York State Supreme Court judgeship. The family enjoyed friends and acquaintances like Gov. Tom Dewey, the Rev. Norman Vincent Peale, Lowell Thomas, Edward R. Murrow, and Frank Smith, often mingling at the prestigious Quaker Hill Country Club in Pawling, New York. Having originally enrolled at Princeton to study engineering, Tom quickly decided that was not to his liking and changed gears, transferring to Cornell, where he graduated in 1945. After college, he completed the U.S. Navy V-12 officer-training program, including service as a midshipman deck officer on a troop transport. That was followed by a position as an industrial salesman for Texaco. He then went back to school, earning his graduate degree from the Harvard Business School, discovering along the way that solving business problems suited him very well. Fresh out of Harvard, he worked as an account executive with the Kenyon & Eckhardt ad agency, entertaining clients at "The Ed Sullivan Show," marketing Lincoln autos, Dove Beauty Bars, and other products. But quietly, he yearned to be making his own big decisions, instead of executing those made by others. Tom Murphy, or "Murph" as we all know him, gave a poignant overview of his business philosophy and career choices when addressing the Harvard Business School graduating class in 1985. An edited excerpt follows:

"Since I had been told I would make a pretty good salesman, I decided to go into advertising. I went to work for $3,000 a year at the Kenyon & Eckhardt Agency, who lent me to Lever Brothers where I got three years of experience. Then came a turning point in my life. I went to a cocktail party at the home of the late Lowell Thomas, noted explorer and newscaster. It was Labor Day in 1954. At the party, I ran into a little guy — 5 feet 3 inches tall — named Frank Smith, who was a business associate of Mr. Thomas. He came up to me and said he was going into a little crapshoot in broadcasting, and was looking for someone to run it in Albany, New York. He said he was looking for a good salesman who wants to run something, and if the crapshoot worked out, that person would be earning a $250,000 a year in five years. ... So much for happenstance, so much for luck. If I had not been home that weekend; if I hadn't gone to that cocktail party, I would never have ended up at Capital Cities.

So I took the job, because it gave me a chance to run something for myself. Now, 30 years later, the company is no longer small, and if you wonder how it happened, well, there is no mystery; we just did it day to day. The bankrupt stations lost $360,000 the first year, and we did not turn the corner until our third year, after going back to our stockholders twice for $150,000 each time. There were 39 employees running radio and TV, and we learned one important thing — we needed only a few people to keep things going. That experience was worth a great deal to Capital Cities over the years. It helped us avoid building up huge staffs. We believed we should hire the best people, pay them well, and never have more people than necessary. Even to this day, we have no corporate counsel, no vice president of personnel, no public relations department. When my boss said the building needed a paint job, I had them paint only the sides the public could see ... not the sides facing the woods and the Hudson River. Today our stations have the latest equipment and facilities. But I remember one time at our original station when a film clip dropped through the projection room floor because it had not been properly threaded onto the take-up reel. It disappeared through a hole in the floor, and was finally retrieved from the basement so the show could go on.

I am going to end with some personal advice from this old warhorse. Be sure to pick a business you enjoy. Do not go for the biggest buck, but go where *you will be happiest, because if you are happy, you are successful And do yourself a favor, get yourself involved in your community. Put something back. When you do well, do some good also. You will feel better about yourself. As my father used to say, do not do anything that would cost you a good night's sleep!*

And finally, in your business career, don't do anything that is ethically questionable. You will lose more than you could ever gain."

In 2012, as our then retired Chairman, Tom sat for a long video retrospective with his friend Don West at the Library of American Broadcasting. Murph's character came through in characteristic style, modestly deflecting a lifetime of near universal praise and accolades from both his colleagues ... and his competitors! That video is available through the Library or on YouTube. Over the decades, as someone who had an intimate working relationship with Tom Murphy, I have often been asked to explain what made Tom tick. If one simply measured the man by his intelligence, person-to-person skills and business smarts, he would already rank among the best. But those who know Tom recognize that his brilliant operational acumen and business philosophy were always rooted in the highest degree of integrity. Tom built a company based upon certain honorable principles and only recruited partners who shared those principles and considered them gospel.

While I confess to an unbridled bias, I join many of my peers who seek the right way to describe a man so imbued with high personal standards, so completely candid, warm, compassionate, and unassuming, that words seem somehow inadequate. What I can add unequivocally is that those who worked for and with him were fortunate beyond measure!

CHAPTER SIX

Heroes Big and Small

Living with Papa Sykes was not the *"get away with anything"* experience most pampered grandkids enjoy. He was not an affectionate man — I never sat on his lap, there were no bedtime stories and we didn't play catch. He gave me occasional chores around the house, like weeding the garden, but was only casually interested in my completing them.

One of the few activities we did do together consisted of frequent Saturday summer trips to the Englishtown, New Jersey, open air market where Papa sold his array of drill bits, connectors, hinges, and all manner of junk from the makeshift table hanging off the back of old Lizzie. Once we were set up, Papa often left me in charge of the family treasures so he could disappear for several hours of important meetings with his pals, Johnny Walker and Jim Beam, who, by the way, never made any appearances at our home. My grandmother was a 5-foot prohibition force. For watching and selling our wares, I was rewarded with real watermelon and ice cream. Wow, did I ever love selling!!

I was well behaved, but Papa Sykes was ill-equipped to tackle the challenges of raising a young boy, along with the inevitable unforeseen events that entailed, like the one terrible incident on a summer day when my then 5-year-old brother Gene had come over for a visit. We were just hanging around the junkyard while our mom and Papa went down the street to do the week's shopping at the local A&P. The yard was filled with the ever-present stacks of newspapers, tires and rat pack stuff, all waiting to be sold; and we were treating this minefield like our homemade jungle gym. Nestled among the rubbish was an old gas can with a large round pouring spout. Somehow, from out of somewhere, Gene had found a match and curiosity led him to light the match, drop it in the can, and peer in! POW!!! Flames leapt up, totally engulfing Gene's face. I ran over to find him laying on the ground, screaming, holding his face, his hair all singed. Oblivious to the fact that the yard was also on fire, I focused solely on Gene. To this day I do not know what compelled me to react as I did. I guess I thought that hot could be fooled by cold, so I dragged Gene into the kitchen, turned the cold water spigot on in the sink and stuck his head under the water, splashing him over and over and over. Neighbors ran down the street to the A&P and soon the Tin Lizzie came flying into the yard and Gene was off to the hospital. Next time I saw him he was bundled up and bandaged just like the invisible man. Fortunately, he never scarred; though for years whenever he got angry, a red outline of the burn would appear on his face. But, in time, that too disappeared and Gene grew up to be the handsome devil we all know him to be! Apparently, the cold water had a positive palliative effect and I got some credit for my quick reaction and speedy actions, whether deserved or not. For a kid who did not run or walk well, that incident did a lot to boost my self-confidence, which had been severely challenged up to that point in my young life.

Papa caught holy hell for the state of his junkyard and the hazards it presented for his family, not to mention the entire neighborhood! He vowed to clean it up, but never did.

Our house was not a culturally enriched one, nor was it cluttered with toys and kid's stuff, so the 5-cent New York Daily News Sunday edition was our eagerly awaited weekly treat. The newspaper and the radio were my sole contacts to the world outside school. I loved all the comic book heroes, but in our household, Superman had trouble maintaining his superhero status. The radio would blast, *"Faster than a speeding bullet! More powerful than a locomotive! It's a bird! It's a plane! It's ..."* and Papa would shout, *"Bullshit,"* and change stations! He preferred listening to the war news, especially the solemn recitation of the fallen dead: Private Edwin Johnson, Sergeant Stanley Romanowski, Corporal Lewis Thompson ... name after name as Papa puffed furiously on his cigar, shaking his head in angry despair and filling the room with billows of smoke. I managed to retune to my programs as soon as he left the room, but he always returned for the news whether from Gabriel Heater, Lowell Thomas, or Walter Winchell, whose signature sign off, *"With lotions of love,"* attained near ritual status in the house.

My mother finally broke down and bought me a most cherished gift — my own small plastic Farnsworth Bakelite radio, which I kept for years. (I believe my daughter, Jane, now 45, still holds it as a family heirloom!) By fifth or sixth grade, I was hooked on the radio and comic books. Sure, I appreciated reading "Treasure Island," "Adventures of Huckleberry Finn" and other classics in school, but at home my favorite reading came from another more "popular" source — a writer named Chester Gould. Gould was the cartoonist who wrote and drew "Dick Tracy" on the Sunday News cover page. I am certain I was his biggest, youngest fan! I anticipated each cliffhanger episode on Sunday mornings, becoming fanatically familiar with all the villains he drew; Flattop, The Mole, Mumbles, and Pruneface come to mind. His character names were so creative, like B.O. Plenty and Sam Catchem. Tracy was my hero. He and Chief Patton always survived with bravado and daring to triumph over evil in full color on the front page every single Sunday. I liked the fact, naively perhaps, that Mr. Gould demonstrated, week in and week out, that crime did not pay! Gould was, in fact, ahead of his time, joining a small cadre of forward-looking writers who used electronic devices to thwart the enemies of their day. Tracy had a two-way wrist radio in 1942!! I still, to this day, own one of those Sunday front pages, which is now 75 years old.

As important as the Sunday comics were, "Jack Armstrong," "Gangbusters" and "Superman" were a great complement on the radio. My listening habits began to diversify as I grew more interested in baseball. The voices of Mel Allen, Red Barber, and Russ Hodges were instantly recognizable to me. I followed the rivalries between the Yankees and Red Sox, Giants and Dodgers intensely, learning about the great legends as I draped myself in the game. Fascinated by the unique relationship between the players and fans, and the broadcasters who forged and nourished those relationships, I got to the point where I too wanted to be a radio announcer, just like my favorite, Red Barber. I can still hear him now. Over the background crowd noises at Ebbets field came Red's singular voice, *"Bases are FOB. Full of Brooklyns ... Reese, Duke, and Reiser take their leads ... Erskine, with a five run lead ... sitting in the catbird seat. Now, here's the pitch ..."*

Looking back, it was Red Barber at the mic and Pee Wee Reese on the diamond who, among others, supported integration when Jackie Robinson broke the color barrier, changing the game forever. The winning magic of the Yankees turned me into a lifelong fan of the team. So, when Red switched over to the Yankee booth in the early 1950s, I felt complete, listening faithfully straight into my college days. I was known to have the best collection of baseball cards in the neighborhood, all stored and catalogued in neat white pine Kraft cheese boxes. What fun! Being a fanatic about baseball and baseball trivia paid some unexpected dividends a few years later.

In 1948, when I was 16, my brother Gene and I went with Mom on our annual trek to Howard Clothes on Journal Square, New Jersey, to pick out our *"go to church Easter Sunday outfit"* — usually one checked jacket and two pairs of solid pants. Mom had an account at Howards, to which she made small payments each month. On this particular visit, while Gene was being measured, I noticed a counter sign announcing a contest. The store was offering a $500 merchandise award to anyone who could correctly predict the final season ranking for all 16 teams in both the American and National leagues. Hmm ... interesting, I thought ... and right up my alley. I began scribbling out my calculations, moving teams around; pretty sure I was getting close. I remember hesitating whether to place the Browns or the White Sox in last place. I made my choice and dropped the entry into the box.

That October, during the Port Richmond High School assembly one morning, I was addressing the student body with an appeal to save the tinfoil from their parents' cigarette packages so our school could roll a bigger ball of silver than our nemesis, Curtis High. Henry Dehart, a classmate and friend, grabbed me as I left the stage and told me he'd heard my name on TV the night before. Could it be?? When I reached home, there was a telegram addressed to my mom, informing her that I had won the contest, as the only person to have named all 16 teams in perfect order, and inviting us to the Jimmy Powers show on WPIX-TV!!!

So there we were, at the studio a day or two later, unaware that the best was yet to come. We were escorted into a waiting room and there were the show's guests, Jackie Robinson, his wife, and my all-time radio hero — none other than Red Barber! Wow!!

Red Barber then started a conversation with me that went on for many years. He started by asking me, at 16, what I wanted to do in life and I immediately answered, *"Just what you do, Mr. Barber."* Apparently it came out, *"Jest what ya do, Mr. Barba!"* And his reply was, *"Well you're going to have to get rid of that accent, young man."* My response was something like, *"But you have an accent, don't you?"* *"I am the only one,"* he replied. I left the studio on cloud nine and felt fundamentally changed. My love and passion for baseball had granted me access to something I never dreamed could happen, allowing me to not only witness my heroes, but to converse with them. Golly what an eye-opener that was! My mom was beaming with pride and love. My brother Gene was in awe of his older brother. All our relatives got Howard Clothes for Christmas for a number of years. And I had a new lifelong objective — *get rid of my New Yawk accent!*

Red Barber's path and mine happened to cross again a number of times over the ensuing years and each time, despite my best efforts, he would always smile down over his bifocals, purring in that delicious Southern drawl of his and say *"You still have a ways to go!"*

A lovely man, indeed.

CHAPTER SEVEN

Reunited

Eventually, Mom decided it was time to bring us all together in our own place. Grandma had died, Gene had joined us in the Sykes house and Papa was aging and relieved to see us move on. Gene and I needed a more normal routine and were both ready for better schools. Mom got a job as a buyer for a department store in Port Richmond, on Staten Island. No more commuting to Manhattan!

We moved into a second floor, three-room apartment in a two-story house, sharing a bathroom at the top of the stairs with the landlady, whom we will call "Lucy." Her bedroom was on the second floor in the front, behind which was our living room. Gene and I slept there on a sofa bed. Mom had her own bedroom in the back, and there was the kitchen in between. Later, every time the opening of "All in the Family" showed Archie Bunker's house on TV, I would sing out, *"Looks just like our house!"* A southern belle of the first order, Lucy had a military husband, who seemed indifferent to his wife's active dating life. Lucy finally did run off with Jimmy the milkman! Things at that point were getting marginally better for us, but we were still living on a bare bones budget. Mom cried a lot about lack of money. The Herald Tribune newspaper chose us as a qualified family and I was sent on one of their programs for underprivileged kids. Placed on a train alone at Grand Central, I traveled to Waycross, Georgia, to the Kirkland family tobacco plantation, where I met a half-dozen kids from New York, with whom I had an absolute ball. All of us got up at dawn to a breakfast of grits and eggs and then picked tobacco till about 1 p.m. before breaking for lunch. The pickers got $2 a day and those who drove the mule sleds got three. After two or three days, I talked my way into the driver's job and loved it! It was a growth experience, being thrown together with kids of different backgrounds, cultures and colors. I think we all enjoyed the mix, and those fond memories remained with me for a long time. On the way back by train two weeks later, I stopped over briefly in Washington, D.C. and saw a headline slashed across all the morning newspapers: "ATOM BOMB DROPPED ON JAPAN ..."

It was August 1945. I was now a 13-year-old with travel experience, a Staten Island Advance paper route, and some neighborhood lawns to cut on a regular basis! That provided my mother with a few dollars each week. Port Richmond High was more than just a place to go to class, study and take exams. For me, it was a chance to break out of a confined, sterile past. I am not sure that I realized it at the time, but the exuberance with which I tackled school and my newfound gregarious outgoing nature, may well have been another compensating mechanism for my awkward gait, which, by that time, had become a less perceptible inconvenience rather than a real handicap. Whatever the reason; I became very active in school affairs.

Certain I was headed for a career in radio broadcasting, I volunteered to do each morning's announcements over the school PA system. And I began announcing the basketball games as well. Anxious to improve my sports writing, I joined the school newspaper, The Crow's Nest, and started traveling with the team to file my stories. By my second year, I was the newspaper's Sports Editor, with my picture and byline above my column in every issue. It did not hurt my credibility with the school athletes that I had won the Howard Clothes baseball contest!!

I met two terrific classmates at Port Richmond: Betty Yost and Harold Olsen, both of whom became important figures in my life. Betty because she was just the most adorable girl in school and I wanted to date her; and Hal because he was my best pal. Active in school, he served as General Organization President, had a consistently quick wit, and a ready sense of humor. Later, connections through Hal's family helped get me into my beloved college, Union, which, in turn led to my subsequent career. The friendship I was trying to forge with Betty was aided by the fact that after Sunday night Youth Fellowship, everyone went to her house for waffles and hot chocolate! I teased Betty for years that I thought her family was rich because they had a waffle iron! Our first date was on Jan. 16, 1948, a very cold, snowy night. After the basketball game was over and I was able to leave the gym, we walked about a half-mile in the snow along well-lit streets to Steckman's, our favorite ice cream parlor for chips and a coke. Then, in still more snow, we walked back to her home near the school. When we arrived at her house, she discovered in shock that she'd somehow lost her brand new wristwatch! She was disconsolate. I convinced her there was a good chance we could find it if we carefully retraced our steps. She agreed to go back, though I could tell she was far less confident than I. After 10 anxious minutes of searching, there in plain sight and clearly visible, illuminated by streetlight, we spotted her watch, sprinkled with a light dusting of snow!! She was thrilled and grateful, and I took it as a sign that our flirtations were blessed. Soon we were *"goin' steady,"* both convinced we had something special together.

In order to provide mom with a promised $13 a week, I worked a lot after school. I had met mom's boss, Mr. Martin Greenberger, at the retail store where she worked. He was a popular, friendly man, who made a point of hiring his employees' children whenever he could, whether he needed them or not. One day, he asked me whether I would like to have a job helping with the inventory. Naturally, I accepted, and down to a terrible mess in his basement the two of us went. It was damp, with a dirt floor and waist high tables stacked with boxes of socks, shirts and pants, none of which looked attractive enough to sell. He asked me to sort through them — this pile for items that needed to go to the dry cleaners, that pile for discards. He had rolls of white paper we used for anything we intended to salvage. One day, as I was sorting through the basement stock, I came across the strangest set of narrow peg-legged, wide-shouldered suits, all in day glow colors: orange, purple, pink, green and yellow. Mr. Greenberger just happened to poke his head down into the basement and saw my astonished reaction. *"They're Zoot Suits!"* he hollered. I made a face. *"But, Mr. G, who would ever buy such a thing?"* His response was classic and has remained with me forever, *"Philip,"* he said in his wonderful Jewish accent, *"Alvays remember, veneva you deal vit de public, 25 percent of everyting you sell must be in terrible taste!"* (Over the years I aired a few programs that met Mr. G's quota, and I thought of him and smiled every time!)

At 16, I got a job at the Post Diner, situated conveniently halfway between our home and the high school. After school and all day Saturdays, I sat on a stool in an alley behind the diner and peeled potatoes and onions. I also washed dishes and later learned to prepare all kinds of eggs, omelets, burgers, etc. I was what is called a short order cook. And except for a minor incident when I sliced off a tiny piece of my finger, which promptly disappeared into an omelet, I acquitted myself pretty well at the grill and steam table. I was the short order cook for two different diners over the next few years, developing a reputation for hard work and honesty, the latter being important in those cash only days. During my first summer break from college, I worked alone each night in an 18-stool diner in a rough part of town. The diner owner worried about my being held up, so the police came over and instructed me in a procedure in the event of a robbery. Simple: *"Put your arms over your head and run like hell out the back door."* To everyone's relief, I was never robbed. Lotsa drunks, but I learned how to always agree with them. *"Right on,"* I would say, and the tips increased!

Before I entered college, the owner of the diner chain, Bob Swanson, who had taught me so much, tried to persuade me to forget about college and join his company on a permanent basis. I really liked Bob and his family, but that was not for me. I did take away a Bob remembrance, however. Whenever he saw a customer trying to get a waiter's attention in the diner, he would shout, *"Rearview,"* as though he was calling a food order. That was his code for prompting waiters to check their sections, because someone needed attention. He would explain from time to time, *"When you are driving, you check your rearview mirror about every 15 seconds. Check your customers that often and you'll never disappoint."* Advice I have applied to other sectors in my career.

Betty Yost was a gal from a large family. Her father worked as an accounting clerk at Port Ivory, the Proctor & Gamble plant on Staten Island. She was smart, pretty, quick-witted, and very popular in school. She had a wonderful sense of humor, often laughing harder and louder than the people around her. We hit it off magnificently because we just plain liked each other, and our families welcomed each of us into their homes. She had to clean the house every Saturday and I would often pedal my way over the 20 or so blocks to her house after work, (on a better bike, by then) to see her and, just incidentally, to get to know her mother. Edith Yost was an outgoing Irish lady who loved her Schaefer beer. We attended a lot of church together, and as the years went by, our teenage friendship got to the point that our mothers — and just about everyone we knew — assumed we would marry one day. They were right ...

CHAPTER EIGHT

Sous les Lois de Minerve ...

Hal and I were close pals all through high school, but came from different sides of the track, one might say. He was a fine athlete, and could swish baskets coolly from the corner on a regular basis. He lived in a big white house in an impressive neighborhood with late model cars in most garages. He also had a television set and would invite me to watch baseball games with his father, Mr. Olsen, or Happy Olsen, as he liked to be called. Mr. Olsen always went out of his way to make me feel welcome, and those visits were a highlight for me. His mother was classy and kind as well. Happy Olsen worked for an investment firm headed by Mr. Frank Bailey, who had held a pro bono position for decades as Treasurer of one of the country's oldest but least known private colleges — Union College in Schenectady.

In addition, Mr. Bailey personally provided scholarships to Union — at the time an all-male college — to the sons of his employees who could qualify academically. Hal's brother, Donald, was such a recipient. Happy Olsen liked me, or more importantly, liked the fact that I was so hardworking. He often joked about Hal's reluctance to get a job. One day, he mentioned Union and asked me where I intended to go to college. I told him my college nest egg amounted to $40, so it looked like Wagner Community College would be my likely choice. His response was, *"Don't go to Wagner, you should attend Union."* That seemed an impossible pipe dream, so more out of courtesy than reality, I replied *"Yes, I certainly would like to apply."* He then set up a meeting between his 80-(plus)-year-old philanthropist boss and this wet-behind-the-ear 17-year-old.

When I showed up in Mr. Bailey's office in Manhattan, I found it decorated wall to wall with Union College memorabilia. I was greeted by a vibrant, short and stocky man, complete with a large handlebar mustache, who reached out and gave me a handshake that almost knocked me over! We sat down and I listened while nervously noting the open bottle of Ballantine's Scotch protruding from the desk drawer at his right knee. Before I could utter a squeaky word, he told me that Happy had said nice things about me and that I was the absolute perfect candidate for Union because too many students were *"spoiled by money, had an annoying habit of racing back to their Long Island mansions on weekends instead of attending team games, had little appetite for work and even less school spirit!!"*

He was so excited, I practically expected him to break out into the school song! That interview is eternally etched in my memory as an important turning point in my life. I had just experienced the first of many kindnesses extended to me by people I hardly knew. I began to think I might be going to Union! A week later, Union's legendary Dean Bill Huntley wrote me an acceptance letter, which came with a Bailey scholarship! (Many years later, when I made my first major gift to Union, it was in Happy Olsen's name.)

Among scholars, and throughout academia in America, Union College, in Schenectady, New York, is known as one of the finest. I will not try to recite its laurels, because I cannot possibly be objective or unbiased. For me it was one of those *"best time and place"* experiences. I mean here I was, an unsophisticated, flat broke, 17-year-old, and I had just been offered full tuition to one of America's leading institutions of higher learning, along with a peak into the fancy well-bred club of upward mobility. I was nervous, but also excited. I knew full well that I was in over my head, punching above my weight class, but that just made the challenge more exciting. I never thought I would have trouble with my grades, since I never had in the past. When Dean Huntley addressed the incoming class he told us to look left and right, warning, *"One of the three of you is not likely to make it here."* I never gave it a thought. I was more concerned about being perceived as a social *"hick"* among all of these slick wealthy classmates, most of whom came from prep schools whose very existence I was unaware of. The Dean was right; the fellow to my left — one of three from Staten Island — flunked out after our freshman year.

The scholarship covered tuition, but I had to pay for my own room and board. Mr. Karl Jonz, who was the President of a small bank across from the Post Diner where I worked, liked the way I served him breakfast, and always took an interest in my plans and future. One day, as a complete surprise, he invited me across the street and before I knew it, gave me a small orange card to sign, telling me that I now had $300 in an account, with my own checkbook!! All I had to pay was some interest each quarter. Another gift right out of the blue! I now had my $40 "nest egg" from my Mom, plus $300. Even so, I had to find a school job. The Rathskeller was an on campus restaurant, and that was a cinch. I got a job there almost immediately, bought some clothes, and moved into a dorm. Everything was working out well, even my acceptance by classmates — Gerry Barandes, Al Goldberger, Bill Burns, Tony Tartaglia and others who remain friends to this day. With Hal's help, introductions and contacts were abundant. I finally pledged Psi Upsilon, because they offered more work possibilities. Hal pledged Sigma Phi, which worked out fine because together we had two of the best houses covered. I, nonetheless, ran out of money about eight months in. The Rathskeller didn't pay enough so I started selling shoes downtown part time. Mr Jonz' money was running low, but I made a point of keeping my interest payments up to date. Across from one of the school's main gates was a restaurant called Eddie Diamonte's, serving pizza, pasta and beer.

I had gotten to know Eddie because I ate there occasionally, ducking the school meal plan as too costly. One night I sat there with Eddie and told him I might be taking a year off because of money. This prompted another gift. *"Didn't you used to work diners in NY?"* he asked. *"Yes I did, for a long* time," I replied. *"You know, my brother Frank wants to get out of his kitchen job. I need someone to run the dinner hour. You know how to do pizza, right?"* he asked. *"Absolutely,"* I lied. Though I had watched hundreds being made, I had never done one. *"Frank can show you how our oven works."* Again, luck shone on me. *"If you run the kitchen from 5 to 10 p.m., and fill in for me at the bar, I can pay you 60 bucks a week, plus all you can eat. I also have a room upstairs where you can live ... and the baker can leave you donuts and milk every morning! What d'ya say?"* Eddie was a lifesaver. He even paid me when the school closed down for holidays. I cleaned out the room upstairs, bought a bed and dresser, and was well situated. Beautiful! I got the house and grounds job at my frat house and finished my first year. That summer I raked Staten Island beaches every morning from 7 a.m. to noon and operated a diner all night alone, with weekends free to spend time with Betty. I made good money that summer, but when I returned to Union, Eddie confessed he no longer had the kitchen job open and, furthermore, a barfly who owed him money was occupying the room upstairs. That was disappointing, but again, luck was breaking my way. I went back to the Rathskeller, working with a good guy named Tom O'Dell, who gave me an important tip. A few months into my second year, Tom had asked me if I wanted his prime shift, because he now had a great job as a page for the local TV station, WRGB. He told me the pages were paid good money to help the station avoid unionization, and he gave me the name of the man hiring — Henry Solomon. A few days later, sitting in Mr. Solomon's office, I learned to my chagrin that the page staff was full. But I knew Mr. Solomon liked me, because he suggested I call back from time to check on the situation. I took him at his word ... to the extreme. I called him like clockwork every two weeks for months. Then one lunchtime at the fraternity house came a shout, *"Telephone for Beuth."* It was Mr. Solomon. When we next spoke in his office, he said that he had never known anyone so persistent ... and he liked that. I could have a page job, but there was a catch. He could not allow pages to leave for summers anymore. He needed someone he could count on 52 weeks a year, and if I agreed to start in May, and stay in Schenectady through the summer, I would be head of the small department by fall. I thought about Betty, hoping she would understand. She did not, of course. In one of the best, hardest decisions in my young life, I took the job. Eventually convincing Betty it was the right choice, I found another page who could cover for me on Fridays or Mondays every three weeks or so to go home. It was just a lowly page job, but I viewed it as a tremendous opportunity to extend myself, and it became one of the most important career moves I ever made. For the next two years, I lived the job, expanding its scope, learning by conversation and action. I worked eight-hour shifts, but hung around many extra hours on my own, absorbing everything I could about this exciting new business. During the daily live dance band show, I sat in the control room, observing directors to the point where I could, if invited, sit in with them. I was probably the longest running page the station ever employed — and all while still in college. What a lucky guy!

Often working the switchboard at night, alone except for the newsroom down the hall, my job included driving the station truck to the train station at precisely 9 p.m. each night to retrieve the "news package" of film footage from NBC News. The Hudson Line train would slow down, swing out a bag, and drop it for delivery to the station so we could have national news to augment our local coverage at 11. Teletype scripts conformed to the film. No matter what the weather, I was careful and reliable, getting an after-hours benefit of watching the news produced, and occasionally running out for pizza as well!

The job also entailed clearing the Teletype machines. Functioning like today's email, Teletype was a major mode of communication between stations and networks. One had to tear off the messages, separate and deliver them to the appropriate person. And since it was serious business, I did it very carefully. One night my attention to detail paid off nicely. While tearing off a sheet, a headline caught my eye. Two guests were due to visit GE and the station, celebrating GE's sponsorship of "True," a prime-time TV series on NBC. They were to tour the GE plant, its broadcast facility, appear on a talk show and attend an executive luncheon. As head of the tour staff, as soon as I read who the guests were, I excitedly assigned myself as guide to host actor (not yet Governor of California, much less President) Ronald Reagan, and more importantly to my fresh eyes, the second guest listed prominently on the subhead, none other than the commercial spokesman for Old Gold cigarettes — Red Barber! Wow!! This was a chance to show off how well I had done practicing my diction. What a lucky guy!

On the tour day, I was at my buttoned down best. The two celebrities were led directly to my golf cart from Mr. Hanna's limo, and off we went. I took them through GE's "backyard" turbine plant, recalling and reeling off just about every detail from the tour factsheet. Finally, when we were all done at the station and riding down in the elevator to leave, I gathered my courage and turned to my guest: *"Mr. Barber, we have met before, sir ... at the Jimmy Powers TV show in New York four years ago. I was 16 and had won a contest."* After a brief pause, he said, *"Yes, yes, I remember ... about baseball."* That bit of chatter brought us to the street as I added, *"That day you gave me a clear bit of advice."* His instant, smiling comment was, *"I probably suggested you lose that New York accent!"* No one could possibly imagine that my path would again cross that of both these men in the future and that my accent would become a running gag between Mr. Barber and me over the ensuing years ...

I was never close to being a star pupil at Union, partly because I had to wing it on exams in classes that were held after 2 o'clock because I worked 3 to 11 p.m. five or six nights a week all year. I never failed a class, as I recall. I am sure I finished somewhere in the middle academically, but never checked on that. English was my major, and I loved it as taught by two professors in particular. Professors Neimeyer and Blodgett have had a 60-year influence on me. The Union College experience helped me feel confident, complete and ready to compete in the marketplace of ideas. The education I received in terms of language skills, appreciation of literature, and the art of effective communication was remarkably valuable, and I will always remain in awe of my alma mater.

It taught me that though I was from a less advantaged background, I could compete — even excel — if I applied myself with diligence, zeal and integrity to the tasks at hand. I could not have made a better choice. I cherish Union as an important part of my life. Minerva, the school's patron goddess, is noted for her devotion to the arts and sciences and, above all, to justice. She smiled on me during my four years at Union. And the school motto, generally cited in the French, *"Sous les lois de Minerve nous devenons tous frères"* translates as *"We all become brothers under the laws of Minerva."* It could not have been more true in my case.

Union was a four-year program, and Betty's nursing degree was three. We both started in 1950, and she visited me occasionally at Union, with her mother, of course. When she finished her degree we married on Sept. 5, 1953. Hal Olsen was our best man. We had a sheet cake and my Uncle Roy had a drink or two, generally unobserved. We received $200 in cash wedding gifts and took off to a nice motel on a lake in New Jersey in a Nash Rambler that a cameraman at WRGB had lent us. Then we toured the Adirondacks for a few days before I reported back to Union. We moved into the married section of the Union campus and Betty got a job at the local hospital, while Hal and I started our fourth year of college. She practiced nursing for only a few years, on and off, until children came along, unplanned, but welcome. Belleview Hospital's Nursing program in New York City was widely acclaimed to be the best, but for many, it carried with it in the 1950s a terribly unfortunate aspect of the profession. Everyone smoked extensively, perhaps brought on by the pressures of long hours. Betty Beuth developed an addiction that lasted throughout her life, with sad consequences. She never did defeat her Kent cigarette dependency, but was a wonderful wife and mother, nevertheless.

CHAPTER NINE

The Nunnery

Ruth Bassett answered the phone and told me that Mr. Tom Murphy, Manager of WROW-TV at Hudson Valley Broadcasting in Albany, would like to see me about a position. *"Yes, tomorrow at 11 a.m. would be fine."* I scooped my few remaining coins off the bar at Hurley's and, after the parking and some gas for my Studebaker, realized I did not have enough money for the 90-cent toll on the recently opened New York Thruway. So I chose the winding but familiar U.S. Route 9W that snakes up the Hudson and spent the night with a fraternity brother in Albany. The next morning, the station's tower was clearly visible off Route 4 in North Greenbush. The access road was single-lane, unpaved and rutted. After crossing farmer Kelb's chicken- and dog-inhabited front yard, I drove another while through barren farmland before arriving at the edifice that housed the studios and offices of WROW-TV, known colloquially as "The Nunnery."

Much ink has been devoted to this Charles Adams structure and its remarkable history. In prior years, it had served as a home for retired nuns — hence the name. An enterprising Harry Goldman had purchased the ramshackle building and promptly pulled out and placed all the nun's 42 bathtubs on the front lawn, where he began selling them for $1 a piece.

Goldman had also converted the chapel into a studio, keeping the oak-stained pews, and he transformed the rest of the building into the offices of his radio and television company. Mr. Murphy, who now ran the enterprise, decided with characteristic frugality to only paint the public side of the building, leaving the backside, which was hidden from view by the dense forest and brush bordering the Hudson River, to languish in moldy discoloration. The building's fire escape consisted of an uncertain two-by-four structure accessible through one of the office windows. And the building's only "facility" was a 6-by-10 unisex bathroom. Our headquarters' motley appearance spawned an unwritten but sanctified rule. *No client visits ... ever!!* And, oh yes, large umbrellas were doled out, not so much to shield employees from the fickle upstate New York weather, but to protect studio camera operators from the periodic roof leaks inside the building! It was a strange ungainly, incongruous operation, but I needed a job, my shoes were shined, and I was excited and ready!

When I arrived at her desk, Ms. Bassett told me that Mr. Murphy was not available, but Mr. Goldman would see me. Not so hot, I thought, not knowing who he was. Black loafers crossed on the desk, green plaid jacket, cigar in hand, bowtie, black glistening hair streaked with gray, Harry Goldman waived me in while shouting into the phone, *"Chester, you are one stupid ass."* As he hung up, he said, *"That's my dearest friend,"* and then he looked up at me, eyebrows cocked in an expression of curiosity. We shook hands and I sat, not sure what to expect. Nervously, I offered my very well prepared resume, compliments of WRGB's new IBM Selectric typewriter. Included was a great head shot of me and just the right quantity of data designed to stimulate interest. What happened next provided us with some humorous retelling for years. Harry studied the single sheet, nodding his head in seeming approval, sucking his teeth audibly, and finally said, *"Very pretty, very pretty. I never saw a prettier resume!"* Then he wadded up the page in his well manicured fingers, pitched it across the room in the vague direction of a waste basket, looked up at me and bellowed, *"But what in hell makes you think you are a salesman?"* Neither of us could ever accurately recall my response, but we enjoyed inventing some creative ones for years. He toyed with me for a half hour, thoroughly enjoying himself, putting me through the paces with questions about what I had done in college, grad school, and at WRGB-TV. Finally he confessed, *"Tom told me to hire you — $60 a week as a film editor. We are only on the air from 7 to 11 p.m., and it is all movies. We have a lot of work to do here and I hope you have some fun. I also hope you can edit film!"* I liked the man, feeling a friendship had been born.

My first day of work at the Nunnery was Monday, Oct. 9, 1955. I was assigned a small cubicle in which there were two sets of 16 millimeter rewinds, a vintage viewfinder, and a couple of wheeled carts, slotted to hold film reels. My job was to prepare these feature films for airtime. It was routine work; not at all difficult and in about a week, all carts were prepped and ready for the next two weeks. A few days after starting, Mr. Murphy introduced himself. He was eager to know how and what I was doing, and he gave me the impression he was pleased to have me there. He then told a story that he repeated often. I knew he loved telling it: *"Bob Hanna asked me to play golf when I came to town. He's a nice fella,"* is the way it usually started. *"He told me he was gonna do me a favor, and suggested we hire you till his hiring freeze was over."* And that's how I became Tom Murphy's very first hire. As far as I know, the freeze never thawed.

Time went on, and soon we were a true competitive presence in the market. I paid back the grad school tuition, $100 at a time, maintained a good relationship with GE, and sent a poinsettia to the Hannas in Shelbyville, Indiana, each Christmas. Once again, I was favored by folks who cared, ready to go the extra mile for me — a lucky guy!

I moved our young family into a nice apartment out in the country, 10 minutes from the station. My dear wife Betty had blessed us with a second boy, Barry, when Phil was 14 months old. The clothesline, full of whites, stretched a long way out the window, tethered on each side by tall pines.

"Murph," (no longer Mr. Murphy), came to visit again, this time asking if I knew anything about Public Service programming. Naturally, I did, and he gave me a $5 a week raise and asked me to add that to my duties. That was it! The two-minute conversation was all the direction I got ... and all I needed. Within a month, I became a producer/director as we expanded our programming. I found a small office upstairs, joined the Albany Junior Chamber of Commerce and began putting faces to the pack of 3-by-5 cards I made, noting contacts from the region's nonprofits. From the arts to the zoo, to all manner of civic associations, we now had a growing file of charitable organizations. That was an assignment Murph was wise to have made. Eighteen months later, our application for a nascent VHF license was being reviewed by the FCC and challenged by Veterans Broadcasting. Those contact cards and the programming we had created provided our lawyers with just the right ammunition to make our case in front of the FCC hearing in Washington. It also placed me — the youngest member of the team — at ground zero for a bunch of fancy Washington dinners with prominent people and a view of a new, more sophisticated, and even wealthier world! When we won our case, Murph gave me a bonus of $350, plus seats to two World Series games, where we were seated right next to heavyweight boxing legend, Rocky Marciano! It also started a new phase for me, as Murph began to give me more and more ad hoc assignments to add to my producer/director chores. I began to feel pretty good about the crapshoot Murph had joined, as the vision for a bold new company began to take shape.

I remember distinctly a presentation we made together to the local TV repair association, where Murph talked about the young company, and I operated the projector. Before the meeting at a VFW hall, we were waiting at the bar. Tom asked if I would join him for a drink. I hesitated, and then said I would have a rye and ginger. *"A what?"* Tom asked. *"Well,"* I answered, *"the only one in my family who drinks is my Uncle Roy, a plumber, and that is what he orders."* Tom motioned to the bartender, *"Give him a Cutty and soda!"* I drank it and discovered an acceptable drink to order for many years! (Incidentally sometime later, Murph gave up alcohol completely.)

Other important events were unfolding for the company far from Albany. While much tribute has been paid over decades to "The Nunnery Days" from '55 to '60, their importance did eventually diminish as the company grew. But for those of us who were there at the outset, when things were fragile, when Murph continually predicted that his dream of a great company where we all could get "rich" was possible, it was a rare, indelible bonding experience. I was one of those lucky ones, along with folks who stayed with us like Jim Mascucci, Mark Edwards, Larry Pollock, Ralph Vartigan, John Stewart and a handful of others, who were able to see the company start to achieve its extraordinary potential. Murph was great at sharing information about the company with our small corps of employees, but he also availed himself liberally of me, as one of his favorite conduits. And I was certainly an enthusiastic and excited messenger. Before long, Murph was traveling almost constantly, busy with a series of acquisitions. In June of 1957, he announced that Frank Smith had bought WTVD-TV in Durham, North Carolina, adding some new talent like Frank Fletcher, Harmon Duncan and Mike Thompson to his roster of star executives. With this new station, (and others to follow), Murph would send me to film an announcement about the acquisition with Lowell Thomas. The first time I filmed Lowell, I put a world globe and a P38 mic on a desk, with flowers in the background. His reaction was, *"No desk ... I stand ... boom mic please."* These news films were sent to all our stations and any others who would air them. Lowell, in front of a world map or desk, would announce, *"Hello everybody, this is Lowell Thomas, happy to announce that Hudson Valley Broadcasting has purchased DUB YA TVD in Durham, North Carolina, joining DUB YA ROW in Albany, New York."* Even later, when we were Capital Cities, and purchased the WPRO stations in Providence, Rhode Island, he did his *"DUB YA PRO in Providence,"* etc. (He never needed a cue card, by the way.)

Back home in the newsroom, while editing the clips, I would get teased about Lowell's approach to the letter "W." My response was, *"You can be sure I'm not gonna correct him."* Over the next few years, I traveled quite regularly with Lowell, and after a while he even learned to accurately pronounce my name! His long time assistant, Electra, was terrific. Lowell was a class act. No talent ever impressed me more, and I was one fortunate dude to enjoy his presence for years!

I began directing and producing all kinds of programs and, as I recall, getting regular raises as my duties evolved. When our schedule expanded and we needed help, I called some former broadcasting classmates from Syracuse. We hired Marvin Mews, George Mitchell and Jim Johnson, all of whom though multitalented, were with us for only a few years. Before meeting Frank Smith, Harry had hired a small core of people to run his struggling station. Included on the team were some who really cared and worked hard to better the company. However, others just put in the time at low pay. Among those who cared was Charles "Gig" Pogan, a fine and talented program director to whom I reported. Even though I had been Murph's personal hire, I was careful to respect Gig's position, and loved working for him. He was well suited to the needs of the station, since he was a walking almanac of movies, stars, and Hollywood lore. I loved the guy! I was not alone in my admiration of Gig. Many Nunnery alums who moved up through the ranks of the company, remained close to him for years, even after he made the ill-advised choice of early retirement rather than a promotion involving relocation.

There were so many unique aspects of the Albany days that taught me important lessons and so many memories of rare events. Lowell had a disdain for crowds, but he also owned a box at the Saratoga Raceway, right at the finish line next to those of Fred Astaire and Jock Whitney. He regularly held forth from his prominent box during weekdays, but never on Saturday, when most of the classic races were run. Guess whom Murphy assigned to handle the box and its tickets for Lowell? For several years, often with clients or our sales team, I filled the box every Saturday in August, hobnobbing with the A list. Some thought I was Lowell's son, until they saw that I did not tip as well as LT! A great memory of a precious time.

Although I was not aware of it at the time, the company lost serious dollars in its first years of operation and had to go back to its investor pool twice for funds to continue. Finally, in 1957, Murphy was able to announce our first profitable year, with pretax surplus reported to be $56,000. At that point, all employees were invited to purchase stock at $5.75 a share. And to encourage participation, the company offered loans with an attractive repayment plan to cover purchase of the first 100 shares. I borrowed the money, bought the shares, and encouraged all to do the same. Because the company did not pay lavish salaries, employee turnover was common. Besides, the industry was bursting with opportunities as more and more stations joined the airwaves. Along the way, we attracted a number of exceptional talents who helped us grow between '56 and '60. Perhaps none was more remarkable than a fellow we hired from Providence who got his start at the Nunnery and then moved on to fame and fortune in Hollywood. He was a man of Polish descent, named Tadeus ...

ꙹ ⌘ ꙶ

First stock issued - March 1957

$5.75 per share

CHAPTER TEN

Mr. Konopka

The entertainment world does not remember him as Tadeus Konopka, nor perhaps by his stage name, Ted Knight, but it certainly does remember him as the hilarious stuffed-shirt (Emmy award-winning) straight man, Ted Baxter, on "The Mary Tyler Moore Show" in the 1970s. I simply remember him as a dear friend.

We met in 1957 when he joined our young, creative production team at the Nunnery, and our friendship remained vibrant until his premature death in 1986. Of all the performing artists I have been fortunate to meet, work with, or enjoy, Ted Knight was at the top of the heap. He was a very talented, kind and thoughtful fellow, whom my family loved like a favorite uncle. Once we expanded our afternoon original programming at WROW-TV in Albany, Ted became a priceless resource who relished the work, especially the multiple hats he wore, including one as a ventriloquist. He had charming hand puppets and worked them proficiently ... so long as the director avoided close-ups of Ted's mouth while the puppets were talking! There is a true story that will linger in the annals of Capcities as long as Nunnery stories are told and retold. One afternoon, when his routines were not getting the reaction Ted expected, he finally complained to the control room. Apparently no one in the booth had noticed that the sound dropped out whenever his prime puppet, Bernard, was speaking. This obviously affected the success of the routines. After a bit of sleuthing, they discovered why Ted was "off mic" each time Bernard spoke. We had recently hired a new boom operator who was diligently redirecting the mic toward Bernard's little sock mouth each time the puppet spoke! The next day that boom operator reclaimed his grocery-packing job at the local supermarket. That is a true story. I was there!! At 3:30 each day, five days a week, Ted became "Officer Ted" on the "Clubhouse" set we'd built in a small room adjacent to the chapel studio. It consisted of a wooden fence painted with stick figure kids, leading to a sentry telephone booth with open windows on the front and on both sides at elbow height. Through these openings, Ted could operate his puppets using his right hand. When Bernard, his star puppet had a "friend" visit, a producer, like me, would operate the guest puppet through the left opening. Marvin Mews, a fellow grad from Syracuse, alternated producer/director duties with me on this daily show. The producer wrote the scripts and worked the studio (and an occasional sock puppet) on week one, while the director handled cameras and mics, etc. We swapped functions every week.

The producer role was the more challenging, but Marvin and I enjoyed all facets of the work. I absolutely loved the job and can recall Betty calling me many times from the bedroom, reminding me it was late as I lay on the living room rug, dreaming up comical situations and pulling jokes from books written by people like Robert Orben.

During the course of the afternoon, we programmed 30 minutes of cartoons, but that still left a lot of original programming time. Marvin and I would prepare our outlines and scripts on yellow legal pads and give them to a wonderful assistant named Beverly Bianco Kennedy to type. Often when I handed the typed rundown to Ted, he would stand in a studio doorway, sometimes weighing the script in his hand, muttering, *"two minutes over."* He would read it while uttering occasional grunts or sighs, and then invariably say something like, *"You mean a man of my talent has to read stuff like this?"* A chorus from our small production bullpen would shout back, *"Just read it, Ted!"* His response: *"OK!"* This was pure "Ted Baxter." He later claimed that his MTM audition was based on a prominent LA TV anchorman, but we knew the truth, having enjoyed exclusive previews and lots of laughs from the very same "Ted Baxter" for years before he ever joined the show. It was a shame that there was no videotape back then because the shows were reasonably creative examples of early live television. Years later, the producers of "The Mary Tyler Moore Show" called me, hoping to find some copies on kinescope. They had cooked up a plot twist where Baxter's twin brother was a weatherman back in Albany. Alas, I had to tell them there were no records of all that original work.

At precisely 4:28 each day, "Clubhouse with Officer Ted" ended with a two-minute cartoon, which was essential, as Ted had to change costumes for the next bit. After the break, Ted would reappear, this time wearing overalls and a Gabby Hayes beard as "Windy Knight," sitting on the porch of a log cabin we painted on 4-by-8 plywood panels. In a salty western twang, "Windy," sandwiched between clips of Roy Rogers, Bob Steele, and other cowboys, would call on his faithful "buckaroos" and "whippersnappers" to mind their mothers, do their school work and practice the Golden Rule. No one seemed bothered by the anachronistic bottle of Pepsi that commonly adorned the set. At the end of each show Windy would waive his hand goodbye through a cabin window ... because Ted was already dressed for his next role as the "Atlantic Weatherman." The local news began with Ted, standing next to a gas pump, singing, *"For business or pleasure, in any kind of weather, Atlantic keeps your car on the go!"* In addition to juggling all those characters, Ted did live commercials and hosted or introduced all manner of movies and specials. On the talent side, he was almost all we had, and we didn't need much more! More importantly, we got lots of positive viewer reaction in the form of fan mail – very exciting for our young station.

Ted was an important part of our audience growth, complementing our recent CBS affiliation. While that growth was accompanied by some staff hiring, wages were still low and Ted was not happy with his salary. He was making about $150 a week and kept asking me what to do about it. Finally, I told him he had to go talk to Murph, who was a very fair man and would level with him. So, one afternoon Ted announced he was ready and was on his way upstairs to have a talk with Mr. Murphy. An hour later, he returned, quite energized. After telling me what a nice man Tom was, he said that he had been told that a raise would be the worst thing that could happen because it would keep him in Albany, when he really needed to be out in Hollywood, working in the big leagues. None of us could argue with that. A month later, many of us joined Ted and his wife Dottie for a picnic in the yard of his rented house. In the driveway was his station wagon, loaded right up to the roof rack with all the worldly goods he planned to take with him as he moved the family out west.

Fortunately, the station had some backup talent to fill the void, including Ralph Vartigan, John Stewart, George Leighton and others who took over and remained on-air stalwarts for many years at the channel. We often remarked that it took three or four talents to replace one Tadeus Konopka. I talked to Ted often over the next months as he hustled himself around Hollywood. He did an episode as a crazed killer in the series "The F.B.I." and a long stint as a military officer on a daytime soap. He also became the answer to a Hollywood trivia question: *What comic actor stood on guard outside the detective's office in one of the last scenes of Hitchcock's, 'Psycho'?" "Yep, Ted Knight"* ... and they showed a photo of him dressed like our dear Officer Ted!

When he landed the Ted Baxter role, I sent a telegram, telling him no one had ever been so perfectly cast. He had been honing that role for years. Then, after he became famous, the fun really started! He never forgot us, wherever our careers took us. After Mary Tyler Moore, Ted helped me with station promotions and benefits in future markets. We even managed to earn a few dollars doing radio or TV station promotion spots together. When people called him, he would refer them to me. We would develop amusing scripts like, *"Hi, this is Ted Baxter … whenever I'm in Boston, I always listen to those great hockey games on WBZ, inning after inning!"* Or, *"My favorite news associate, Roger Rocka, is the best in Central California. Roger Rocka … sounds like a candy bar."* We had a pal named Bob Hesse in LA, who would produce these spots, and a rep would sell them to the stations. This was not a regular thing, and depended on Ted's availability, but for a time between MTM and his next series, I would get occasional calls asking for him. PR agents would ask if Ted could make an appearance on a Saturday at a shopping center or major retailer. I remember one call, asking if Ted could do an appearance at an Eaton's in Toronto, since he was already scheduled to do a benefit in Buffalo. They offered $7,500. I called and asked Ted. His response was *"You know, Phil, I do not go to the mailbox for less than $10,000 anymore."* *"Yes, Ted, yes, I know, but do you want it?"* The answer was always, *"Of course, first class air."* Later, wherever I was based, he was a frequent house and station guest. He liked the down to earth folks in Buffalo, especially the Polish ladies of the Variety Club, who would cluster around him at a venue like the local VFW hall and listen to him tell jokes in Polish! He did a telethon with Burt Reynolds for the Children's Hospital in Buffalo that was a record setter. A lifelong health addict, Ted often chided my wife Betty about her smoking, and was always careful about his own diet. I do not remember him ever using alcohol. Late in his career, in the early 1980s, we loved him as Judge Smails in "Caddyshack."

His death from cancer in August '86 at the age of 62, was a shock. I knew he'd been struggling with health issues, but he dismissed them as minor in our last phone conversation earlier that year. He was one of the many remarkable people I have been blessed to know.

His picture, with my daughter at 4 years old, occupies an important place on the wall of my den.

CHAPTER ELEVEN

Adios Productions

Wow! Those months flew by at an alarming rate during my early years at the Nunnery. Betty and I were wonderfully blessed when a third boy, Bob, was born in November 1957. That completed the hat trick, making things hectic on all fronts. Betty proved a perfect, if harried mother of three boys under the age of 5, handling the home front while juggling the start of a modestly active social life. All indications from Murph were that the company was beginning to gain momentum. He shared the information that both Albany and Durham were meeting cash flow projections. I was reassigned from the afternoon/evening shift to mornings as producer/director. My day began overseeing early news at 7 a.m., followed by "Captain Kangaroo" and "Romper Room" — both with live commercials — then more news. The shift ended at 2 p.m., but I often spent afternoons firming up my relationships at Clubs like Rotary and The Junior Chamber of Commerce, where I held a couple of committee assignments. Continuing to build my Public Service files, I became active with United Cerebral Palsy, and other nonprofits. Along the way, I met hundreds of wonderful earnest, committed, motivated individuals. But as a broadcaster attached to a responsible communications company, I was not only similarly motivated, but more importantly, had the facilities and resources to help make a real difference. That afforded me a unique advantage and considerable leverage in the realm of community work. And while most of the young executives I met were more sophisticated and worldly than I, being in the media allowed me to exude self-confidence. I found myself less and less concerned about my modest roots and upbringing or "station in life" and increasingly confident about the role I was molding for myself in business. At the same time, I was abiding by a founding principle of our company's mission statement, as codified in our broadcast license. Using the power of my industry to do well was now becoming a central part of my DNA.

My salary was also evolving ... albeit slowly. I earned $175 a week, not luxurious for a family of five, even in those early times. So I decided to do some moonlighting, selling shoes on Saturday to bring in extra cash. One day, during a Chamber lunch, I met a man named Joe O'Connor who worked at General Electric. When he learned I was a television producer, he became intrigued: *"Could you help me with a sales problem?"* Joe's assignment at GE was the marketing of a new, computer-driven industrial product, called the Base Plate Drilling Machine. Thus far, according to Joe, in order to sell the cumbersome machine, GE had to bring prospective clients all the way to the plant in Schenectady to view it in operation. It was a massive machine with a level platform that moved a plate right or left, while a drum-like drill press moved up or down to drill various sized holes in the plate. As soon as I saw the apparatus, it was clear that a 15-minute color film that could be sent all over the country as a sales tool might well do the trick. Joe got very excited, *"How much would a film like that cost?"* I sucked in my breath, crossed my fingers and took a wild stab — $30,000, plus cost of prints. Joe had never seen my work. Truth be told, I had only produced one black and white film in grad school! But Joe called me the next day to say GE accepted my offer! I wrote a simple one-page memo on personal letterhead, confirming the project, and then began to think about how I could accomplish what I had so glibly promised.

In our station's tiny film department was a very experienced Dutch cinematographer named Jean Berghman. Jean was older, had been in the Dutch resistance during the war, did superior work, and even had his own small studio downtown. I went to Jean and proposed a 50-50 joint venture: I would write and produce and he would do the camerawork. We shook hands on the deal. Then, I went to Murph to reassure him this assignment would not interfere with my duties. Tom, knowing my situation — a young family, lots of responsibility, a fair amount of ambition — approved. I called the company Adios Productions because often as I left the station at 2 o'clock, Murph would lean out his office window and shout, *"Adios, Philly!"*

We started by painting the gargantuan machine a nice green color, then found some music to accompany the movement of the panels, and gave our station anchorman $100 to do the narration. Some simple animation jazzed up the GE logo and

Jean's brilliant camerawork gave the iron shavings that peeled off the drill into spiral curls sparkling colors! It was a smash hit and delightful to watch. We split the profits and made additional money on the prints we supplied. In all, we netted $13,000 each for a month's work after hours at night. Joe O'Conner became a hero over at GE and later told me his higher ups thought the film was worth twice what they'd paid. When I told Tom I was sorry I hadn't charged more, he graced me with one of his precious pearls: *"Philly, always try to make others look good, because when they profit, so do you. And always leave something on the table."* His words did not fall on deaf ears of his young, eager protégé.

We then got two other jobs; One with the Troy School System, and then a biggie — the main exhibit of the State Department of Weights and Measures at the New York State Fair in Syracuse. This time, a public relations man, whose name I do not recall, phoned me up. He was under pressure to get something done for an exhibit on Labor Day, and asked if we could create a film that would run on a continuous loop during their exhibit. I collected some information, wrote a script overnight, and off Jean and I went, shooting in late afternoons around Albany dairies and farms. It fell together quite nicely, and was our best work by far. The half hour color film, called "The Protecting Eye," showed how the quality of bean and milk production was carefully monitored and guaranteed. The finished program ran on TV channels throughout New York State for years. We charged $40,000 and when the end of the year came, so did a request for new prints, changing the end credits to reflect a set of new state government officials. Lucky again!

By this time, Jean and I were tempted to break out and create our own shingle. It was 1960. Tom was aware that I was doing well with Adios Productions, and that I had just purchased a new home for $12,500. Despite that, I made sure he knew I was committed to him and the company long term. He continually went out of his way to expose me to our Chairman, Frank Smith, and to inform me of the corporation's growing fortunes. I read all I could about our company and began to understand the importance of cost controls and bottom lines. I remembered Smitty's advice: *"The best defense against revenue uncertainties are constant, tight cost controls."*

I felt great loyalty to the company and to Tom, but, at the same time, Jean and I were on a roll and tempted to take on more business. Then, an opportunity arose that put Murph and Adios at loggerheads. Jean and I had seen a lecture by a local doctor who showed off his work with animals in Africa, using a carousel slide projector. After seeing the lecture I sold the doctor on the idea of creating a full color sound film shot during his next African safari. Without hesitation, he accepted … for a fee of $50,000!

Jean had been pressing me to get Murph's permission, as I was tardy getting my ducks in line to make the climb upstairs and seek his blessing. Finally, alone with Tom in his office, I made the pitch. I told him about the Africa shoot and how I could cover my shifts without subjecting the company to any overtime while I was away. When I finished, Tom said something I will never forget:

"Philly, you know you have a job with me regardless ... And I know how much you like to fool around with cameras and such, but I have bigger plans for you. If you want to continue filming in your off hours here, that is OK, but if you want to grow with this company you have to consider what I say now carefully. We are building a great company and we are all going to get rich. I want you with us, not 8 hours a day, but 24 and we want you to grow with us, full time, all the time."

When I said I'd like to talk it over with my wife, he came straight back, *"I did not hire your wife. I want a decision here and now."*

I took a deep breath, got up, reached across his desk, shook his hand and said, *"I'm with you, Tom." "Good,"* he said, *"Starting tomorrow you have a new job and I'm doubling your pay. You will be the Assistant Promotion Manager."* I am sure my delight was apparent and I said all the right things, but I did add a question: *"We don't have a Promotion Department, and why Assistant?"* His response, accompanied by a warm smile, was, *"In time, Philly, in time. I don't want you to get a bigger head than you already have."* Again, what a lucky fella!

Then, for the kicker ... I got downstairs just as Jean ran up to me in a panic. *"You didn't talk to Tom, did you?"* He'd just gotten off the phone with his wife, who was asking him for a divorce! There was no way he could take off for Africa to do the film and he hoped he'd caught me before I went to see Tom.

I breathed a sigh of relief and imagined what it would have been like to trudge back up the stairs to Murph's office with my swelled head you know where!

CHAPTER TWELVE

Running the Table

One night, Tom took me to Frank Smith's favorite New York restaurant, a well-known steak house called Joe & Rose's. We joined Smitty and a couple of his friends for an evening of storytelling at his designated table. I sat and listened, fascinated as Frank held forth; an unlit cigarette in one hand, a tumbler with a couple of fingers of Tennessee mash in the other. One story stuck with me. Frank recalled a night when he and his wife met Mike Todd and Elizabeth Taylor for dinner at that grand dame of New York restaurants, the 21 Club. As they entered, Todd asked Frank if he had a $10 bill, which Frank quickly produced. When they got to ordering drinks, a man came to the table offering roses for each of the ladies, *"compliments of Mr. Todd."* They had been purchased with Frank's 10 spot! Frank told that story often with some degree of irony, because he claimed that although he'd invested with Todd on numerous occasions, none of those investments had ever earned him a dime! Still, he considered himself lucky and successful, because he'd lost less than everyone else who'd ever invested with Mike.

Smitty had a natural, soft-spoken charm, and I was a willing and excited sponge. He had a lot to reflect upon. His crapshoot was going well as the table kept serving up 7s and

11s, allowing the company to score points with the FCC, advertisers, and investors. From humble beginning in '54, good things continued to unfold. In one of Smith's memos to employees in '57, the final paragraph concluded, *"... expect further expansion."* Our three television stations in Albany, Raleigh/Durham and Providence, were all growing steadily and the "partnership" of our loyal band grew stronger as well. The company had jettisoned the name Hudson Valley Broadcasting and was now rechristened Capital Cities Broadcasting (as the three stations we owned were all in state capitals). Although it can be spelled both ways, Smitty preferred Capital with an "A" rather than an "O" because *capital,* in his book, stood for money. And as if by self-fulfilling prophesy, that is exactly what began to flow generously. In fact, cash flow, which became the bottom line indicator for the company's success, had been flirting with a million dollars by '59. Enthusiasm was rampant throughout the company, and Tom, who had his acquisition elephant gun always at the ready, was spending less and less time in Albany.

In my small corner of the world and the company, I kept busy setting up a new promotion operation at the channel. Not so difficult, as it consisted of obtaining fairly accessible collateral print and film materials for our slate of programming, packaging them with a theme, and getting them on the air. We had no print advertising budget, so making sure the newspapers got good information on our activities was important in getting gratis editorial coverage. It helped to know people at the newspapers, so I cultivated those contacts to ensure our network got as much space as possible. Several months into my new position, I was sent to see what could be done to help the promotion department in our Providence channel, only to learn that they were far ahead of us. I was the one who learned from that trip!

I was also invited to attend a management meeting at the venerable Pine Needles Golf Resort in Durham, where I was reminded that my humble upbringing contrasted sharply with the smart, affluent golf and country club crowd. But since I was the youngest, and had apparently handled a few tasks well, I got along just fine, aided by Smitty's always-benevolent attention. I remember that day well. Before dinner, about 20 of us gathered in a large room for cocktails, giving Smitty a chance to spread some of his delicious southern charm. All 5 feet 3 inches of him stood in stocking feet on the back of a sturdy couch, his right hand over his head, touching the ceiling. I stood in the back of the room, eyes and ears wide open, admiring his cool, when, to my complete surprise, he pointed to me with his free hand, and announced, *"Callaway bids are open, and Phil Beuth just made a $50 bid on my foursome,"* prompting raised glasses, and cheers! I had neither that much cash, nor any idea what a Callaway competition was, but that was Smitty, tending to his flock!! He also invited me for a ride in his golf cart, just the two of us for a talk, to make me feel welcome. He told me he was aware of my work and that he felt I was doing a *"fine job."* (Tom had apparently coached him well.) He repeated his philosophy, *"Hire as few of the best people available, pay them well, give* *them equity and autonomy in an ethical company and leave them alone."* Many years later, I saw a copy of a note, quoting Smitty. It went like this:

> *"Some of you fellows may think I tie you to Capital Cities by corrupting you with compensation and stock options. But I've decided the reason you are afraid to leave this company is more because our system naturally corrupts you with autonomy and authority. And I suspect that after living that way for a time, you're fearful that someplace else might not operate in the same manner."*

I don't remember feeling particularly corrupted, but at that point in my career, with five or six years at Capcities under my belt, even in my minor role, I felt I had enjoyed unprecedented autonomy and authority in an ever-expanding ethical and bustling company. It certainly did give me an appetite for more. In the years ahead, from 1960 to 1964, fantastic opportunities, along with the introduction to more remarkable people — all imbued with Frank's philosophy — would contribute to my maturity ... and to my continued corruption!

Late in 1960, Tom asked me to join him for a ride from Albany west to Buffalo. Some 40 years earlier, the Rev. Dr. Clinton Churchill, a televangelist minister, had established a Buffalo broadcast franchise under the call letters WKBW, which stood for Well Known Bible Witness. There was a strong 50,000 watt radio station, WKBW-AM, and a sister station WKBW-

TV on Channel 7. Both stations covered western New York State quite adequately, but as we drove west that day, Tom explained that while Buffalo was the primary target, there might be a bonus opportunity in the city of Toronto, Canada, across Lake Ontario.

By this time in its history the Churchill group's programming had become notably less religious. They were one of the area's most popular radio and television sources and, as an ABC affiliate, carried a wide range of entertainment and news that attracted thousands of viewers from Canada. Buffalo's live kids programs were particularly popular north of the border. Back in 1960, Television in Canada was in its infancy. It would be years before Canadian stations would grow dominant enough to properly serve their own constituency, so, for the time being, many Canadian households looked southward to the U.S. for their television programming. Out the window of Tom's Thunderbird, I got my first sight of the magnificent spectacle of Niagara Falls. And sure enough, when we got to the Canadian side, we came upon an overwhelming landscape of rooftop antennas, all pointed south! The possibility of luring more Canadian viewers to the Buffalo network seemed a tempting proposition. In addition, we discovered that the packaging for many nationally advertised TV brands was identical on both sides of the border — a fact we would later exploit to good advantage.

Frank and Tom captured this prize radio and television package for $14 million and received FCC approval in May of

1961. That opened a new chapter in the company's history, one that brought a trove of legendary on-air, sales and management personalities to the company. Over the next 10 years, people like Herb Mendelson, Jim Arcara, Warren Potash, Norm Schrutt, Tony Rocco, Tommy Fenno, Bill Campbell and Dick Rakovan did the management and selling, while on-air talents like Danny Neverath, Tom Shannon, Stan Roberts, Dick Biondi, Joey Reynolds and others fueled up a dynamic radio powerhouse. The climate was one of *"a will to win"* by an aggressive team of tough competitors. Down the hall, the TV gang with Bob King, Dick Sheppard, Irv Weinstein, Rick Azar, Tom Jolls, Cliff Fischer, Steve Zappia, Nolan Johannes, David Boreanaz, Peter Kerr, Liz Dribben and Ron Martzolf, were beginning to build their part of a broadcast machine which would go on to finance and staff many of the company's ensuing acquisitions. I may be wrong, but I am certainly close when I claim that at the time, no single Capcities operating entity was more responsible for generating profits than the Buffalo stations. The primary target had been Buffalo TV, along with its collateral Canadian viewers, but the unexpected windfall came courtesy of the robust and growing success of the radio station.

Buffalo may have been the butt of jokes in the press and on late night talk shows, but in Capital Cities management meetings, the laughing was all the way to the bank. Many of those who served there were impressed with the quality and strength of a diverse western New York population that had suffered through and survived the demise of the Rust Belt economy. Most of the original Capcities team looks back fondly on their Buffalo history, knowing that many future acquisitions were financed by freshly minted Buffalo nickels!

Frank Smith made some industry headlines in 1961 by obtaining the exclusive television rights to the Adolf Eichmann trial in Israel, and offering it to all stations at no charge. Tom plucked Marc Edwards from WTEN-TV to be the show host, proving again that he had faith in the young talent rising from our ranks.

Then, the company purchased WPAT-AM and WPAT-FM in Paterson, New Jersey, for $5 million in October 1961, giving us access to the New York market and advancement opportunities for people like Pete Newell, Aaron Daniels, Hal Deutch, Tom Cuddy, and Gary Berkowitz — all shining trophies for Smitty's talent showcase. The radio teams all continued to set records in sales and profits. In '64, we bought the Goodwill stations, WJR radio in Detroit and WSAZ-TV in Huntington. KPOL radio was added in '66, giving us six radio and four television stations.

Meanwhile, Murph continued to toss me varied company assignments. He called me to New York in October 1962, this time for a morning meeting at the Waldorf Astoria Hotel. In the room were several well-known political figures, including Leonard Hall, Chairman of the Republican National Committee. Also present were a half-dozen persons from Gov. Nelson Rockefeller's reelection campaign whose current target was a substantial plurality in the upcoming election, preparing him for a Vice Presidential run. The group announced that Richard Nixon, campaigning for Governor of California was planning a "Dial Dick Nixon" telethon the following weekend in San Diego; and they wanted some advice from their television "connection," Tom Murphy. Tom began by introducing *"one of the best telethon producers in the country"* — Me! Here we go again, I thought. I had produced maybe three telethons at that time, and none to write home about: *"Sky King and The Green Hornet? Please, Tom!"* Next thing I knew, I was buying a new shirt and tie, calling Betty to say I was heading to San Diego with Tom, including, to my delight, a stopover at the Sands Hotel in Vegas! On arrival, Tom gave me a $100 bill so I could try my luck in the casino, while he went to meet his pal, the hotel's manager, Jack Entrata. The money lasted a scant half hour, but the walk through the luxurious hotel was a revelation and a thrill. I was amazed at all that conspicuous consumption, the noisy gamblers and the free flowing money — a fancy adult playground for the rich!

The next day in San Diego, we were welcomed by more Republican officials and introduced to Mr. Nixon, who was pleasant enough, though reticent and remote. We watched an undistinguished telecast, contributed little more than moral support and moved on, having scored a few political points for the company. Back in New York, the committee thought it would be advisable for me to travel with the Rockefeller campaign and produce the "Ask Nelson" telethons in

Schenectady and Buffalo. Ironically, the first telecast was from my college workplace, WRGB-TV, and the second from WKBW-TV, which would become my home 14 years later! The Buffalo broadcast was scheduled for the night of Oct. 22, 1962, the very same night the Cuban Missile crisis erupted. President John F. Kennedy had just made his famous speech. Most questions understandably centered around the crisis, but Gov. Rockefeller did not want to talk about that. He handled himself well, stating privately that he had no facts, and would not shoot from the hip in such a critical situation. Pretty reasonable I thought. So, I began to pull questions about taxes, education and health from previous broadcasts. The Governor seemed to appreciate that. Otherwise, the Rockefeller telecasts were uneventful, except that they undoubtedly helped score political points for the company and they provided an unusual experience for me ... *"one of the best telethon producers in the country! Just ask Tom!"*

CHAPTER THIRTEEN

Red Skelton

As my work progressed, my duties proliferated and my future looked ever more promising. Our family of five settled into a new white Cape Cod in the comfortable Albany suburb of East Greenbush, where we joined the Methodist church and got our first dog, Skippy. As a church volunteer, putting together a brochure for a successful capital fundraising drive came naturally to me, as did coaching the East Greenbush Tigers to a Little League championship. My sons, Phil and Bob, along with a great little pitcher named Eddie Withkowski, helped us field an undefeated team. The Albany Times Union printed the team's victory picture, which proudly adorned my desk.

Tom continued to generously share news of the company's expansion and gave me total autonomy in my new sales and audience promotion job. When he became Chairman of the CBS Affiliate Board, he involved me there as well. He sent me as his stand-in for a weekend retreat at Saratoga Lake, where I was the only guest without VP stripes. I mingled as an apt listener while high-ranking CBS executives reviewed the network's affiliate affairs. On a break, I met a delightful man, who saw me fishing from the banks of Saratoga Lake, and asked for a few tips on handling a spinning rod. Dick Salant, President of CBS News, and I caught more than a few black bass that day! And I came back with other fish stories that likely contributed to my continued head swelling.

Shortly thereafter, I got a call from Tom asking — in typical cryptic fashion — if I would come to New York for a meeting at CBS. I was introduced to Kidder Meade, Executive Assistant to Frank Stanton, longtime President of CBS and the man widely considered the "conscience" of our industry. I learned that Mr. Stanton was to celebrate his 50th birthday and Tom had offered to help out with the organization of the event. We conferred with Kidder Meade, who'd been prepped by Tom's hyperbole, introducing me as one of the industry's *"best live event producers."* And that's just what was needed as this was not going to be any run-of-the-mill birthday. The event centerpiece was a live 90-minute extravaganza starring Red Skelton, whose weekly CBS show made him a TV superstar and household name. The show also starred the David Rose orchestra, the Skelton dancers, with comedy bits by Carol Burnett, Don Knotts, and Alan King — all held in the main ballroom of the Waldorf Astoria Hotel before a glittering black-tie audience of TV execs, socialites and politicians!

I was a bit apprehensive, but perhaps less so than Kidder Meade, who, I later learned, had hedged his bets by placing some of his seasoned watchdogs in the preliminary planning meetings. By show time, Kidder must have thought I was cutting the mustard, because on show day, I sat alone behind the director's console with no one behind me to snatch the headset in case of a screw-up! The show went off without a hitch, thanks in large part to a crew of experienced technicians, who I am sure kept wondering who the hell this new guy was at the control panel.

Red Skelton and I had only two short meetings. He was extremely kind. He had a joke in one of his routines that ended with his stomach being upset, so on cue, a close up of his face had to be drenched in a ghoulish green light, courtesy of gels from a couple of super trooper follow spots. The timing had to be right — this was comedy after all. It was simple to call but was all that concerned him. It went perfectly, as did the entire production. After the show, I asked Alan King how it felt to follow Carol Burnett. His answer was, *"I could follow Jesus Christ!!"*

After the show, although utterly exhausted, Red Skelton made a point of moving around the studio, thanking all the technicians. We stepped into an empty elevator together, just the two of us, heading for the top floor where CBS stars and senior brass were gathered for the after-party celebration of Mr. Stanton's birthday. But Red got off early, at his floor, thanking me and warmly shaking my hand, saying it was not for him. What an impression he made on me!

Burt Reynolds, who, at the time, played Quint on the CBS show, "Gunsmoke," greeted me at the door, and I had a drink or two in a room crowded full of CBS stars. I received a number of kudos (probably more than were merited) and was back at the Nunnery the next day.

Tom had given further evidence of his confidence in me. Good things seemed to be falling into place as I was working well with my peers, and enjoying some real success. What a lucky guy.

CHAPTER FOURTEEN

Bermuda

I had begun spending more and more time with the outgoing owner of our Albany channel, Harry Goldman, who was running out the clock on his consulting agreement with our company. Harry and I had developed a real fondness for each other. He treated me like a son, but always with a lesson. Harry, just as colorful, extraverted, mischievous and well-connected as ever, had kindly introduced me to a number of influential people in Albany and New York, but he seemed particularly anxious for me to meet a friend of his in Manhattan who *"would be of invaluable service to me for years."*

In or around 1958, Gig had bought a huge film package from MGM films, creating a need for more on-air promotion, which suited me just fine. It led to new duties, and also gave Harry Goldman the perfect opportunity to entrust me with an important assignment. Harry recommended I pay a visit to his highly respected source of 8-by-10 movie stills in New York City. Let's call him Milton Weiss. Mr. Weiss, famous for his collection, was someone I should know and impress, Harry urged. If I had the good fortune to get an appointment with him, I should show up looking sharp and make sure to take him to the 21 Club for lunch. *"Entertain him as I would and you will be doing yourself and the station a world of good."* Surprisingly, I was able to make an appointment quite quickly with Mr. Weiss' secretary, and then carefully reserved — *for my first time ever* — a table for lunch at 21. On the day of the meeting, I got myself decked out in my Sunday best and showed up at his West Side office at the appointed time. As I walked up the stairs, I was impressed by the classic Hollywood posters lining the walls.

At the top of the stairs, I entered a surprisingly ramshackle office to see a large unkempt woman sitting behind a desk. I identified myself and told her I had a luncheon appointment with Mr. Weiss and that I was there on the recommendation of Mr. Harry Goldman. She leaned back and hollered over her shoulder, *"Miltie, sumbuddy here!"* It quickly fell into place as I pictured Harry howling back in Albany. "Miltie" came out — all 300 pounds of him — laughing out loud, wearing a sweat-stained T-shirt that did not reach his pants. *"How's that Jew Bastard, Hershel?"* We never got to 21, preferring Reuben sandwiches from the local deli ... but I did buy a ton of movie stills at 20 cents each!

Harry always hugged me, and even kissed me sometimes gently on the lips, like a father. I remained close to him, occasionally visiting him in Pompano Beach until he died. He was a great teacher, a man one does not easily forget, and a loveable prankster of the first order.

During his time as owner of WROW, Harry had regularly thrown an annual August junket called, "A Day at the Races." It consisted of a chartered DC-3 that flew radio time buyers from LaGuardia Airport to Albany, where ground transport whisked them 40 minutes north to the famous Saratoga Raceway. After lunch, and a day at the races, buyers were bussed to dinner at the Shaker Ridge Country Club, before the private DC-3 returned them to New York. By 1960, just before concluding his consultant contract with the company, Harry had invited me in on the planning of these junkets, and then promptly abandoned me to run them on my own. Another multitask assignment, and I loved it! Enlisting the aid of one of our newest producers, a handsome fellow named Jim Masucci, we built upon Harry's concept and added a few flourishes of our own. Skip Parsons' Dixieland band now welcomed guests at the track and serenaded them again later at the club. Jim added a novel element, which we used to great effect for years on all manner of station promotions. Guests were filmed by our crew as they arrived; stepping off the plane, betting, drinking at the club and cheering their favorite horses at the afternoon races. Then the footage was rushed back to our Albany station, where it was intercut with an already prepared laugh reel of ridiculous canned material — everything from Tarzan, to the Three Stooges, Groucho Marx, Hitler, along with several dozen other silly, stupid clips. And the Skip Parsons' Dixieland band provided the soundtrack! We got the finished film back to the country club, and screened it just as the buyers were finishing dinner, by which time (and throughout the afternoon) they had imbibed generous amounts of liquor. We probably got a serious assist from the alcohol, but the reaction in the room when the buyers saw themselves up on screen, clowning around alongside these slapstick comic legends, was all but hysterical. That home movie roast trick worked like a charm every time we rolled it out and Jim and I, along with photographer Gene Collins, milked that gimmick and other silly stuff for years. By the way, Jim Masucci moved steadily up through the ranks of the company, assuming a number of roles, culminating with his being named President of our prized Houston station, KTRK-TV. Collins, about whom there were many high jinks stories, was our unofficial photographer. He always seemed to have a camera in hand, and distributed hundreds of his photos generously to all our appreciative guests and co-workers.

During this same time period, I developed an on-air sales kit to give our promotional campaign some semblance of art design. It was a simple piece of artwork consisting of a blue frame resembling a TV screen. Inside the frame, we could display clips from movies or advertise a range of our shows and products. After a while, it became a signature device that the sales department used to pitch clients. Before long I was not just doing on-air promotion, but also creating an assortment of sales tools, using our now recognizable blue TV frame. Occasionally, we'd get some of the office secretaries to mimeograph the contents and put a spiral binding around it so our sales team could have hard copy presentation pieces. That's how I found myself in sales as well as audience promotion. And all this from my 10-by-10 Assistant

Promotion Manager cubbyhole that also served as the building's sole second story fire exit. In case of fire, employees were instructed to climb through the window of my office out onto a wooden porch to escape conflagration. Luckily, we never put that dubious evacuation plan into action. For my promotion/sales duties, I began visiting supermarkets, asking for printed product material from their displays or buying six-packs of Pepsi to get the collars around the bottles. Reproduced on our mimeograph machines and pasted into the blue TV frames, they became product logos to wow our buyers. It was the beginning of our own in-house art department!

With Harry's consulting agreement winding down and his presence steadily declining, Tom asked me how we could jazz up his "Day at the Races" concept. Our General Sales Manager, a seasoned professional named Bill Lewis, was responsible for selling the national TV spots that were purchased by important media buyers, mostly out of New York. National spots brought us more revenue and sometimes, when inventory was tight, preempted cheaper local commercials. As we grew and our programming began attracting more national advertisers, this put Bill in conflict with our popular head of local sales, Dom Vignola. Bill Lewis' clients were agency buyers who controlled large pools of ad dollars devoted to moving nationally advertised products. Agencies and product managers allocated their TV dollars according to market sales, inviting stations and their national reps to pitch for all or a share of the budget. Our rep, the Blair Co., was regarded as one of the best. Schmoozing the buyers, some young and impressionable, others more seasoned and wary, was the name of this high stakes game. Salesmanship was paramount and "favors" were not uncommon, sometimes to the detriment of media value. It helped if you sold by the numbers, but the sway of relationship perks or "sophisticated entertainment" often carried the day. I trusted most buyers who had been in the business a long time, but saw many well-intentioned younger ones taken in by the charm offensive. Bill Lewis asked me to replicate and enhance Harry's captive audience junkets to help put our fledgling, three-station company in the spotlight.

From my vantage, it seemed that the power of television was so overwhelming that most campaigns successfully increased product sales, despite a possibly flawed process that sometimes saw millions of ad dollars placed in the hands of inexperienced, impressionable buyers. In later years, I preferred to deal directly with product managers. However, at that time in the company's evolution, we needed to get on the map. It was all well and good to have a solid firm like Blair in our corner, but we wanted to reinforce the message about our startling growth, successful stations, and talented sales force directly with our buyers. Our promotion budget totaled $50,000, which could easily have been swallowed up with a few ads in the standard industry trade magazines, but I wanted a more personal touch, reminiscent of Harry Goldman's classic jaunts. Anything less would have been ineffective or wasteful, and wasteful was not part of the Capcities lexicon.

One night at my home, I spread a map out on our kitchen table and traced a 75-mile radius around Manhattan to see what popped up as a possible venue. It had to be a destination close enough to New York to get our guests there and back in one day. The Jersey Shore and Long Island were logical choices, but our selected date in March made those beaches less than appealing. While I was mulling beaches, I noticed that Bermuda might be within striking distance. On a lark, I called an artist acquaintance named Jim Fisher at his home. Jim and I had met at a promotion gathering. I always found Jim's touch intriguing, and had used his creative work from time to time for promotion. I explained my challenge and the moment I mentioned Bermuda, he broke right in with, *"The Bermuda Commuter Club!"* I knew right away we were onto something. The next morning I rushed into Murph's office, announcing my concept, promising I could pull it off on our budget. His face lit up with obvious glee and I was off to the races (well, not the races) for an adventure that now lives in the annals of Capcities lore. When Smitty heard the concept, he added his inimitable twist. *"Let's promise each invitee they'll be covered by a million dollar insurance policy!"* I loved that idea, included it in the invitation, and proceeded to seek out the 250 airline seats Bill Lewis needed. My first call was to Pan American Airlines, which served Bermuda extensively. In the process, I met a bright, eager Pan Am salesman, named Bill Campbell, who happened to be just my age. Our pitch was that world famous broadcaster, Lowell Thomas, wanted to charter two DC-8's, carrying 125 passengers each for a round trip to Bermuda on March 8, 1961

— departing at 8:30 a.m., returning by 11 p.m. We'd be flying out of Idlewild Airport (it became JFK in 1963).

Within a week, I got a telegram from Campbell: *"One Pan Am DC-8 confirmed ... Cost $8,000 ... March 8, 1961 ... Seeking second jet."* A week went by and so far, no second jet. And therein lay my dilemma. Bill Lewis said one plane would leave him with 125 disappointed buyers. It had to be two or nothing. Bill Campbell and I became a team. We researched and queried every possible airline with our pitch, realizing rather quickly that airlines did not have these highly mortgaged expensive airplanes just sitting around hangers waiting for two guys wishing to book a day charter! I insisted we keep hunting while I proceeded to put other elements of the trip in place. This was too big an opportunity to miss. I flew to Bermuda where I was welcomed like royalty by The Bermuda Trade Development Board. Through them, I met a fellow named Peter Rosario, manager of the Elbow Beach Club, with whom I made a very good off-season deal for food and beverages. I wanted the jets to be met directly on the tarmac by several buses, which would shuttle guests straight to Elbow Beach. But, the Bermuda taxi drivers union had other ideas. They insisted we hire taxis, despite it being horribly impractical. I met with the union leader and discovered they only had 10 drivers on the clock at that time of the year. There was no way 10 drivers could handle 250 guests. It would take hours to shuttle our guests to the hotel. That seemed to make little difference to the union boss. When I learned that the drivers' daily income ran to about $12 a day, the solution appeared. I told him I'd pay each driver $15 for the day and arranged to have them carry signs identifying each taxi as a "Capital Cities Touring Car" that offered free rides to anyone on the island. And I reminded the headman that tips would likely be larger because of the free ride. So that placated the taxi union. And, courtesy of the Governor, whose friendship with Lowell came in mighty handy, we arranged tarmac clearance so our buses could drive right up to the planes, thus avoiding customs in and out of the island. We also arranged to have the official uniformed Bermuda Marching Band play for our guests as they boarded the planes for the return trip at 9:30 p.m. At each of the tourist venues our guests would visit, like the Perfume Factory, we placed a large Capital Cities punch bar, free of charge to anyone who entered. Jim Fisher and I had creative invitations ready to go. And when Rosario called to say he planned to line the beach with umbrellas welcoming us, I knew we were set to have a swell time. Everything was in place — except the second plane! Bill Lewis had set a Jan. 1 deadline to find that second plane. It was now the second week of December, with the Christmas holiday looming and pressure mounting.

I thought of Frank Smith, who had always been cordial and complimentary, and had offered to help if I was ever in need. I phoned Smitty and explained our dilemma. Everything was buttoned up, but it would all go sideways if we couldn't lay our hands on a second plane. He said he would get back to me.

At about 4 p.m. that same day, I got a call from a very excited Bill Campbell. *"What in hell did you do?"* he asked. *"I have a telegram confirming a second Pan Am jet from the office of the Chairman, Juan Trippe!"* I took a deep breath (to be perfectly sure I was still breathing), and told him I would call back. I put a call in to Frank Smith, who calmly said, *"Well, Phil, I told you I might be able to help. You may not know this, but Juan Trippe's daughter recently married Lowell Thomas Jr.!"* Now that I knew our side had pulled the strings, I called Bill back and told him *"Well Bill, I just got tired of dealing with the disciples!"* We both had a good laugh.

The twin DC-8 Constellations, glistening in the bright Bermuda sun, touched down at 9:15 the morning of March 8. The party had already started for some, with cocktails in hand and a mood of hilarity settling over the cabins. As our 225 guests deplaned, they were handed a local newspaper, carrying a front-page story about the trip. Bermuda tour guides on the buses escorted our guests to the hotel. Lunch on an outside beach terrace was followed by beach time, taxi tours and considerable libation. Everyone was having a genuinely great time and telling us so as well. Pals clustered together, celebrating, especially during the dinner entertainment, and the crowd was quite well mannered and behaved. Harry Goldman had been invited and was enjoying the day with Tom and some Pan Am representatives, including a gentleman named Ralph Down, who had impressive Pan Am management stripes.

At about 8 p.m., when people were spread far and wide around the hotel, Ralph came to me and quietly told me weather conditions were shutting down Idlewild; our 9:30 departure was in jeopardy. There was even a chance we might not get out till morning. He followed that up by saying that after 9:30, all costs for food, beverage or lodging would be picked up by Pan Am. I told him no thanks. It was our party and we would absorb any additional costs. I went to the table where Harry and Tom were sitting and told them about the Idlewild situation and that the hotel had a manifest and was beginning to book the guests, two to a room, men in one hotel, women in another. Pete Rosario had that aspect covered since every hotel had vacancies. I felt I had to tell the guests about the delay, but Harry disagreed, fearing it would kill the party. Tom, not surprisingly, said, *"Whatever you think, Philly."*

I took the microphone, told our assembled group about the delay and promised, *"they would all be home ... by Easter!"* Great cheering ensued! I also pointed out that telephones were available in the lobby in case anyone had to call home regarding airport pick-up schedules and I told them that hotel rooms were being assigned. Since this was a non-spouse trip, that spurred some interesting casting around. The hotel opened the nightclub and our high-spirited guests formed a conga line into the famous Horseshoe Bar, as the drinks flowed even more copiously.

In all that activity, I had totally forgotten about the Bermuda Marching Band, set to play us off at the runway at 9:30. Pete

Rosario brought me to a phone to speak with the Band Commodore, who was already at the airport awaiting our arrival. I explained the weather delay and asked if there was any way the band could come to the hotel to play for our guests. He informed me that was impossible as it was strictly against protocol for the official Bermuda Marching Band to perform in any commercial establishment. I took the opportunity to remind him that the Governor had made a number of exceptions to policy and rules, including the waving of customs for our group. I further assured him I would commend his actions highly to the Governor. There was silence on the line. Finally, I added, *"Commodore, it would be such an honor to have the band play for my guests, would you consider accepting a gratuity on behalf of the band? I have a brand new $100 bill in my pocket." "Yessir, we'll be right over, sir,"* was his crisp response.

The band came over, playing the "Colonel Bogey March," right through the crowded Horseshoe Bar, and out onto the Terrace Beach Bar, where they regaled us with an hour-long concert. During the festivities I got word that the weather at Idlewild had cleared. We were finally able to depart shortly before midnight, with everyone on board feeling no pain.

While I was pleased that all had gone well, that we had thrown a great party, come in under budget, and that we had made a mark for our company in the industry, what impressed me most were the leadership traits that Tom exhibited once again during that trip. When he said he trusted his people and left them alone to make decisions across the board, he meant it. Murph allowed me, not yet 29, to call all the shots, fend for myself and figure it out. And when Ralph Down told Tom I had taken the decision to assume all overage costs, even though Ralph had offered to cover them, Murph said he agreed completely and was pleased I had made that judgment call. Frank Smith, who had not joined us, called with his personal congratulations, but since he had an aversion to flying, he asked Murph if all future sales promotions could be organized without airplanes.

We followed that up in '62 with the "Capital Cities Cruise to Nowhere" aboard the SS Oslofjord, which I planned and executed. By '63, Marc Edwards, my successor in promotion, took over the second cruise party. Marc went on to a distinguished career with the company, capped by the Presidency of KFSN-TV in Fresno. When I took Marc to meet the Captain of the SS Oslofjord for the first time, the Captain was amazed at how young we both were. He told us, between shots of Aquavit, *"To give such authority to those as young as you is truly exceptional."* I told him we were fully aware of that, and that we did, indeed, *"work for an exceptional company."*

৯ ⌘ ৶

CHAPTER FIFTEEN

Burke: *"Watchful, Quick & Wise"*

Tom began to spend more and more time away from Albany, telling us he was hunting for new opportunities. It became obvious he needed an operations guy to replace him for the day-to-day duties at WTEN-TV. An extensive search ensued. When Tom settled on his choice, he again chose to favor me by introducing the mystery man before he met the rest of the staff. He called one Sunday night, asking me to join him the next morning for breakfast at Albany's Dewitt Clinton Hotel. Over tomato juice and scrambled eggs, I shook hands with Dan Burke for the first time, and was immediately impressed by his casual manner, obvious smarts, and solid sense of humor. We had a nice hour together, exchanging information about our families. I learned that Dan had been born in the Albany region and that his brother and Tom had been classmates at Harvard Business School. It did not take much imagination to see that Murph had made a brilliant choice, and I was feeling pretty good by the time we were ready to leave. Then Murph suggested I drive Dan to the Nunnery where the rest of the staff was waiting to meet us.

That 20 minute drive was memorable as Dan shared his concerns about being on the "other side" of the business; now selling TV instead of buying it as he had in his former capacity at General Foods. Murph had somehow convinced Dan that I could be of help to him, but I doubted that this very smart man would ever need my help. As we arrived, Dan turned to me with those piercing steel blue eyes I would get to know so well and shocked me by saying, *"Phil, I am going to depend on you. And I want you to know that if I make it, so will you."* Pretty heady stuff from a man I'd known a few brief hours. Like Tom's words in the past, Dan Burke's candor and trust had an unsettling and empowering effect on me. My already lofty spirits soared to new heights.

We settled in very well together and began to forge what became a lasting, learning bond, and a strong personal friendship. I was not the only beneficiary of Dan's skill and leadership. It extended to a long and growing list of exceptional future colleagues. For, throughout the company's trajectory, but particularly during our exhilarating growth in the 1960s and 1970s, Murphy and Burke displayed an uncanny talent for stringing together some of the most talented men and women one could ever meet to help them realize their vision of a unique apolitical media partnership. My timing was just right to have been there at the outset and to work so closely with both men. I had a privileged front row seat, beholding the beginning of the "Murphy/Burke" phenomenon, as their partnership came to be known.

Working with Dan was a wholly different matter than working with Tom. Tom delegated easily, and did not always have time to work directly with me in getting things done. Dan, on the other hand, was involved on a much more granular level. He gave me more demanding assignments as the station grew and he enjoyed jumping into the trenches to work side by side when the need arose. We had great fun tackling a slew of challenges, for while there were signs one might call promising; the facts were that Dan inherited a station with lackluster ratings, meager revenues and spotty reception in many rural areas. Working on those problems with Dan was remarkable. And he took a keen interest in the development of my business management and leadership skills, personal maturation, and even my golf game! Like many who worked with and for him, I never stopped learning from Dan Burke. He also put up with Murph calling me away for special assignments ... for a while, that is.

Early in our relationship, we encountered an incident that tested and unified us still further. The Goldman & Walter Advertising Agency, run by Harry Goldman's younger brother, Jack, was a growing local powerhouse, helping advertised brands gain visibility in the Albany region. The agency had recently increased their clients' TV investments and presently held the account of our largest local advertiser, RCA. Sometime in early 1962 our National Sales Manager, Bill Lewis found himself at an unexpected semi-social get together with these important RCA clients over cocktails. Prompted certainly by a few too many whites, the meeting went off the rails and culminated with Bill Lewis leaning into the face of the RCA rep, holding his pinky finger threateningly in the air and then placing it on the tip of the rep's nose, saying *"This is how much your account matters to Channel 10."* Needless to say, Bill was fired several days later. And then, as if on a rampage to purge the department, Dan called me into his office and told me to go down the hall and fire Dom Vignola, our local Sales Rep! I protested, *"He doesn't work for me, Dan."* *"Yes he does,"* was his reply. *"You are now our Sales Manager. You have been writing their pitches. You might as well deliver them too. Now go give him the broom!"* Two minutes later Dom was at Dan's door. All Dan said was *"Take it up with Phil."* That is exactly how I became Sales Manager. The next few weeks were hectic, with Dom gone, no organized sales department (except of course, for me), a mimeograph machine and my empty TV screens. Rather unimpressive! Shortly thereafter, Vignola got a job as ad manager for Pepsi, another of our major accounts! Woe is me, I thought …

We were heading into strong headwinds and the pinky incident still lingered. I really needed the local business Jack Goldman controlled, so Dan decided we should tackle that situation head on. We made an appointment with Jack and his VP, Norm Tillman, close to the Christmas holidays. Jack had the same kind of pot-stirring, *devil sitting on his shoulder* disposition as his older brother. In fact, they were much alike, but for some reason (that I was not anxious to learn) they did not get along. When Dan and I walked into Jack's office, he was loaded for bear and delighted in taking the two of us apart over the Bill Lewis incident. We sat in front of Jack's desk and took it on the chin for maybe 10 minutes. Finally, Dan said, *"Jack, face it. We need each other and right now we are at your mercy. Bill*

Lewis is history, you have dealt with Phil and know him to be a straight shooter ... and you can count on me. So let's have a fresh start." "We will see," said a stone-faced, noncommittal Jack as we gathered up and left. Walking down the stairs, Dan turned to me, "Did you see that empty billboard across the street, through the picture window behind Jack's back?" I said I had. Dan looked at me like the cat that ate the canary. "Think you can figure out something to do with it?" Another choice assignment! It so happened that Harry Goldman owned that billboard. Getting it painted for us was a thrill and right up his alley as he liked getting one over on his brother. Plus, being sworn to secrecy about it was pure fun for Harry! What I developed was a full-color 16-foot billboard, featuring an RCA TV set decorated with a Christmas bow. In the middle of the TV screen, appeared a poem, which read:

"If this were only live TV,
How more effective it would be
To wish a prosperous '63
To Mr. G. and Mr. T!"

Naturally, we pretended to know nothing about its origin. Jack suspected it was us, but I denied it and so did Dan. There were a few weeks of speculation, especially amongst the other agencies in this small town, so we kept it on the QT. One afternoon, several weeks later, at a club that was known to be one of Harry's haunts, Dan and I were at the bar, when a couple of people brought up the billboard again. An agency guy whose name I cannot remember, declared, "There is only *one guy who could dream up something like that, and that is you, Beuth!"* I laughed and shouted back, *"Not a chance!"*

When we finished our drinks and got out to the car, I could tell Dan was upset. *"You took credit in there,"* he said. *"How do you figure? I denied everything,"* I said. *"Yeah, but your intent was clear. You admitted it with your tone. And you should have said it was the two of us."* And then he went on to chew me out over another task that I thought I had handled well. I had just gotten an insight into the workings of my new boss and a taste of the famously short Burke fuse, sparked by his brilliant, but complex mind. I was in the doghouse for a day, not really clear why. On another occasion, I committed the faux pas of inadvertently interrupting Dan during a meeting. When the meeting adjourned, Dan asked me to stay, closed the door and proceeded to rip me apart, which he could do with great skill. I was devastated and reported as much to my wife at dinner before heading back out for an after-dinner meeting. When I got home, Betty said Dan had called and wanted me to call him back regardless of how late it was. When I reached Dan, he was full of apologies, saying no one who had done so much for the company deserved to be spoken to in that manner. The next morning it was like it never happened. A few years later, he asked me and another exec, who shall remain unnamed, to have a drink at the bar of the Drake Hotel in New York. For a half hour he was mercilessly critical of every aspect of this fellow's life, behavior and even his appearance. When he finished his verbal lashing, he turned to me and said, *"Take care of him, Phil."* and left.

Tough, but oh so gentle was our Dan. Over the years, those were the only such incidents I personally witnessed, but Dan's short temper became legend; experienced and feared by many, but always tempered by our overwhelming affection for him. He was a distinctly effective executive and an extremely likeable boss. I admired him as much or more than anyone in the company, and was hardly alone in that regard.

During the early 1960s, in order for WTEN-TV to compete with WRGB-TV, we had to establish satellite relay stations to the east in Pittsfield, Massachusetts, and to the west in Amsterdam, New York, requiring a constant association with area TV servicemen. Then to help promote coverage, Marc Edwards and I put together a "Channel 10 Caravan" on Saturdays to cruise through poor signal areas. Over a multiple-week period, Marc and I launched a parade of service vans calling on homes of designated customers. Our van had a pneumatic device that could raise a variety of antennas on the street. I would go into the home, open a window near the television set and Marc would pass a cable through the window that was connected to different antennas in the truck. When the right antenna was found, customer reaction was recorded, and the week's local newspaper would tell all that Mrs. Anderson of 3200 Morgan Lane exclaimed, *"I can finally get Red Skelton."* I called it BADD — Building Audience Door to Door. Burke would sometimes join us for dinner at VFW halls. Twelve dollars: *roast beef, spaghetti on the side*, was the way it was promoted.

Shortly after the Goldman & Walter meeting, as things improved, Dan asked me a question out of the blue, while in his office. *"Do you know what equity is?"* I told him I did, and proudly mentioned the 200 shares of company stock I owned. He answered with one of the most generous recommendations ever made to me. *"Gordon Banker — yes that is his name — is the President of the Union National Bank in Troy. You need to go see him."* Mr. Banker knew what the meeting was about before I even sat down and got directly to the point, asking if I had any collateral. I told him about the 200 shares of stock. He asked if I had an insurance policy. I told him I did, remembering that my mother had diligently paid 25-cent premiums for years. When, a day or so later, Mr. Banker had read the policy, he called me back to his office to say that he could lend me $2,500 based on its value, *"as long as I was not going to use it to buy stock."* I didn't see the wink, but was sure it was there. *"Sign this yellow card,"* he said. The routine continued for years. As the stock surged, so did my loans. Mr. Banker, with quiet pride, greeted me on many future visits, reveling in the stock's continued growth as he collected it to serve as fresh collateral. Much later, satisfying our option debts with appreciated company stock became a unique and ongoing Capital Cities perk, particularly for a few of us early employees.

Years later, after Tom retired, he mentioned in a video interview that Smitty had set him up with the same bank, from which he'd been able to borrow $20,000. I wondered if Tom had, in turn, set Dan up as well!

In 1964, at age 32, I was relocated to West Virginia, transferring a debt of $100,000, most of which had been spent on our stock, or options. At the First Huntington National Bank in West Virginia, my new loan was for $104,000, the extra $4,000 to cover the interest for the first year.

Later, much later, I was asked to go to New York with the purchase of ABC. I went without a word about compensation, but did write a tongue in cheek letter to Dan, noting the change in cost of living between Buffalo and New York City. I mentioned that as my cholesterol was a tad high, my doctor had prescribed bran muffins. I pointed out that those muffins were three for $1 in Buffalo, but $3.50 each in Manhattan. The letter made no reference to compensation. A note came back from Dan with the word "Bullshit" stamped across the top. He, apparently, was not a fan of my creative writing, but folded into the envelope was a healthy six-figure check! I need not write more here about compensation, except that I rarely ever talked about it with either Dan or Tom. Increases and valuable options came to all of us, in step with performance. Generations of Beuths are grateful that Murphy/Burke put together such a success story, executed by loyal, responsible people who dedicated themselves not only to winning, but also to the high standards of Capital Cities, proving that doing it the right way can pay off.

Back at the Nunnery, building a new sales team was not such a difficult task. I had met Jack Ryan and Ted Mueller, a couple of sharp candidates, at the Albany Junior Chamber of Commerce, which I joined when Murph asked me to handle Public Service years earlier. The companies where Jack and Ted were on the sales force for were no match for us, as WTEN-TV offered more upside potential and a superior commission structure (that I'd copied from WRGB). I still have the first memo Dan sent to me with our sales objectives. He established a clear dollar goal for us, and I relayed that to the sales staff. By the end of 1962, with the Goldman & Walter matter squarely behind us, we had blown past our sales targets, so Dan sent us and our wives — the Ryans, the Muellers, and Beuths — to New York for a couple of nights on the town. The trip kicked off with a cocktail reception in our new offices at 24 E. 51st St., the former headquarters of longtime Archbishop, Cardinal Spellman. Lowell Thomas' personal office overlooked New York's famed St. Patrick's Cathedral. The walls of the oak-paneled office traced the legendary career of this intrepid explorer and newsman, known to those who knew him well as "LT." One could study those walls for hours, tracking his fortunes and adventures all across the globe. A world map covered the whole south wall, which, when raised, revealed scores of photos. Also adorning the room was a set of 4-by-6 illustrations of six of the Seven Wonders of the Ancient Greek World, including the Hanging Gardens of Babylon, The Temple of Diana at Ephesus, The King Mausolus Tomb at Halicarnassus, The Pharos Lighthouse, the Pyramids of Cheops and Sphinx, and The Colossus of Rhodes. The seventh wonder, the Statue of Zeus, was not included for some reason.

I happened to have been in his office, waiting for LT on the morning these six brown wrapped paintings arrived and was an audience of one as he excitedly tore off the wrappings and described each illustration in vivid detail. LT delighted in sharing his intriguing stories. He told of King Cheops' construction of the Great Pyramid and the beacon of fires that beamed through the open eye-sockets of the Colossus standing astride the harbor of Rhodes, or the 100-year building of Diana's Temple. His knowledge was phenomenal. Again, what a lucky guy!!

Frank Smith hosted our intimate sales department reception, unlit cigarette in hand, spreading his charm to this young, eager group. He had even taken the time to learn what we all drank, even Ted Mueller's wife, Judy, whose drink of choice was rather exotic. Smitty had a cherry heering aperitif on hand just for her. Then we were all treated to a Broadway show — "Bye Bye Birdie" — and some nice New York dinners, before my sales team and our grateful wives all returned to Albany, inspired anew.

I was building a local sales department and mostly relying on the men and women of Blair TV, our sales rep, for national help. Dan knew it was not prudent for me to work both local and national sales long term and, so, he began a search for a second sales manager. As the search got started, the green stairs up to Dan's Nunnery office hosted a parade of experienced pros, all of whom seemed willing to endure the desolation of North Greenbush for a shot at a job with Capital

Cities. A slew of well-credentialed sales executives made that pilgrimage up the Hudson over the next several months.

And, throughout the process, John McCarthy, the sales manager for our radio station, would periodically pop into my office, pushing me to insist that Dan give me the National Sales job. I told John my plate was full with local and that I had no appetite for change. Finally, Dan made his choice, and called me into his office to meet the new hire. I walked in expecting to see a *"Mr. Television, square-jawed executive sales type."* There, sitting on top of a long table at the back of the room, swinging his legs back and forth, was a nice ordinary looking guy, kind of thin, with a full head of black hair, black horn-rimmed glasses and a big ready smile. His name was Larry Pollock. We shook hands as Dan said something like, *"Philly, meet your new partner. Larry this is Phil. You each report individually to me. Larry, you get some sizzle from Phil, and Phil will get research from you ... Together you will make a good team."* He was right, although I do not think Larry was yet on board and I doubt Dan had spelled out the job to him as he had described it to me. Larry and I quickly formed a bond that survives to this day and we shared years of triumphs, together and separately, each in the other's corner when necessary.

However, Larry did not make an immediate stellar impression on the staff. It was obvious he had a lightning quick mind, but was somewhat impatient with those who were not as sharp. Some of our very capable team players, as they readily admitted, had trouble keeping up with Larry. John McCarthy dropped in again after Larry got hired and uttered a comment that ricocheted around the office for several days: *"Dan looked high and low for Jesus Christ, and settled for Woody Allen!"* I tried to protect Larry from some of those unkind and unwarranted remarks and did my best to establish a good working relationship with my new partner. We did not always agree on sales approaches, however.

One day I invited him to accompany me as I pitched the owner of the local Rayco Seat Cover franchise. Larry and I were both well dressed and met the client, who sat in his rather unkempt office, leaning his oily hair back against a grease-stained chair. As soon as I got started, the man cut me off with *"You know I don't have an aerial to get your Channel 10."* I told him we would send a team right over to install an antenna and went on to say that I believed he could measurably increase business by sponsoring our late news at $350 a broadcast, three nights a week, for 52 weeks. He could follow "The Jackie Gleason Show" one night, "The Carol Burnett Show" another night, and if memory serves me correctly we were broadcasting "Gunsmoke" the third night. He looked stone-faced. Then, I followed up with some ratings information, to which he still didn't react. I realized he was not a numbers guy, so changed tactics while Larry sat in silence. I told him there was a bonanza in those 11 p.m. shows because a lot of very smart men were paying millions and millions of dollars in production costs for all three 10 o'clock shows to build ratings and viewership that served as the perfect lead in for the shows

I was proposing he buy. He could inherit all that success and for a fraction of the cost! He said he would think it over. I handed him my blue TV-screen pitch document and Larry and I left.

In the car, Larry told me that I had made a terrible pitch; that I should have given better numbers and that, in the future, we had to be more professional in our approach. Nevertheless, that afternoon, I wrote up and submitted the new Rayco order: 52 weeks at $1,050 a week direct, with no local agency commission — a new $50,000 account for the team! We never made a pitch together again, but we did develop a wonderful friendship. Larry became one of our most prolific income producers and a stable asset to the company for decades. He played by all the rules and won constantly, teaching many who worked with him that the Capital Cities adherence to ethics and integrity was the right path to success. The perhaps unlikely choice of Larry Pollock was a testament to Dan Burke's stewardship and uncanny instincts when it came to forging the right team. Larry went on to many great things at the company and his crowning achievement (and where he had the most fun) came when he was named President of our Philadelphia powerhouse, WPVI-TV.

Our WROW radio was going through some dramatic format changes and hired a new manager named Bob Peebles, a tall engaging fellow who became a long-term favorite friend. One day Dan and Harry Goldman decided that Bob and I should join them for lunch at his club, followed by a round of golf. Neither Bob nor I had ever swung our hastily acquired clubs, but we agreed. At lunch, Harry placed a three-pack of balls at our place and began to set handicaps. Bob had previously played only one full round. I'd had a lesson from Dan at a driving range — nothing more. When Harry gave Bob 20 strokes, I asked for 30. *"No, no, Philly,"* Harry insisted, *"20 each."* It was a crowded tee off time and I was up first. I flubbed badly and hit the ball into the rough 20 yards to the right. I hit another, this time straight, but not very far. While we all were looking for my ball, Dan asked what I was hitting. I answered, *"Tillhouse? I think."* Harry picked up my Titleist and immediately shouted, *"OK, 30 strokes!"* Of course, I proceeded to shoot an 80 on the next six holes! I privately noted that my background had not adequately prepared me for what lay ahead and recognized I needed to catch up!

Over many years, I continued to observe the unique Murphy/Burke leadership style and, like many of my peers, grew in the appreciation of its application. Capital Cities employees wrote few resumes and all would attest to the extraordinary talents of the Murphy/Burke combo. There is a specific quote my Capcities partners heard over and over during the following years from our friend, Warren Buffett:

> *"Tom Murphy and Dan Burke were probably the greatest two-person management team the world has ever seen, or maybe will ever see."*

Few, if any, who ever worked for the company, would disagree. I was singularly blessed by time and events to have worked with or for each for perhaps longer than anyone, thrilled, like most, to be on the Capcities team. Tom led an apolitical group by example of excellence, honesty and devotion to tasks that might have seemed unbelievable or even corny to outsiders, but was gospel to his team of proud followers. Dan, for his part, developed a set of maxims that he sprinkled into his discussions over the years.

Phil Meek, who came along later to head our print division, collected some of them and would quote them eagerly. Here are some of Dan's most notable:

"You just have to let your managers know someone is watching."

"Be careful what you say to subordinates. You will forget in 24 hours, but they will remember it word for word forever."

"Always be careful who does the hiring. Mediocre people tend to hire mediocre people."

"Avoid the echo effect. Line managers besieged by MBA-laden corporate staffs hire their own MBA's, so they can talk to one another."

And my favorite:

"Never tweak the nose of a bear ..."

The hiring of Dan Burke was certainly one of the most significant events in our company's history. Important growth and activities over the next several years included the development of our newspaper division and the increased attention and respect we garnered from Wall Street and the FCC. Employees had been given the opportunity to buy shares of stock at $5.75 a share in 1957 and it had grown to more than $21 by July 1963.

Burke was a remarkable people person and a brilliant teacher. He could cut to the essence of a matter quickly, and loved to challenge us to reach beyond our own perceived abilities. He was ever watchful, quick and wise.

One day, out of the blue, a package showed up at our home from Steuben Glass. Lifting the surprisingly heavy object out of the box, I unwrapped a 5½-inch crystal depiction of an owl mounted on a crystal base. Its eyes were large, round and penetrating. Accompanying the piece was Dan's personal card, on the back of which he had written, *"No comment necessary!"*

℞ ⌘ ℟

Price of stock – July 1963

$21 per share

CHAPTER SIXTEEN

Seven-Year Itch

The purchase of two Goodwill Stations — radio powerhouse WJR-AM in Detroit, Michigan and WSAZ-TV, an NBC affiliate in Charleston-Huntington, West Virginia — had us nearly maxed out on our FCC station ownership cap, but also offered the prospect of new job openings.

1964 through 1968 brought this country through a period of remarkable change and upheaval. While the nation was excited about space exploration, The Beatles and Muhammad Ali, it was also ravaged by race riots in Chicago and Watts, torn apart by Vietnam, and challenged by the Voting Rights Act and Dr. Martin Luther King Jr.'s march on Selma. Neither of our new markets was exempt from the generally difficult times America was experiencing. Appalachia became the poster child for the nation's poverty belt and Detroit suffered severe racial strife.

While I consider myself fortunate to have been a part of the remarkable success story told in these pages, there is one decision for which I feel great lingering regret ... and for which I have only myself to blame.

The Goodwill purchase brought two new job opportunities for me: radio with Dan in Detroit or television in Charleston-

Huntington. In retrospect, I now know that staying close to Dan would have been a far better path; that learning from and following Dan should have trumped all other considerations. Declining Dan's invitation to go to the Motor City was a hasty and flawed decision, albeit one made with the best of intentions. Likely blinded by a mixture of ego and defensiveness, I believed I could contribute more to the company by staying with TV, where I felt comfortable, convinced it better suited my talents ... such as they were. But I was also uneasy about the radio sales management job in a market as sophisticated as Detroit, where much of the business of WJR was conducted hobnobbing and networking in the golf and country club scene. Though I'd made inroads and incursions into that upper crust world, it still wasn't really my universe and, more importantly, I still did not play golf!

So, I opted for the TV job and moved my family from Albany, New York, to Huntington, West Virginia. What can I say about Huntington? West Virginia today, blessed by Mother Nature and by the infinite beauty of its mountains, valleys and streams, is a scenic delight with highways that treat tourists to miles of breathtaking scenery, mountain lakes, popular campgrounds, and national forests. But such was not the case in the mid-1960s, when the state was mired in a backwards "Appalachia" mentality that only came to public light after John F. Kennedy's presidential campaign visits brought a media circus to the state. The resulting harshly negative (and largely merited) coverage spread like wildfire and endured for decades. Scenes from rural

144

communities outside the few major cities created a postcard of poverty littered with tin-roof shanties, ashen coal miners, toothless farmers and highways bordered by the gaping scars of strip mining. Even the famous Greenbrier resort, constructed on the eastern side of the state for easy access by the Washington power elite, lacked acceptable highway access for any residents from the less affluent western side.

Looking back, I know that while I did a good job at WSAZ-TV — a relatively easy assignment by our company standards — my skills were, if I can be objective, relatively wasted in Huntington. But far more troubling, was the fact that the move caused unwanted stress and lost opportunities for my children and family. Murph and Dan would never have wished that, and I can't lay the blame at their feet as it was solely my decision. One I lived with ... *for seven long years.*

My station duties were new and challenging. I was appointed General Sales Manager, working under Jack Lee, who'd recently been transferred from Providence. Jack was a smart man, but preferred to be a "Mr. Outside." Before long, I found myself handling many of his insider chores. We got along fine, but after a short while our boss, Joe Dougherty, saw what was happening and promoted me to General Manager of the station, while Jack left the company and retired. This was a feather in my Capcities career, as I became one of, if not *the* youngest Vice President in the company.

But, on the homefront, and much to my chagrin, my family's environment was less positive; in fact, extremely challenging. I never imagined what a culture shock West Virginia would prove to be. I was unprepared for the Appalachian temperament, the slow-paced everyday living, the inadequate education, the anti-Yankee sentiment, and the apathy, ignorance or outright hostile resistance to the new Equal Rights Act. This was 1964, after all, and West Virginia was, in many ways, the heart of the rural south. The region could not unglue the labels left by the JFK campaign tour, which resulted in headlines like *"soft coal, hard life," "hillbilly haven,"* etc.

I was surprised to discover that when I tried to buy a couple of button down business shirts at Huntington's largest department store, not only did they not carry buttoned down shirts, they had never heard of them! Neither did they accept outside credit cards, only their own.

Trying nonetheless to get well settled, Betty and I met a lovely builder named Granville Morrison who had three finished homes for sale — all in the $50,000 range. We chose one in a modest, new neighborhood, called Pea Ridge, just off the Guyan Country Club golf course. I told Mr. Morrison I would like to move in as quickly as possible and would visit the bank right away to prepare my loan papers. He said there was no rush, and if I paid him 10 percent down, I could move right in and get the mortgage later. I did so, moved in, and applied for a mortgage at the First Huntington Bank the following week, around Labor Day, 1964. By mid-September, we still had heard nothing about our loan, so I called a nice woman at my bank named TC (I will use fictitious initials so as to not embarrass anyone). TC told me there would be some delay. When I replied that I needed to pay Mr. Morrison, her answer was so charmingly West Virginian that I wrote it down:

> *"Well Mr. Booth, don't you make no never mind, about that! Mr. Morrison don't need the money! Yur application is here, but Lucille can't git to it cause the poor dear, she broke her wrist a-skeein, and can't type for a while. They's a pile of applications waiting for her, but I will put yurs right on top."*

Betty and I then turned to furnishing the house. We purchased two white leather recliners, promised by mid-October. When only one showed up several weeks later, I called inquiring about the second. The manager explained, *"Well, truth is, ever time we get a holiday shipment they's always two whites, but for some reason, only one come in."* I asked him if he'd ordered two when I bought them. *"Neva thought it needed a call, but I sur will call now!"* was his response. The second recliner arrived months later. Late December of that year, I got a call from my bank, saying my mortgage had come through. I'd already been living in my home for three months. And so it went.

These amounted to minor, sometimes amusing, sometimes irritating cultural details that I wrote off to the tempo of Southern life. However, the more serious matters concerned a school, church and community environment that simply was not ready for three young *"northern Yankee-boys."* Boys who were similarly unprepared for the challenges they faced in this very different and not always welcoming community. Betty and I had always been careful to school our boys in proper manners. They were well spoken, bright, and did well in school. Phil, the oldest, who was 10, played baseball well. He had an outgoing personality and always ranked high in his class. Our middle son, Barry, was exceptional, and different in many ways. He never received less than an A, and was a voracious reader, customarily burying himself in books while his brothers were shooting hoops. Barry was also a self-taught pianist and organist who went on to learn more about opera than I will ever know. As one might surmise, he was even at age 8 — the family's independent thinker. Bob, the youngest, was a total delight. He loved Rocky the Flying Squirrel and could always be counted on to provide some novel artistic behavior. He was 6. The boys all shared a common trait. They had been taught to respect people for who they were, regardless of their color, religion, background or social station. In Albany it was not unusual for them to be around and enjoy all manner of people from different stripes. These new rural surroundings proved a shock in that regard, as they were confronted with prejudice from every quarter. And what was particularly disturbing is that the most racist views often came from those in positions of authority, who all seemed to think we were still fighting the Civil War or as Dan Burke put it, *"... did not know Lincoln had been shot."* The boys and, consequently, Betty and I were confronted over and over with ugly racist and bigoted views from teachers, Scout masters, Little League coaches, and yes, from church officials and their flocks. This proved for difficult times as my family grappled with such backward thinking. After a few early clashes, we largely stopped trying to impose (or even share) our view of justice with the community and sadly resigned ourselves to accepting the pervasive ignorant, regional behavior and views that seemed to permeate all of West Virginia life.

I want to emphasize that at no time did we ever experience anything but good will and respect from my colleagues at work. In fact, we made friends at the station, some of whom we are in touch with to this day. But, I will relate one or two incidents that were particularly trying for our family.

Our youngest, Bob, came home in distress one day claiming that his fifth-grade science teacher at Pea Ridge Elementary had called his Dad a sinner. When Bob protested, defending me, he was sent to the principal's office. It seems that his Mormon teacher — let's call her "MJ" — while teaching elementary science, somehow began talking about filthy magazines and how those who read those magazines were all sinners. Bob raised his hand and said his father read *Playboy* because it published articles by a number of good writers, and he didn't believe his Dad was a sinner. Next thing you know, Bob was on his way to see the principal. Prompted by what I considered an injustice, I wrote to MJ and to the principal and included copies of articles by prominent American authors and thinkers (pointedly including Martin Luther King Jr.). In my letter, I further questioned the rational for discussing popular magazines in a fifth-grade science class. I learned that my letter became a hot water-cooler topic amongst the teaching staff. I privately wondered if I aroused curiosity among any of the teachers with the penetrating articles I sent along! I will never know, as I did not get a response to my letter. Over time, my reputation as one of the community's premier sinners gradually dissipated.

While my boys were bright and well behaved, they were far from pushovers. Like the few others who were *"not from these here parts,"* they were characterized by the locals as *"northern hoodlums."* In junior high school, there was a mandatory woodworking class taught by a man whom we will call "JB." Every new class was treated to a ritual which involved Mr. JB dropping his pants and lifting his boxer shorts to display his World War II shrapnel scars on his upper thighs, *"That's to show y'all who's in charge here!"* was his message. None of my kids was impressed. They just considered him a crazy old coot. Each year the entire class was given the same assignment; to make a wooden lamp. Bob and a friend took it upon themselves to alter the design and created a lamp in the form of a peace symbol. Mr. JB went ballistic, sent the two boys to the principal's office and threatened to have them suspended for spreading the *"witch's foot"* sign of the devil in school! Such subversive activities could not be tolerated in Huntington Junior High! That incident prompted another letter to the principal's office. The lamps got made as per Bob and his friend's design.

In Little League, Phil demonstrated consistent batting skills in practice, but was hardly ever put in the game. I kept telling him to hang in there and persist. He got his chance to bat in the last game near the last inning ... and sent the ball careening high over the right field fence. I have never been a proponent of the middle finger, and it may not have been popular at the time, but if he had raised it over his head as he circled the bases, I might have considered it appropriate! Barry had no trouble in school because he aced everything. However, several teachers used his good grades to chide his older and younger brothers, Phil and Bob, about why they were not as smart as their brother. Barry's difficulties came from the Boy Scouts of America that were at that time, in that community, a bastion of intolerance. Our kids were on the front lines, constantly defending what many locals referred to as *"that no-good, amoral, unpatriotic Yankee family!"*

When Martin Luther King Jr. was assassinated on April 4, 1968, Betty and I (along with much of the nation) were shocked to our core and deeply saddened. That day, we decided, as a family, to attend Sunday services at the First Baptist Church downtown, which was so full we had to sit in the very first row. After the services, we spoke to and shared our grief with a couple of our black friends. Then, we traveled across town to attend Sunday services at our own Pea Ridge Methodist Church. In the car on the way over, I recalled a song we used to sing at the Methodist Church when I was growing up in Staten Island:

"Jesus loves me, this I know,
For the Bible tells me so.
Black and yellow,
Brown and white,
All are equal in his sight ..."

We settled into our pews at Pea Ridge Methodist and, at this grave moment in our country's history, I naively expected some sentiment reflecting Christ's love of all people of every race. The sermon was about how the rocks cried out to Jesus. Needless to say, not a word was said about the assassination of Dr. King.

As we left the church and were shaking hands with the pastor, I said, *"Reverend, those rocks you spoke about. They were crying out for you to talk about our country's great loss this week."* He took me aside, leaned in and said, *"You are from the north and do not understand that I just could not do that in my church."* I doubt the Jesus loves me song was ever sung in that Sunday school, but I will never know as we began to seek out another congregation. Similarly, when I brought a black friend from the Urban League to the Guyan Country Club, where I had been a member since becoming the station's GM, I was advised that my guest was not welcome. I became the first GM of the town's leading TV station to ever resign from the country club, thus forsaking some of our town's old-fashioned southern hospitality.

These cultural rifts were a true test for my family and though some were minor, even comical, others had deep and serious ramifications. Over time my boys developed thick skins, but

152

they were never thrilled with that period of their education and you can imagine the pain it caused me, knowing my decision forced them to face the kind of racial hatred and bigotry that was contrary to everything we had tried to instill in them from birth. As the company grew and some of my peers were moved around to various markets, they too faced similar challenges, some even more difficult than ours. We finally sent Phil to private boarding school at Western Reserve Academy in Akron, Ohio, and would have sent Barry as well had we not been "rescued" by the next round of Capcities acquisitions. More on that later ...

Probably as a coping mechanism and because I've always had an inclination for hard work and new challenges, I threw myself fully into the task of building the station into an even more important part of the Capital Cities portfolio. I was operating, however, in a marketplace that was hardly ready for change or upward mobility. WSAZ-TV was strong in audience share (and promotion where I might have made a difference had that not been the case). I found it very easy to work with the staff, which was generally professional, though not as sophisticated or motivated to excel as I had hoped. Resting on the laurels of the station's dominance in the market, the staff was fairly complacent about striving for more success. WSAZ-TV was a powerhouse whose strength came early in the TV business, primarily from a monopolistic signal, over which was aired a very credible news operation and a popular programming schedule. Bos Johnson, an over-qualified pro, ran a fine newsroom. Bos and his wife, Dottie, could have fared well in a much larger market, but they were committed to Huntington; a sentiment I respected. And there were a number of other talented on-air performers at the station, including a man called "Mr. Cartoon," who'd been a local legend for years. His name was Jule Huffman — a genuine talent and unforgettable guy. I also fondly remember a woman named BJ Schroeder, who competently presented the late night weather. BJ did not like it when I asked her to stop signing off her popular weather report by saying *"nite-nite."* Too many viewers took her at her word and went to bed! I needed them awake to hold up our late night ratings! Though it was obvious the staff was competent, it was just as clear they had never faced serious competition. There was no rival network signal on my home street in Pea Ridge and infringement from cable or new antennas was spotty. Walter Cronkite, the most trusted man in America, was an unknown quantity in Huntington, West Virginia!

And though we had a dominant market share, our advertising rates were under par and national advertisers were scarce. So, the job I set for myself was to discover why and fix it. WSAZ served large swaths of three states, as parts of Ohio and Kentucky were also in its licensed coverage area. To say it owned the market was an understatement. What resulted were huge audiences, but practically no advertisers, as they saw no need to pitch their wares to a depressed marketplace. What we call "CPM's" (cost per thousand impressions), the rate at which advertising dollars are calculated, were dismally low despite our wide coverage and market domination. This situation meant very little pressure on our inventory. I quickly learned that the market in general was not perceived as fertile enough to be of real consequence to advertisers. The big shows like "Country Caravan," a syndicated country western show with stars like Porter Wagner, were sold out, mostly to regional advertisers, but at rock bottom rates.

And then, as I dug deeper, I found that dozens of national brands, active as they were in other regions of the country, were totally absent in West Virginia. Amazingly, it looked like the big national brands had decided to skip over Charleston-Huntington, dismissing the market as one that didn't count, or worse ... didn't exist! Further research began to reveal the reasons why. The first, obviously, was the impoverished image of Appalachia itself, which, far from a mirage, reflected an inescapable market reality. But, the second had to do with marketing research and its shortcomings at that time in the region. While national advertisers were becoming increasingly sophisticated in improving their demographic marketing research in major markets in the early 1960s, they were not applying some of those new testing methods to West Virginia. In fact, when I attended a couple of meetings of food brokers and regional food reps, I got an earful of claims that they were being fed incomplete data about their product sales. Their complaints to headquarters were generally ignored. This was an irresistible challenge! At the center of the problem was a disconnect between where products were actually being sold and where the advertising designed to convince those consumers to buy the product was being placed.

155

Let me explain. The detergent that I could readily buy in my neighborhood Kroger supermarket was not delivered straight to Huntington; rather it was trucked in from Columbus, Ohio. So the computers in Columbus credited the sales to Columbus, not Huntington! As a consequence, advertising based on those numbers, resulted in increased commercials for those detergent products all over Columbus TV stations, instead of where the consumers were purchasing the detergent — *in my coverage area for WSAZ!!* And this was true across all sectors and for all kinds of products, including leading brands from companies like P&G, General Foods, SC Johnson, and others. Our market was being short-changed while Columbus was the beneficiary of a windfall of unwarranted advertising coin! I now had a story to tell. And boy did I love telling stories. Our rep, The Katz Agency, provided me with dozens of companies who bought advertising in Columbus, but bypassed us, giving me dozens of prospects. I developed a map showing trucking routes delivering products from Columbus directly to supermarkets in our coverage area, unreached by Columbus TV stations! And I started an endless trek; not to the ad agency time buyers, but directly to product managers for hundreds of nationally advertised brands from Atlanta to Battle Creek, from Cincinnati to Detroit, from Chicago to White Plains, and Rochester to Racine (where the winters, by the way, were far from pleasant). I spent lots of time on the road and scored some early successes, as recognized by the National Television Bureau of Advertising's naming my innovative sales strategy and pitch *"the year's best!"*

It took a lot of effort, but we brought dozens of new products like Tide, Toni Home Permanent, Martha White spinoffs, Wrigley, and others to the market. Some huge gains came from SC Johnson in Wisconsin, whose broker boasted how we had dramatically changed his business, adding a whole bevy of household products to our region's shelves for the first time ... and for decades to come.

In addition to all the traveling, I was anxious to assure our local sales staff that despite some increased pressure on inventory, their work provided an important foundation to the station's earnings and to their own profit sharing. I brought folks in from the Television Bureau of Advertising to conduct sales coaching workshops, which were greeted with little enthusiasm by our staff of seasoned execs. Bill Watts and Bob White were the veterans, backed by Bob Harris and Harold Hall, the latter having answered a TV spot we placed on our station, seeking salespersons. All were dedicated and I enjoyed generally good relations with the team. It was true, however, that Bob White, our most senior and experienced salesperson seemed decidedly unexcited about adopting new sales approaches, especially those that brimmed with the optimistic suggestion that there were prospects all around us! Bob politely brushed off my efforts to revamp the sales strategy, but I finally got the better of him, in an unorthodox way. I accompanied him on one of his sales calls through the rural back counties of West Virginia, including a visit Bob assured me was a complete waste of our time. The call was to an old pal of Bob's who ran a company manufacturing coal-mining equipment. In my typical gregarious fashion, I asked the owner to give us a tour. Before we knew it, a frowning, reluctant Bob and I had been outfitted with safety helmets (over our business suits) and were visiting an actual working mine! I asked the owner if he'd ever considered selling his custom built rail cars, using commercial time on TV. And, while Bob scoffed, I further offered to produce that commercial free of charge to him in order to test the idea. Some weeks later, our cameraman was lying on his stomach, with his camera and lights on the floor of a moving pallet, capturing a ride into the bowels of the mine. We successfully aired that spot campaign, selling the mine owner's equipment; the first of its kind in the region! Bob, in spite of himself, had to admit my methods were not all that hair-brained.

About two years into the job, a friend of the company named Reid Shaw, called me with the news that my college station, WRGB-TV wanted to interview me about the General Manager position there. I called Dan Burke and told him. After the usual *"hang tight, nothing is happening now, but changes are on the way ..."* conversation, Dan suggested I go ahead and take the interview anyhow. The man doing the hiring; let's call him Mr. Andrews, was in charge of General Electric's Consumer Products Division. He oversaw a budget of many millions of dollars including the TV station, but also GE's washer/dryers, refrigerators, and all sorts of other GE retail items. How excited could he be about a measly $5 million or $6 million from one TV station, I wondered. I flew to Syracuse one very cold winter morning and, after 10 minutes with Mr. Andrews, who was outfitted for a day of skiing, I figured out why Dan wanted me to take the trip. Mr. Andrews knew very little about television operations; and his questions made it clear that he was not in the Capcities league. When he asked me who this man I kept referring to as Tom Murphy was, I felt hard pressed to keep him from the slopes any longer. I told him Mr. Murphy ran the company that represented his primary competition in Schenectady. I thanked him graciously and told him I was not interested at this time. Reid Shaw apologized for wasting my time. Dan had taken a page out of Smitty's book. I was, by this time, thoroughly corrupted by Capital Cities. Years later, GE made another inquiry about my possibly joining them, and so did Cox ... I respectfully declined both offers.

By mid-1966, although the company was doing very well, unwelcome events were just ahead. Revenues were approaching the $25 million mark, when the company suffered severe, sudden leadership losses of more important dimensions than numbers. Harmon Duncan, owner and co-manager of WTVD in Durham suffered a heart attack in August of 1966, and died, shocking all of us. What happened next was that Frank Smith, who always rejected air travel, decided to attend Mr. Duncan's funeral by car. On the return trip from Durham, he, his wife and his driver, Jack, stopped for an overnight break at a motel in Maryland. That night, Aug. 6, 1966, Frank Smith suffered a heart seizure, and died. He was 56. The Capital Cities Board promptly named Tom its Chairman. Smitty's death went by without fanfare or wide public notice, as those who knew him expected he would prefer. His legacy was clear. Capital Cities was poised to take on the best.

Tom wasted no time in crafting the company's continued growth. According to a report produced by the Harvard Business School, from the time Tom replaced Smitty, the company's stock growth over the next 30 years returned $203 for every dollar invested. That Harvard report was accurate of course, but it addressed growth from the date Tom was made Chairman in 1966, and does not reflect growth since the original stock price in 1957 of $5.75. Footnotes in this book track that growth, assuming one held onto the original shares. That growth was astronomical.

In 1967, Tom engineered the purchase of KTRK-TV, the ABC affiliate in Houston, Texas, with the help of a fine, colorful Texan named Bill Wallbridge, whose appreciation of Tom persuaded the owners to choose Capcities. Bill became a valuable, popular asset to the company, and a wonderful personal friend and mentor to me.

In the early 1990s my dear friend, Walter Hawver, who served our company well in Albany and Houston, took a suggestion I made, and wrote a wonderful book about the company called "How the Minnow Came to Swallow the Whale." At his request, I collaborated with him, and among other stories, provided him with an anecdote that got around the company rather well. Tom Murphy, on one of his infrequent visits to

Huntington was sitting in our home and happened to call his secretary from the Beuth dining room table. After what seemed like an interminable wait on the phone, he learned that his secretary was having trouble finding a flight to get Tom back to New York. Tom set the phone down and asked, *"Philly, how the hell do you get out of here?"* Betty Beuth, without missing a beat, replied *"We have been asking you that for years, Tom!"*

There is a sad and ironic postscript to the Huntington story. Some of the biggest events on the calendar in Huntington were the Marshall University football team's away games. Particularly one toward the end of the season with one of the league's outstanding teams — the East Carolina Pirates out of Greenville, North Carolina. A charter plane had been booked to carry the team, the coaches and 25 local "boosters" to the much-anticipated game. Two weeks before the game, a college friend gave me two tickets for the plane and the game, and Betty and I debated using them. As the GM of WSAZ-TV, I presented the news and stocks at the Rotary lunch each Thursday. After my short report, a popular local politician named Mike Prestera, whom I liked a lot, saw the tickets sticking out of my breast pocket, came up to me and pulled them out saying, *"You won't be using these will you?"* I said, *"Not if you really want them, Mike."* Well, the team lost their away game to the Pirates, but that was not the tragedy. On the return trip, on the night of Nov. 14, 1970, the Southern Airways charter carrying the entire Marshall University football team, its coaching staff and 25 fans crashed trying to

161

land at the Huntington airport. All aboard perished, including Mike (who had taken my tickets), along with many other good folks. Just the thought of it remains painful.

My wife and I were not big boosters of Huntington. How could we be, given the discomfort the environment posed for our children? As a consequence, we were not devoted fans of the Marshall football team. If we had been, and if we had loved our town more, we'd have surely been on that plane and surely would have perished along with all aboard. After the tragedy, I was contacted by Martin Umansky, GM of a Witchita, Kansas, TV station, who reminded me that the Wichita State basketball team had recently suffered a similar crash. We conspired, and making a long story short, co-produced a telethon in the Wichita State gymnasium, fed to a hastily crafted network of 50 stations with Bill Cosby as host. We raised $400,000 for the crash victims' families. I am told that it took years to distribute the money.

So, to many of my fellow broadcasters and friends, some of whom have passed, thanks for some good memories. People like Jack Lee, Bob Franklin, Bos Johnson, Jule Huffman, Lew Click, John Clay, Mickey Curry, Jack Williams, Mickey Roth, Bob Harris, Bob White, Fritz Leichner, Bob Bowen, the whole Apgar family, Bill Watts, Bud Dailey, Harold Hall, Bob Brunner, Bill Kinnard and Shawkey Saba. You all remain in my thoughts. I am sure that one day, while reading this, I will remind myself of some nice folks I failed to mention! The bottom line was that West Virginia was simply not the right place and time for us and in many ways had an unfortunate and unwelcome influence on my family and me. We did have a magical moment on July 12, 1970, however, when our daughter Jane arrived.

As far as the West Virginia economy goes today, a friend tells me that since Gov. Bob Wise brought in slot machines to practically all bars and grills, things are "perking!" May God bless!

CHAPTER SEVENTEEN

And the Seas Parted

At some time in 1969, my boss changed from Joe Dougherty to Bob King, who had come to the company from Metromedia to be General Manager of our Buffalo station in 1961. No one who worked for either of these men would regret a single day. Joe was more laid back than Bob, but both had great personal skills. My memories of Joe include many short notes commenting on so many details that I knew he was paying attention. He referenced sales increases, cost controls, hires, and was not above leaving notes tucked into my tennis racket ... once even accompanied by new stock option grants!

Bob King was more likely to handle those items over a beer or two at a local jazz club. Both men were prize bosses who radiated Capcities style and personality. On about the sixth year of my "temporary" assignment in West Virginia, Bob King called with welcome news. The company had just concluded the purchase of radio and TV stations in New Haven and Philadelphia from Triangle Broadcasting, owned by the distinguished Walter Annenberg, who was at the time serving as our Ambassador to the Court of St. James, U.K. The purchase meant a likely sale of one or two of our television stations to satisfy FCC limits. Bob King assured me the deal was great for the company, and that good things lay ahead for us … and for me. He intimated the company would likely want to move my family and me to another post. That night at home there were mixed emotions about leaving friends we had made, but the overall feeling was that it was indeed time to move on. West Virginia had been a less than ideal assignment. Although the job went well, the toll on my family had been considerable.

The anatomy of the purchase, the largest in broadcast history, was significant for the company, and spoke eloquently to the reputation and esteem the Murphy/Burke team had established in the industry. Murphy had long targeted the Triangle properties, especially their premier operation, WFIL-TV in Philadelphia, an important ABC affiliate. Ambassador Annenberg had developed a broadcasting and publishing empire over the previous 40 or more years, including such prizes as The Philadelphia Inquirer, *The Daily Racing Form*, and *TV Guide*. Murph's previous discussions with the Ambassador had always been cordial, but had produced no indication of interest from the Triangle side. And so, one Saturday afternoon in February 1970, when a call came in from London, interrupting a basketball game Tom was watching with his son, Murph was pleasantly surprised to hear the Ambassador's voice. The purpose of the call was simply an invitation for Tom to visit Annenberg at his Philadelphia office the following Friday afternoon; an invitation Tom readily accepted. And I'm sure his mind went straight to the elephant gun he told us was always at the ready! The essence of the meeting and its repercussions over the following days became

Capcities folklore. I have personally heard all versions and retell it now as accurately as I have heard it recounted by Tom.

Murph brought with him the prominent Republican of CIA and SEC fame, Bill Casey, who was a Capcities Board member. Murph recalls the meeting as short and businesslike, sparing all but the briefest pleasantries. Murph said that the Ambassador first remarked on the high regard he held for Capital Cities and quickly followed up with his willingness to sell Tom his properties in Philadelphia and New Haven; those being WFIL-AM and WFIL-TV, along with WNHC-TV, at a cost of $100 million, $29 million down, with the balance to be paid off in eight years at prevailing prime. Tom, delightfully stunned by the enormity of the opportunity, walked across the room without a word and shook hands on the deal, which was set to close in March of 1971. When they adjourned, Bill and Tom found themselves in the elevator. Bill turned to Tom, *"You just met Santa Claus."* It was a quick and surprisingly uncomplicated transaction, a testament to the transparency, business acumen and class of the Ambassador.

But as conservative radio talent and right wing pundit of the time, Paul Harvey might have pointed out, there is a *"rest of the story,"* which I know to be true, but which has not yet been recorded accurately elsewhere to my knowledge. The next day Tom chaired a conference call in which I participated. As Tom was telling those of us on the call about the Annenberg meeting, he was interrupted by Ruth Bassett Fitzgerald, who advised him it was the Ambassador's office calling. Before he took the call, Tom said to us all, *"I hope he hasn't changed his mind!"* As we held the call (and our breath), we could clearly hear Tom's side of the conversation, peppered with a few *"yes sirs"* an *"I understand completely"* and, finally ... *"The answer is yes."* After he hung up, Tom rejoined the conference call, asking, *"Where in hell is Fresno? That was Annenberg's finance guy. We just bought their Fresno TV and radio for $10 million! The Ambassador decided he wanted to sell Fresno, and we now have it in the deal."* Decisions, even major decisions, sometimes come as an afterthought and lives can change in an instant ... as I was about to learn.

A few weeks later, Bob King predictably asked me to think about New Haven. He was sure I was the right man for WTNH, an ABC affiliate. I immediately subscribed to the New Haven Register, had it mailed to Huntington and began scanning the real estate sections. Murph and Dan, meantime, were under time pressures, since the Ambassador had given them a year, until March 1971 to close the deal. They faced potentially deal-breaking obstacles in the form of minority group challenges and station ownership swaps to meet FCC rules. It became obvious almost immediately that my station, WSAZ-TV would be sold.

As we approached the closing, Bob began to tell me that although New Haven was still an option, there were new discussions, considering each station's needs, pointing to Fresno for me. Bob began to sell me on the idea that I was a better fit for Fresno because it badly lacked the kind of help I could provide in programming, news and especially promotion. New Haven did not need a new start, but Fresno did. That turned out to be true, but at the time, I was focused on New Haven. The clincher came when Bob suggested that Fresno was Dan and Tom's preference for me as well, and that moving to a smaller market would not affect my compensation, a factor that was far from negligible for my family of five.

I accepted Fresno and did not talk to either Tom or Dan prior to the decision. Years later, both told me I would likely have been a better fit for New Haven.

CHAPTER EIGHTEEN

Into the Valley

By 1971, Dan and Tom had put the Triangle acquisition to bed and were looking at broadening our interests into the new world of publishing. Fairchild Publications was about to become a distinguished, profitable print companion to our maturing broadcast operation. Fairchild would be the first of several publishing acquisitions that ultimately not only matched or exceeded our broadcast earnings, but more importantly, added a corps of talented men and women to our roster. More on that to come ...

Meanwhile, Betty and I, the three boys and their baby sister, Jane, were settling in to sunny California! Fresno is north of Los Angeles and Bakersfield, and a two-hour drive east of Monterey and Carmel. The San Joaquin Valley claims to be the number one agricultural producing region in the state and Fresno County promotes itself as the largest agricultural county in the country. It is hot and dry and is framed by the majestic Sierra Nevada Mountains to the east; an hour drive north is Yosemite. Fresno was, I have to say, a most welcome change. We found local theatre, good schools, better newspapers, modern shopping, gorgeous homes, and dozens of lifestyle amenities absent in Appalachia.

I was told by my boss, Bob King, that the station, KFRE-TV, had been labeled the worst CBS affiliate in the country, making it *"perfect for you, Phil."* It may well have deserved that moniker as it was a sort of black sheep of the Triangle family, separated geographically from its sister cities. Managed from Philadelphia (more than half way across the country), it was being hammered by the competition. First was the NBC affiliate, KMJ-TV, owned by the McClatchy organization and the long time audience leader in the Valley. Retlaw Broadcasting (Disney), which ranked second, had an ABC affiliation, and an independent station, KMPH-TV, was third. KFRE-TV, renamed KFSN-TV deserved its fourth place position. It aired in black and white, transmitted from a small studio in a seedy part of town, had very little syndicated programming, a slim news department, a skeleton staff, and a weak program lineup. Its run rate was a $12,000 deficit per month. *"... See, perfect for you, Phil."*

I set about the task eagerly, spreading the Capcities gospel to the staff, assuring them their jobs were safe. It was not a tough sell because of our reputation, combined with their neglected orphan status of the past. I was aided by Dick Appleton, the Sales Manager I inherited, who decided to join the station once he heard Capcities would be involved. He left a good sales job in LA because he knew our reputation; and he had preconditioned many on the staff with high expectations. About 6 feet 4 inches, and a veteran of Duke's basketball championship seasons, Dick made a fine impression. His choice to join another winning team paid off as he had a long career with the company, becoming a dear friend along the way.

Arriving in town just before my 39th birthday, and two weeks before the next rating period, my first department head meeting tackled the program schedule. After a daylong session, I announced we were making immediate, dramatic changes. Program Manager, Lee Jason, a man I came to admire greatly, made a strong case that we didn't have enough time to buy syndication and build a proper promotion campaign. I agreed with his concern, *but too bad — we were going ahead!* A half-dozen syndicated salesmen showed up immediately, and a brand new afternoon line-up, catering to kids and young adults, materialized almost overnight. We bought "Petticoat Junction" and "Lost in Space," changed the time of the local news, and added some creative promotion. I sent our maintenance guy down to 20th Century Fox in LA, where the "Lost in Space" robot sat in mothballs and had it abducted and brought to our studios. We added an on-air contest about outer space, and were absolutely knocked over when, two months later, the ratings book showed growth from a six share to a 48 share! Wow, that got everyone's attention, including management in NY. Dick and I had been sure our moves would bring some growth, and had convinced our reps in LA and San Francisco to boost commercial rates, just in case. It worked as though a magic wand had been waved over the station. Shocked, we had far greater growth than expected, right out of the gate! We held a full staff meeting, brimming with anticipation, at which I suggested we had released an emergency brake that had been holding the station back! In a real sense, it was true. Monetizing our growth was an active advertising agency group — something I had sorely missed in Huntington. I immediately became active in their Ad Club, interfacing with folks like the Sturgeons, The Cliff Davis Company, Looney Advertising, Walter Daley, Mike Theilen, and others. The agencies were a receptive group to our local sales team, led by Tony Twibell, Bob Dutra, Ray Carrasco, Dudley Few and Dick Wagshall.

Years later, as a guest speaker at the Club, visiting from my post as head of GMA, I was introduced as *"the man who woke up the advertising business and then, four short years later, skipped town!"* Local revenues increased as the staff was encouraged to get more involved in community. I asked the employees to place the station on *"the tip of an arrow, aimed at everything that was happening in town,"* an image I had effectively used in the past and continued using for a long time. During the first few months, my activity consisted of interviewing community leaders to get a feel for the city. Along the way, I learned that Fresno suffered from a subtle, unspoken inferiority complex about being the unwanted stepchild of Los Angeles and San Francisco. People actually loved their city, but were shy and reticent to express it. I took that little piece of information and insisted that all station identification, both visual and audible, announce, *"This is Channel 30 Fresno, a GREAT place to be!"* That television cue reminded viewers they were watching a great station in a great city and it became more than just station identification; it became a rallying cry. I was told time and again, it just made people feel good! Selling can take many forms, I thought, remembering Jack Goldman and the Christmas billboard ...

Spurred by a strong start, audiences grew steadily and consistently. Jeff McCracken, our head of news, gradually upgraded the reporter corps, gaining momentum as we added some new and distinct promotion. Ted Knight remained a true friend, who was gracious enough to come up from LA to help with gratis air promotion for our main anchorman, Roger Rocka. His copy likening our anchorman's name to a candy bar, zipped around town nicely.

Each of the three main anchors wore obvious hairpieces on the air, giving me an idea. I asked Roger how he would feel if he never had to wear the rug again. *"You mean I'm fired?"* *"No, Roger, you're not fired. What if we take off your hairpiece ... live, on the air!"* I replied. He loved the idea and the next night he did an *"only my hairdresser knows"* routine and as he lifted it off, cheerfully commenting, *"The lid is off Action News."* Viola! Positive reactions came from everywhere, and the other competitive anchors could never duplicate that stunt!! As time went on, adding full color and better syndication from 7 to 8 p.m., we just kept growing.

The station had a long-term talent called Al Radka, who was our local "Mr. Television." Everyone in town knew who he was, but many considered him a borderline buffoon. He aired long, live, hyper commercials for his pals who ran dry cleaning

175

stores or pizza shops. He dressed casually, and carried — *I kid you not* — a rubber chicken around his neck! Al insisted it was his trademark and essential to his image. I insisted differently. *"Throw away the chicken; trade it in for a shirt, tie and jacket, Al, and you will be a new man!"* I claimed. Predicting doom, telling me I was ruining his cherished career, he finally relented and cleaned up. The public loved it and he lasted many years as the new classier Al Radka! He later thanked me, *"On behalf of my many fans!"* he boasted.

The station quickly became connected and involved with the community. We helped regenerate interest in a stalled Cerebral Palsy Center, attracting much public attention and praise. I joined a couple of high profile organizations and launched a 15-minute "Let me speak to the Manager" show at noon on occasional Thursdays. Always candid about programs I thought were good or bad, I corrected an occasional news gaff, and worked on improving credibility. I also started responding by hand to viewer mail, a practice I continued for years going forward. Good, persistent selling never stopped.

One of our lighter moments involved a live musical stage show for the public about Fresno's fictitious drought, and its need for a lake reservoir downtown. It was presented by the Ad Club. Chuck Carson and I created it, and with the help of Frank Wells and his orchestra, Tal Jonz, Ken Owens, Dan Pessano, Art Bender and other outrageous hams, we pulled it off to unexciting reviews. I was awarded their Member of the Year honor for two years running; something I understand had never happened before or since. Socially, Fresno was a revitalizing gust of fresh air. We built a lovely home and entertained often. Our friends were from inside and outside the business, including a few celebs from LA.

Our memories of Fresno include a man named Frank Sinatra, who happened our way in 1974. One of Bob Hope's wartime traveling buddies was a guitarist named Tony Romano, who lived in Fresno and operated Romano's Italian restaurant. He had a pal named Frank Wells, who'd been a musician of some distinction before moving to Fresno to work at the NBC station — my competition. I met and liked Frank immediately. One day in the spring of 1974, Tony called on me with an idea. Sinatra was in retirement and wanted a station to air and test new material for his comeback, billed as "Ol' Blue Eyes is Back" on the NBC national network in November. Tony had a charity he wanted to help. He proposed that the station promote and produce a Sinatra concert with proceeds going to charity. Frank Wells' station had apparently turned it down. We jumped at the chance, booked the new Fresno convention center, promoted it extensively — to the sellout point — and had a smash hit. I oversaw the promotion, the accounting and the normal freebee tickets. I finally met The Man himself on the morning of the show. He was certainly cool — black turtleneck, sharply creased slacks, loafers, teeth a brighter shade of white than seemed possible on a human being. He was just simply *"It," in one!* I expected he would be casual and he was. I expected he would be in charge and he was. He had a stack of charts handled by a few sidemen he had brought with him, and joked with the crew as if they were old friends. When I asked how things were going, he smiled and said, *"Just fine, boss!"* When I started to assure him that we had a good fix on the charity and mentioned our expense controls, he reassuringly said, *"There are no expenses, we'll handle all that."* After the concert, Tony invited Betty and me to his restaurant for dinner with Frank and his team. We were thrilled. When we got there, Sinatra graciously escorted Betty to a private dining room where she was seated right next to The Man himself. Joining us was a fellow I did not expect, who just happened to be in town. Accompanied by an oversized glass of vodka, no ice, "F Troop" star, Forrest Tucker sat down with us. The jokes were great and terribly raunchy, but the laughs rolled along for an unforgettable couple of hours. I can still picture Betty and Frank at the end of the table, smoking and laughing. The next time I saw Sinatra was about 10 years later. I was sitting with some of our salesmen having a drink in Peacock Alley at New York's Waldorf, when I noticed a stir a few tables away and saw a man sit at Cole Porter's famous piano. Next came Sinatra and a half dozen of his pack. He sang for more than an hour to an audience of maybe 75 enchanted people — what a thrill!

Station revenues continued to grow, and within a year we were able to anticipate modest profits, due to the turnaround in audience and station prominence. At the annual CBS affiliate convention in 1974, compliments about the station's rebound came from the podium. The fact that by then I was a member of the network's affiliate board may have had something to do with the praise! A few Fresno stalwarts like Lee Jason, our gentlemanly golden-voiced program manager, Ed Mayo, head of the CP Center and Ed Sturgeon had passed, but we stay in touch with their wives, Ann Mayo and Pat Jason, plus the charming irrepressible Vonny Sturgeon. We also enjoyed updates from a guy I call old reliable, Bob Tyrcha. Rebuilding audience and sales was exciting and fun. Managing a challenge to our broadcast license would prove less amusing, though it soon came to dominate our agenda.

A year before we took over in Fresno, our attorneys and management were seriously pressed to satisfy FCC ownership rules and meet the Annenberg closing deadline for the Philadelphia, New Haven and Fresno purchases. Just months before the deadline, a petition to deny the new licenses was filed by a minority group. Their position, justifiably, was that blacks, Hispanics and Native American Indians in the affected three markets were not adequately represented in programming and hiring practices in the predominantly white broadcast industry. They took this opportunity to make demands of Capital Cities as the clock ticked, providing them considerable leverage. Negotiations continued until Capcities made an unprecedented offer. The company pledged $1 million from the three stations for minority programming, training and hiring, in coordination with community groups from each market. *Broadcasting Magazine* characterized the proposal as pacification ... *"buying peace with dollars."*

The agreement was very loosely structured, making it rather vague for all parties. General Managers were expected to fully comply, but, in keeping with the company's autonomous operating philosophy, were not given specific guidelines or a master plan. Joe Dougherty simply told each of us, *"Make it work!"* We had hired an African-American man named Andy Jackson to help make the plan succeed. Andy came recommend to us by a TV executive at Metromedia whom the Capcities team greatly admired (and who would later join our ranks and ultimately become our CEO), John Sias. John had spotted Andy when he was an early TV entrepreneur and pioneer in UHF TV and radio in Michigan. Sias directed Dougherty's attention to articles in the national press about Andy's local programming innovations. Andy joined us with the assignment of making positive things happen between the minority groups and the stations — uncharted territory, indeed. He was to be our *"go to"* guy if things got sticky and if wrinkles in the plan needed smoothing. Smooth was one apt and dandy word for this cool fellow who joined the party and soon became the company's only genuine rock star. He brought a bright, curious personality and a sharp sense of humor to a situation where tempers would periodically flare. Over the course of a few years, his reputation became richly enhanced by his ability not only to meld community activists and company staffs, but to attract unusual and high profile acquaintances. Meeting Andy in New York for business dinners or a libation often brought surprises in the form of unusual, sometimes glamorous "friends." His coterie of minions, models, matrons, and masters of Zen constituted a moveable groupie retinue. I always enjoyed his infectious personality and company, though I also wondered how all that personal entertainment squared with the notoriously rigorous Capcities expense accounting system! I did not always agree with Andy, but spending time with him was always a treat and he was, after all, the gatekeeper for the pledges we had all made to our minority constituencies.

As the community outreach Committee formed in Fresno, it became obvious that membership came with a variety of ambitions and motivations. Our group had several factions: The black group contained both moderate community-minded men and women and younger, male aggressive types of initially questionable intentions. The Hispanic group held local businessmen and women, plus others who were attracted by their experience as protestors against Fresno State University's minority shortcomings. Thirdly, there were a few Native American men who attended sporadically, in varied composition and numbers. Ironically, they had perhaps the most legitimate reasons to be attentive because their plight of unemployment, desperation and homelessness was completely ignored by the local media. Unfortunately they were not really equipped to take advantage of this opportunity.

It was decided that we would meet every other Monday night, except during school breaks and holidays. That pattern continued for several years. Our Program Manager and Business Manager attended the bi-weekly meetings with me, as did other staffers from time to time for sensitivity training. Several mandates emerged from our first meetings. Each ethnic group insisted they could and would meet privately amongst themselves, but I insisted no official business be conducted outside our regular full meetings. Each feared losing out to another. Further, the Hispanic group was divided by nomenclature according to persuasion. Aggressive members wanted to be called "Chicanos" and moderates called "Hispanics." The Hispanics were insulted by the term, Chicano, and refused to attend meetings in the Chicano barrio. Minutes identified each faction separately. Fissures and fractures were normal, and few actions were unanimous. I was visited by two men from the FBI who expressed interest in the group. They asked only a few questions about the program and intimated they would continue to monitor our activity. As our meetings became regular events, I wondered if there was any kind of infiltration, but saw no evidence of such at any time, and never heard from the FBI again. Station initiatives, such as assignments to watch and comment on our training or employment, were given only casual attention, despite our continued inclusion as items on the agenda. One positive result came soon, however. Our station staff was being sensitized — an absolute necessity if we were to accomplish anything of consequence. Early on, intimidation was a strategy commonly employed by young male members, who showed up bare-chested, necks ringed with multiple chains, even bearing swastikas. Raised voices were common, but amounted to little except noise. Conservative blacks were embarrassed, especially a religious, God-fearing woman named Mrs. Sudie Douglas, who finally resigned, calling the group "sinful." She reported information we already knew, like fictitious receipt books for cash reimbursements and other potential rip-offs. I encouraged her to remain, assuring her that we were monitoring and rejecting the most obvious attempts at chicanery. Over time, Mrs. Douglas satisfied her conscience, calling me secretly to fill me in on high jinks, most of which I was aware of. I never asked her to spy, or to obtain a single piece of information.

We, for a time, rented an abandoned supermarket, and set up a few editing booths and camera equipment to train young students. The group preferred blaring wild music for dancing, with a lookout posted to warn of a station vehicle, or my car coming to visit, at which time the editing booths were hastily reoccupied. After a while, the abuse forced closure. Meanwhile, we were interviewing and hiring with special intention to adding minorities. We hired a talented Hispanic female reporter and a well-educated Hispanic man named Bob Rios as our business Manager, but the committee was not satisfied with his background. He remained and did fine work. News made special efforts to increase content addressing minority concerns, but our actions rarely seemed to satisfy this fractured group.

Throughout our experience, my most frequent contact was with Ricardo Duran, the most effective and committed Chicano on the Committee. Smart and handsome, his long black hair and black eyes recalled popular artistic illustrations of Jesus Christ. I suspect and hope he is still active in his cause. Had he chosen a more traditional career in business or politics, I believe he could have been extremely successful. As we spent more and more time together we established a sound working relationship and mutual respect, though we had gotten off to a shaky start. As the program started, in my small office, Ricardo, and a few of his associates, proceeded to tell that they knew all about me, and they proceeded to lecture me on why I was unqualified to understand their plight! They said my background in New York public schools, an upstate "rich man's" college, work in Albany and West Virginia, had hardly prepared me to understand the concerns of disadvantaged Mexican immigrants. They claimed that the books I read about Mexico demeaned them as fat, dumb cartoon characters, usually sleeping against a tree, sheltered from the sun by an oversized sombrero! And I had to concede, they were largely correct! Those schoolbooks are criminal, they added, saying I should know that those Mexicans only appeared to be sleeping. In reality they are resentful of the gringo and boiling with rage ... and that one day they were going to rise as a force and blow up this station! At that, they punctuated their warning by slamming their fists down on my desk, before sitting back down, visibly angry. I recovered somewhat and told Ricardo neither of us would benefit from such a threat. But they had made their point and articulated their rage.

The second incident occurred months later during one of our Monday night meetings when Ricardo and I got into a heated debate and Ricardo knew he was not making sense. The next morning, he marched into my office all riled up to emphasize one specific point. He wanted me to know that regardless of who was right or wrong, he would never give in. This time he slammed his flat, open hand against the wall, as he shouted, *"For my people I will be a wall!"*

I could discern his hand imprint in the drywall for as long as I had the office. I spent more time with Ricardo than with any other member of the Committee, usually at his invitation. We'd meet across the tracks in the barrio, where we walked the streets together. On one occasion, he took me into a movie theater where the audience consisted primarily of unemployed men. He wanted to show me how Hollywood emasculated Mexican men by purposely showcasing large-busted, blonde, white women in movies made for distribution in Mexico. During the first few months, when the Committee realized we were not rolling over to fulfill their every extraneous demand, they insisted they would no longer deal with me and demanded to speak directly with Mr. Murphy. Murph flew out to dinner with the group and set everyone straight with a simple speech. *"The station and its decisions are entirely Mr. Beuth's responsibility. If anyone calls me, my response will be clear. Talk to Mr. Beuth."*

Over time, Ricardo and I developed a reasonable degree of mutual trust. I really liked the man, and respected his work. The fact is that we could have achieved more, just the two of us, without the Committee. Reflections even after these many years cannot diminish the waste of time, money and efforts resulting from the extortion-imposed plan. I believe that if a simple directive had been issued requiring measurable performance and a better-vetted committee including some objective oversight from outside the market, more would have been accomplished. However, the history of past inertia seemed to rule in favor of this more litigious confrontational course of action. But, the station did increase minority hiring, sensitized the news and entertainment programming, and devoted more attention to a large sector of an othewise disenfranchised population.

Another example of frustration, despite meaningful efforts, is worth telling. In February of 1973, an incident took place at Wounded Knee, South Dakota, that immediately galvanized the attention of our generally quiet Native American members. Some 200 Oglala Lakota Native Americans stood in defiance of the FBI and U.S. Marshals, citing long-standing issues of injustice. Since several of our Native American members had learned how to do news reporting, it seemed an appropriate opportunity to test their newfound skills by sending them out into the field. After a bit of research, planning and help from the station news department, it was decided to underwrite the cost of sending two crews, with cameras, audio and mics on assignment to Wounded Knee, where the standoff continued. They were to report from the viewpoint of the Native Americans who were opposing FBI tactics. Teams were prepped, cars rented, and because the crew had no credit cards, petty cash was provided for hotel rooms, food, etc. About $1,200 as I recall. Two three-man crews left for Wounded Knee.

About a week later, Dan Burke, by then our Chief Operating Officer, happened to drop in to Fresno for dinner after a day in Los Angeles. He had never been to the station, so the next morning at about 10 he paid me a visit in my office. As we were chatting, I looked out towards the lobby to see one of the production teams, just back from Wounded Knee. I anxiously waived them in and, without introducing Dan, asked them how things had gone. *"Not very good, Mr. Beuth,"* one man answered. *"How much did you shoot?"* I asked. *"We shot a lot, but don't have none,"* was the answer. *"What do you mean?"* I asked. *"Well, we stopped in Visalia for breakfast this morning, and lost what we shot. Somebody stole it. We went in to breakfast and while we were in the diner, somebody stole the car."* *"Did you leave the car unlocked?"* I asked, now not knowing what to expect. *"We left the keys in the car."* *"You what? What else did you lose?"* *"Well, the cameras, the money ... everything."* *"You left cash in the car?"* I interrupted. *"Yes, everything, including all the receipts"* ... then silence. *"Fellas, I cannot believe that and I am not sure the committee will believe it either."* I suggested they write it up and report the stolen car to the police. Burke sat, staring in disbelief. I expected him to explode, but he did not. Neither of us ever believed their story. The committee did an investigation and decided that it happened because the young people were *"unfamiliar with responsibility!"* These men were in their 20s! Their story was so ludicrous that I suspected they did not shoot anything acceptable and sold the equipment. The police found the rental car, abandoned. At first, I wanted the police to cross examine the three men, but I knew the result would damage the program, so I chalked it up to just another disappointment in an overall frustrating experience. The second team came back with some good video, which was used on air. They also had a receipt book, with creative expenses listed, but few formal receipts. And the "game" played on, to my dismay.

I trust that today overall conditions for minority persons have improved in the Valley. On par, I was proud of my contribution to whatever progress was achieved despite the continual frustration. At the same time, I was deeply dissatisfied with the process, which, had it taken a different form, could have been far more productive. I was also struck by the irony of my abrupt transplant from Huntington, West Virginia, where my views were considered too progressive and too liberal to this new environment where I was constantly being chastised for a worldview considered racially insensitive and close-minded, even bigoted! Only in America ...

But after four years, it was time for a new assignment. I was relocated, this time to WKBW-TV Buffalo, and replaced in Fresno by Walter Liss, a man who was moving rapidly up the ranks from spots like Buffalo and Philadelphia. We would hear lots more from this bright man and I was about to have a great run in the Queen City.

❧ ⌘ ☙

CHAPTER NINETEEN

In the Black (ink)

All during this time, starting in 1967, Tom Murphy was actively seeking new revenue sources to add to the growing broadcast group and he now settled on publishing — specifically newspapers and magazines — for two reasons. First, he had hit his threshold of station ownership, so every new acquisition had to be offset by the sale of an existing asset. And second, as broadcasting was an advertiser-supported media, owning another of the prominent advertising platforms made good economic sense.

Like any skilled hunter (and Tom was a superb marksman), patience and agility proved his strong points. He had been keeping a watchful eye on one of America's oldest and most distinguished family-owned fashion publishing houses. Fairchild Publications was founded in 1892 by Edmund Fairchild, a peddler, who took over the Daily Trade Record (later the Daily News Record), a failing newspaper that covered the men's clothing business. Ed Fairchild built that newspaper into a successful venture and in 1910, took what was originally an insert in DNR, and created a powerhouse stand-alone known as *Women's Wear Daily*. Aside from these two blockbuster publications, Fairchild boasted a handful of other fashion trade papers.

When Tom caught wind that Fairchild might be shopping for a buyer, he thought he might have found the right match for his broadcast group. And when Tom knocked on their door, his reputation preceded him. He found a warm reception from the Fairchild family who welcomed Murphy and the prospect of a well-run, structured company like Capital Cities. Similarly, Murph welcomed Fairchild's $20 million in gross sales. Fairchild, a company unaccustomed to fiscal discipline and lofty profit margins, needed a top-to-bottom restructuring in order to conform to Capcities business practices. Tom convinced Dan Burke to leave Detroit for New York to take on a set of challenges in a brand new industry. Fairchild, then led by John "Fashion Personified" Fairchild, responded well, as John ironically enjoyed more editorial autonomy than when the company was run by his own family. His staff of veterans also appreciated that the new *"fresh-to-print"* ownership team respected the lore, history and traditions of the magazines. Despite a few early bumps in the road, mutual respect developed rather quickly, producing some strong, long-term "partners." The Fairchild acquisition proved complex, but the benefits were sustained and far-reaching, especially as Fairchild brought a strong bench of seasoned professionals to a company thirsty for a broader executive team. From the ranks of Fairchild alone, dozens of talented assets found their way into our management; people like John Fairchild, Jim Brady, Bill Dwyer, Dan Newman, David Branch, Dick Lynch, Steve Stoneburn, Phil McGovern, Octavia Thompson, June Weir, Michael Coady and Marty Rosenblum, among others. Many of these executives participated in subsequent

Capcities/Fairchild ventures, like the launch and immediate success of *W Magazine*. In addition to Fairchild talent, the purchase also introduced changes and additions to the Capital Cities executive ranks. Burke named Bill James to replace him in Detroit. Joe Dougherty's role was expanded as he found himself involved in several print purchases as well as broadcasting. In a master stroke, the Murphy/Burke team hired brilliant businessman, personality, and occasional wag, John Sias — the very same John Sias who had recommended Andy Jackson to be our community outreach liaison in Fresno. Sias spearheaded a number of successful ventures for us and his trajectory was always peppered by a bucket load of colorful anecdotes. Sias became president of Fairchild in 1971. His creative energy, combined with an elfish prankster persona blended well with like-minded original talents that could always be found in the fashion publishing world. John's history with the company spanned many years, beginning with a tremendously profitable venture into specialized publications at Fairchild and the expansion of their core fashion papers. Sias' career with the company was a memorable mix of humor and brilliance, and fortunately for this writer, included a full run in television.

Now, new profits from publishing began to fuel continued expansion, just as earlier acquisitions in radio and television had provided cash infusions in prior years. And as the print side of the business gathered momentum, Dan Burke, now head of publishing, completed the purchase of The Pontiac Press in Oakland, Michigan. This opened another door, through which strolled an acquaintance of Dan's from the Detroit days named Phil Meek. Phil, who came from an entirely other industry, was named publisher of the Pontiac Press in a baptism by fire, which included contending with circulation drops, a weak staff, subscriber cancellations, and union problems. As this book was being researched, I asked Phil Meek to reflect on those early years. What he wrote follows:

"Having spent years in finance at the Ford Motor Company, I was accustomed to analyzing and reviewing the decisions made by others. Now appointed Publisher of The Pontiac Press — at age 32! — I was expected to make decisions with little involvement from above. Within three months, Dan Burke concluded I was having difficulty. 'I sense in you,' he said, 'a reluctance to decide something until you have all the facts, so you keep delaying to get more information to make sure you're right. We don't have time for that. Look at what you can, seek your people's ideas and views, and then do something. Remember, Ty Cobb still holds the all time batting average at .420, so he was out more than half the time! You're smart enough to be right more than half the time.' That turned out to be a liberating moment although it took me longer than it should have to get the hang of it. Yes, I made my share of mistakes, but learned from them and went on. So much of what made Capital Cities special was embodied in those word: Do not let lack of experience stand in the

way of hiring the right person. Counsel and work with subordinates. Don't send them off to some seminar on decision-making or leadership. Be patient with the people who work for you. Let them make mistakes but expect them to be smart enough not to make the same mistake twice."

Phil's reflections speak clearly to the powerful central tenets of the Capital Cities operating philosophy.

Meanwhile, in Pontiac, union battles, walkouts and strikes brought us Bob Ballow, a tough labor negotiator who remained our chief counsel for years. Ballow, Meek and others who followed eventually worked out a settlement with the Teamsters, changed the paper's name to The Oakland Press and restored larger readership. When Meek was transferred to Fort Worth, Bruce McIntyre, a seasoned pro, became Publisher and was joined by young talents like Rich Connor and John Coots, who provided additional armor in ongoing labor disputes and helped spur the paper's circulation growth. Despite soft economic times, the team survived until the auto industry revived, allowing them to prosper and eventually break the union's stranglehold.

While this was going on, Tom trained his sights on another well-established, family-run newspaper, The Belleville News-Democrat, which had been in the Kern family in Illinois since the 1890s. Tom, again, chose one of our company's brightest and most promising 30-year-olds, John Shuff, who had spent a short time in Oakland, to be publisher. The Murphy/Burke duo was certainly and constantly raiding and restocking the talent deck! Later, when Shuff was named chief financial officer for the company and sent to New York, even more changes took place in Belleville. Darwin Wile, Gary Berkley and later Rich Connor took over, setting circulation and profit records for years. They made circulation shifts to follow population changes and made wise investments in people and equipment. A new Sunday edition and innovative layout design ushered in new readers and resulted in profits greater than those of many other company-owned papers. These and other outstanding performances, one after another, demonstrated to the industry and to Wall Street that Capital Cities management consistently operated acquisitions more profitably than did the former owners.

The purchase of a Fort Worth newspaper was the most compelling and complicated Murph had ever experienced. In order to buy the famed Star Telegram, Capcities would first have to divest itself of the sister broadcast properties held by the seller, the Amon G. Carter Foundation. They were WBAP-TV, WBAP-AM and WBAP-FM. Tom tapped his former CFO, Don Pels, who had purchased WFIL-AM in the Triangle deal, as a possible buyer. Pels made one of the best purchases of his remarkable career when he bought WBAP-TV for $35 million. The Star Telegram had tremendous circulation "deep in the heart" of West Texas, and had readers who revered it as gospel. It had been run for decades by a giant in Forth Worth named Amon Carter, who passed away in 1955. The paper, however, had been on a multiple year decline, making it ripe for a Capital Cities restructure. Amon Carter Jr. was an amiable man who became publisher upon his father's death, relying on his father's old hands to run the paper. By 1974, after prolonged difficulties, the required FCC matters were finally settled. Warren Potash, a Capital Cities radio veteran, was named manager of the AM and FM stations. Potash, one of the company's most creative radio programmers, invited Joe Somerset, another company radio whiz, to join him in a makeover that excited the industry. Potash had cut his teeth on exciting promotional concepts in Buffalo and Providence radio, and was just as unorthodox at Fort Worth, introducing some new, nationally recognized sales and programming approaches. The results were record-breaking profits for years. Meanwhile, at the newspaper, Murph took good care of Amon Jr., protecting his image and appreciating his value, while Dan concentrated on operations, inviting some of our other publishers and Joe Dougherty, as well, into planning discussions. To our extreme delight, along came a man named Jim Hale. He was as genuine a newspaperman as one could find. A Baylor University Journalism alumnus, he had done it all in newsrooms all over Texas. Some remarked that printer's ink ran through his veins. When he was named publisher of The Star Telegram, he had no idea that he was beginning a long and distinguished Capital Cities run. He knew the business, and worked at it with great vigor, improving operations and profits immediately. Murph's talent roster was growing and changes were in the wind. Soon Meek was in Fort Worth, succeeded at Pontiac by another comer, Rich Connor.

By the time Meek arrived at The Star Telegram, Jim Hale had already resolved many of the union problems and begun to bolster the paper's profits, which did not seem to be a particular priority of the paper's former Publisher. Meek continued Hale's work and met West Texas population growth by stretching the paper's news presence in those fringe areas that were facing shrinkage in circulation and readership. At the paper, both Hale and Meek were viewed as "outsiders," who had to convince the staff that decisions would continue to be made locally, without interference. Burke came up with a simple solution and opened the company's financial books to the Telegram management. It was the first time such specific information had been shared, making it clear Capcities would operate with trust and transparency. Meek still had union issues, but positive market conditions were on his side. He increased editorial content and staff, playing the population growth like a maestro conducting a new brass section. He spent money on news bureaus, advertising, and a $75 million printing and distribution center, all of which produced substantial returns. The paper also earned two Pulitzer Prizes. By 1985, profits at The Star Telegram exceeded $40 million. Meek later moved on to become president of the division. He remains our retired print "Guru." And he also has helped this writer with many of the important details of the company's newspaper history, as did Walter Hawver's previously cited book.

From the 1970s through the 1980s, other properties like the Oregon-based Jackson newspaper chain were acquired, along with Connecticut's Shoreline Newspapers and Penny Power Shopping News in the Midwest. These gave people like Glen Cushman, Tom Cronk, John Coots and others an opportunity to add to our revenue and profits while competing for readers with traditional dailies. Over the years, more community newspapers were added. By 1992, group head Wes Turner was presiding over a total weekly circulation of more than 2 million homes. In subsequent years, The New England Newspaper Group evolved and provided attractive alternatives to the regular city papers in Hartford and New Haven.

While those additional enterprises became future treasures, nothing by 1977 appeared more promising to Murph than the Kansas City Star/Times. Murph paid a whopping $125 million to acquire those publications, recognizing that these highly respected newspapers would substantially elevate the company's profile on the media landscape. From its first issues in the 1800s, and through the Depression, the Kansas City Star/Times was known for publishing highly acclaimed papers. But when Murph came on the scene, the venerable enterprise was suffering a serious shortfall and lacked the bailout cash to keep operations afloat. Historically, management had opted for the "security" of a stock plan that benefited just the very few senior executives. A pattern of low wages and a management team that treated employees as chattel provided Murph with a turnaround possibility that would be employee-friendly and restore some of the security the larger staff had been denied. Tom started boosting morale by offering to buy employees out at 2½-times book value — a move that was not universally supported. But, it did have the effect of healing old wounds as it proved an exceptional windfall for the staff and some retirees. Murph knew that Jim Hale would be the right match for the Star and named him Publisher as soon as the deal was finalized. Jim Hale made his usual, unorthodox management shifts and his strong presence sent the message that the paper would not be run by New York. Hale engineered a multiple-year restructuring of the staff management, marketing, editorial policy, and business approach. He enlisted highly skilled newspapermen and women from outside the market, updated the presses, re-established ownership of delivery systems, and regularly raised rates. His legacy set standards and engendered levels of respect and loyalty that are the envy of the industry to this day. Profits reached new heights and the paper won two Pulitzer Prizes. Jim had a favorite maxim: *"I know of no good newspapers that are broke, and no broke newspapers that are good."* I was lucky enough to get to know Jim at our management meetings, and he always took time to engage me in a friendly conversation over a libation ... or two. I enjoyed his lively, independent spirit immensely. He retired in 1992.

A Harvard Business School report, written in 2000, on which Phil Meek and I participated, made these bullet point observations about some of Capital Cities' publishing performances during the first three years of the company's ownership:

- *Fairchild's operating profit margins tripled.*

- *Cash flow doubled at The Kansas City Star and The Star Telegram.*

- *Operating profit margins at The Kansas City Star reached as high as 35 percent.*

- *While cash flow at the paper grew from $12.5 million in the mid-1970s to $68 million in 1996.*

Tom Murphy chose his targets patiently and carefully, reviewing their profit and operating histories. And when he moved forward with an acquisition, it was because he was confident that his team could successfully infuse the Capcities philosophy and business savvy into the new assets. Almost across the boards, the response from the newly acquired entity's employees was positive, gentlemanly, collegial and enthusiastic.

That was about to change dramatically, with unpleasant consequences. In midyear 1978, Tom Murphy bought the Wilkes-Barre, Pennsylvania daily, The Times Leader for $10.5 million, making what historians have labeled his only significant management error. The purchase opened an unfortunate association with an employee group whose union history stood in stark contrast to Capcities' reputation, management style and operating philosophy. The union ran the newspaper and made all the decisions, period. The paper was plagued with languishing readership. The ink had hardly dried on the purchase when the union called a strike, and the battle lines were drawn. Dick Lynch, a major executive at Fairchild was named Publisher, but was unprepared for what faced him, later likening the situation to "World War III." That was hardly an understatement. Strikers barred entrance to the paper, union leaders refused to respond to management's offers to meet, a 10-foot high chain link fence was built around the building, and private Wackenhut security guards were hired to quell violence and protect the staff. Battles ensued, attracting national headlines as our employees in vans were unable to drive through the mobs of strikers. The paper did not print Monday through Thursday that first week. Dick Lynch, warning that employees were in danger of being hurt, returned to Fairchild after a brief, torturous period on the job. He was replaced by Rich Connor who was joined by Bruce McIntyre and, together, they endured incredibly contentious years of acrimonious community and union relations. Those years were extremely difficult and costly for the company, exerting heavy strains on a swath of executives from several Capcities properties. Despite losses and bad press, the Murphy/Burke support and intransigence was unshaken. Both were widely quoted as being in it to the end, confident that the company could turn the matter around and become a positive force for good in Wilkes-Barre. Connor and McIntyre were joined by other company personnel, including Red Newby from Fort Worth, who volunteered to pitch in for a while and ended up staying more than a year. All three, and those who preceded them, faced unrestrained violence, vandalism, reader boycotts, police complicity, terrorizing threats to advertisers and readers, and personal attacks. Throughout the onslaught, their attempts to improve the paper's quality proved surprisingly successful. The battle was pitched on the streets and in the courts, where numerous injunctive measures were reviewed by the courts, often with considerable delays. Meanwhile, the strikers created their own competitive paper, whose circulation and revenue continued to grow. By 1980, as the siege dragged into its second year, the company's losses approached $15 million. Connor's persistent strategy included inviting Dale Duncan from Pontiac, who had volunteered his help during the early strike days to help staff and improve editorial content. Finally, by 1981, aided by long overdue but favorable court rulings, the unions were finally decertified and the tide began to turn Capital Cities' way. Duncan succeeded Rich Connor, and began to see modest profits, enough to launch a Sunday edition, which, in time, became very profitable. It was not until 1993, a decade later, that The Times Leader was able to start sending headquarters several million in profits, and Capital Cities' objective in Wilkes-Barre was finally accomplished. The paper finally fulfilled its charter once again, becoming an important contributor to a better community.

CHAPTER TWENTY

Shuffle off to Buffalo

The company's growth during the 1970s was phenomenal. While television and radio operations were scoring high profit margins, the print side of Capital Cities would, in rather quick fashion, contribute to a doubling of our size in people, places, and profits. Our reputation as a strong, respected communications force grew in parallel step, attracting increased attention from Wall Street and Washington. The stock, watched closely by each of us, was experiencing rapid growth and would soon become the grist for future financial writers.

For my family and me, Fresno flew by. Station audiences grew and business relationships were solidified. New agencies and advertisers flocked to the station because of our surprising audience growth, aggressive promotion, and strong community presence. The station was no longer an embarrassment. Business was good for a market our size, budgets and cost controls were in place and 51st Street was pleased. Betty and I had bought a weekend home on a lake in majestic Yosemite, an hour north, and were pretty much settled in. I reported to Bob King, another boss I greatly admired, who visited often and kept a keen eye on our progress. We were close to firing on all cylinders when, about three and a half years into the Fresno assignment, Bob surprised me with a new proposal. Would I like to move to Buffalo and run WKBW-TV, one of our prize stations? My first inclination was *"absolutely!"* However, the family did not weigh in with equal enthusiasm. All three boys were enrolled in California colleges. Phil had chosen San Jose State, Barry chose Berkeley, and Bob selected Fresno State, quite taken by its theatre department. None wished to leave California, which suited the boys to a "T." Jane was still a child, so her vote counted less.

To many, Buffalo's weather might have been a negative, but that was not a deterrent to Betty and me. Plus, I knew the city well, was familiar with the outstanding station and staff and knew, firsthand, the resilience and diversity of its audience. Betty and I also shared a homing instinct for New York. California had been special in many respects and we had developed a wonderful group of friends in Fresno, but the time had come, and we made the decision to move. Barry was a specific concern, but he was firmly committed to San Francisco. Bob, already dedicated to a career as an actor, remained out in LA and Phil's law school plans kept him on the West Coast as well. So, the unit returning to the East Coast was Betty, Jane and me. It was 1975, and I was 43 years old.

Once in Buffalo, we took advantage of Tom Murphy's voluntary role as Chairman of the Board of New York University hospital and arranged for a review of Betty's addiction to cigarettes and pulmonary problems. We met with a number of prominent COPD physicians, going through multiple tests. The lead specialist, whose name I recall as Dr. Fox, spent hours with us, summing up with a large screen X-ray, which demonstrated in dramatic detail, the hundreds of cilia-like stems through which one brings air into the lungs. He likened them to plastic rope, which coagulates, closing inward when burned. He did not mince words. He told us that Betty's smoking had closed many of those essential paths to her lungs, and that if she did not stop smoking immediately, her situation would deteriorate, drastically shortening her life. It was devastating news, but not unexpected. We all hoped the message would stick. Unfortunately, despite many attempts with prescribed remedies, Betty's addiction was never curbed. She continued smoking, a slave to the little white pack of Kent cigarettes; sometimes kept out of sight, but always there, even during her increasingly frequent hospital visits. We all tried to stop her, but failed. I consider the fact that I could not convince her to stop, a personal failure. Her habit became a lingering, contentious-but-loving family-wide issue.

Rather quickly, we found a lovely two-story brick house in Williamsville, a popular Buffalo suburb. The city was an excellent fit for Betty, Jane, and me and remains a favorite of mine to this day. There was a well-respected Catholic elementary school close by, and although we were Methodists, we enrolled Jane and, much to our delight, she took to it magnificently. She had been learning sign language in Fresno, and was happy to continue signing with the nuns. The boys visited on regular college breaks and Betty enjoyed being the ever-gracious, popular corporate wife. The notoriously troublesome winter snows, were nonetheless tolerable because Erie County handled them so efficiently. One historic storm in 1977 buried our home right up to the roof with only the chimney poking through the huge snowdrift! The station covered the news that day on rented snowmobiles we called *"Snowsevens"* and anchorman Irv Weinstein dramatically opened the show on horseback. The staff celebrated the fact that not an hour of work had been missed! Another story for the grandkids.

Being the President of WKBW-TV in Buffalo, which had been brilliantly nurtured under prior managers, like Bob King and Larry Pollock, was a rare privilege. Our audience was large, as was our commitment to responsibly serving the public. At that time, in the mid-1970s, before the FCC eased up station ownership, channels 2 and 13, were powerhouse facilities. Our Channel 7 dominated the western New York and southern Canada markets to a degree matched by only a score of stations around the country.

We enjoyed audiences that were the envy of most stations, especially in news. My challenge was clear ... do not screw it up!! I had no concern in that regard, however. A strong staff, and the station's rich history and high audience shares, gave me all the assurances I needed. My first actions were to satisfy any apprehension on the part of the staff regarding new management. That was easily accomplished as I was already known to many of the employees, and the company was highly regarded. Regular meeting with department heads was routine for the seasoned pros I inherited. My style was a bit looser than that of my predecessor perhaps, but our goals were identical. We all wanted to win, please stockholders, employees, and advertisers, while, at the same time, being good citizens of our community. And the job came with audiences galore — huge audiences — that helped buoy everyone's spirits!!

Over the first few weeks, I recalled a simple motto I had previously used in my meetings with new employees. I called it *"Sinatra in One."* I had always been fascinated how Sinatra could stand alone on a stage and mesmerize his audiences, totally enveloping them using only the power of his persona and voice. Sinatra's God-given talent demanded excellence, as though it were on loan, and I wanted our viewers to identify us, in similar fashion, with only the very best. When broadcasters acquire a license, it gives them a rare privilege to serve the public, combined with an obligation to provide the very best service possible. So I encouraged our staff to become *"Sinatra in One,"* and to make the audience feel special by delivering unparalleled excellence, believing that it would be identified and appreciated as such. Every time we had the opportunity to attract viewers to Channel 7, the content should be meaningful *to* them, and *for* them. Seeking their loyalty, as their primary *"go to"* station for news and entertainment was one of my single-minded audience goals. Fortunately, the station had a long history of providing excellence in news and entertainment to a loyal audience, and

I knew my input was essentially preaching to the choir. Again, I was surrounded by talented people, similar to the Fresno folks, except that my new staff was accustomed to success, *"standing O"* style.

Soon we were unpacked, and working together. Immediately, without missing a beat, progress became almost a ritual in the hands of a talented, motivated group of people who loved being number one. Local news maintained its audience dominance for the next 10 years, regularly refreshed by Irv Weinstein, his remarkable Assignment Director, Nancy Sanders, and the best team of reporters, and videographers in the region. We brought in the country's most creative promotion genius, as well as the consulting team of Frank Magid; two new expense items that paid off nicely. We noticed that "Wheel of Fortune," then on NBC daytime, was the only daytime program beating us, so a quick call to King World resulted in WKBW becoming among the first stations to program Pat and Vanna in early fringe. By 1979, having done some enjoyable tweaking to an already fine operation, our position was more secure than I could have hoped. Maintaining or increasing our audience dominance however, meant increasing and protecting that ever-precious viewer loyalty to the station. My predecessor had done that to a reasonable degree by catering to one of Buffalo's chief passions; hockey, whose fans had grown to love Channel 7. Positioning the station as an important adjunct to a viewer's life is a viable strategy. I had used it to good effect in Fresno. News can be an effective vehicle. Adding a personal connection to the news, showing how it directly relates to the viewer is a natural audience builder. Complementing hard news, feature reports, which include human-interest elements, also generate high viewer response. Firemen collecting for charity at traffic stops might be a good feature story, but a better one might be the Boy Scouts running back and forth bringing them lemonade! Covering a parade is one thing, but shooting it from the point of view of a child on his father's shoulders can be a totally different viewer experience. Involving people is a strong connector and Channel 7 was well connected, indeed. Our product mix of news, entertainment, and promotion was clearly superior. Our pride was clear and infectious, and our staff was thrilled to hear my prediction that we could take the station's popularity to even greater heights. And the record of excellence I inherited was surpassed consistently, year upon year.

Of course, occasional accolades came to me over time, but I took great care and pleasure in crediting my staff, including those who had built the station from early Capcities days: Martzolf, Zappia, Sheppard, Fisher, Dudley Few and later folks like Mike Randall, Linda Pellegrino, and John Di Sciullo, and so many others who made me look good! I described myself as a turtle on a fencepost, claiming, *"Do not ask me how I got here, the recipient of all this credit, because the truth is my staff put me up to it!"* I used that visual image occasionally, even later in my work. It was true; I was always blessed and lucky to work with good people, about whom I cared deeply. I had been taught years earlier by Dan Burke that it was smart management to let your employees know you believed they could succeed beyond even their own expectations. He had employed that tactic with me on many occasions. WKBW-TV overflowed with gifted people and more of them should be acknowledged here. I think they all knew how much I appreciated the team and I hope they too have fond memories of those days. As a unit, we continued to outperform year after year, partially benefitting, as did some of our other company operations, from sunnier economic news around the country. Through the late 1970s and early 1980s, three stations regularly led all other ABC affiliates in the country in audience share: Philadelphia, Houston and Buffalo! All three were Capcities stations. The late Peter Jennings loved the fact that his mother watched Channel 7 from her home in Canada, and that we were number one long before many other ABC affiliates distinguished themselves by leading in their markets.

I was the new man in charge of the strongest electronic media outlet in town and, at the same time, an associate of the legendary investor Warren Buffett, who was not only an unofficial adviser to Capcities, but also the owner of the town's leading paper, the Buffalo News. That was a happy coincidence, as we occasionally paired the two business staffs as collaborators to the benefit of the general public. Buffalo was a rust belt city that had been severely battered by economic storms, but which was now showing signs of resilience and resuscitation. To ramp up and reinforce our effort to tie the station to the viewers, I created several alliances by involving myself in nonprofit groups. Many such groups needed increased identity awareness, like the dollar depressed Buffalo Philharmonic, the historic Sheas Theatre, The Urban League, and the Buffalo Children's Hospital. Getting involved with charities is easy for a media manager. As I had learned in the early Albany days, no community-minded person in any profession can do more to provide charitable media publicity than can a TV station manager.

One illustration of a community connection stands out because it not only provided an audience catalyst as important for us as hockey, but also because it is a program that has endured now for more than 40 years. The station had, for a long time, carried a traditional telethon, associated with *"Tent Number 7,"* a Buffalo Variety Club International charity. The local Children's Hospital was the beneficiary and important funds had flowed through to the Hospital from the multiple hour show. But by 1975, despite the tenacity and energy of Jerry Lewis' fight for Muscular Dystrophy, the country had, in large part, tired of telethons. And WKBW's program was leagues behind the indefatigable Lewis show. Local telethons were in trouble and ours was no exception. Money was just not flowing in as local show formats proved less and less appealing. The easy call would have been to drop it, but a strong volunteer base dedicated to helping the Children's Hospital persisted in perpetuating this endangered venture. I joined the Variety Club and, as the new General Manager of Channel 7, was asked to be the speaker at their next function. The audience was almost exclusively blue collar and economically diverse. The constituents, mostly union workers, government employees, educators, and ordinary citizens, were witnessing shrinkage in their ranks and, likewise, a lessening in the number of individuals willing to volunteer and sustain the charity. I learned that revenues from the telethon had steadily declined, and were currently hovering at about $250,000 a year. I started my talk by applauding the previous year's funding efforts, but quickly segued into a warning that future fundraising was in serious jeopardy. No one disagreed. Then I outlined a plan that I had already been pre-warned would likely get a cool reception. I told them they must follow Jerry's formula and go more commercial; something they considered unethical, and unacceptable. I cited an example: A prominent bank had been handling the money and tabulation on the show, thereby benefitting from commercial identification. I suggested they require a donation from the bank in return for that valuable exposure. The suggestion was met by universal grunts of disapproval. I gave them examples of certain other commercial possibilities. More grunts. Finally, without mentioning that the station's participation depended upon it, I strongly advised that going more commercial was their best avenue toward future solvency and I, further, predicted that, if they heeded my advice, they would be able to raise their annual hospital contribution to $1 million within five years. I also promised them additional support from the station. After a smattering of polite applause, rancor exploded. Nonetheless, an hour later, they voted to accept my challenge, and the bar stayed open late that night as we excitedly debated ways to reinvigorate the program. (They didn't have to wait five years. They hit the $1 million mark two years later.) About a week or two later, I announced that while the former bank had declined to accept the fee, a competing bank had stepped up with a gift of $10,000 for the privilege. Liberty Bank had not previously been a television advertiser, but as a result of this initial exposure, was soon spending regular ad dollars with the station. In fact, they eventually became the station's largest local advertiser. At the same meeting, I announced a $10,000 gift I had obtained from a man named Richard Fors of Burger King. (Mr. Fors has remained a friend for 40 years). Then, the three biggest supermarkets in town joined when the station created a Chairman's Committee, including brokers and national food brand regional managers, chaired by a different supermarket each year. This committee still raises money, with key executives holding volunteer positions. And by the way, all are fans of Channel 7! I was enjoying the sales aspect of this civic promotion and developed a speech I called *"Contagious Synergy,"* enticing businessmen and women to get involved in their communities. The concept grew quickly, to the point where our efforts spawned the largest volunteer association of its kind in Western New York. Over the years, its numbers swelled to thousands of supporters of Channel 7's Children's Hospital campaign. Involvement of that group continues to this day and every March, a "Telethon," which I preferred to call a *"Thank You Parade,"* is presented on the station, consistently earning over $1 million for the Hospital, even during stiff economic times. All those thousands of ordinary good citizens, who either volunteered their time, donated money or convinced their companies or colleagues to contribute, shared a love of their community, and all held an abiding affection and respect for their favorite Buffalo television channel at the center of it all — WKBW-TV Channel 7! Once more, by doing good, we had, in fact, amassed a huge fan club.

I instigated another charity-related station program after seeing something similar carried out in Philadelphia. I made a call to the Buffalo Courier Express newspaper and "Kids Day" sprang into being. Each year, on a cold February morning, newspapers were sold on street corners 7 a.m. to noon by volunteer executives — all to benefit kids' charities. My corner, for years, was Main and Church streets. The program exists to this day, now taken over by The Buffalo News, after the Courier Express ceased printing in 1982.

Events ran smoothly at the station. Business fluctuated with the economy; the staff was stable, excited by audience growth and energized by the handsome profit sharing. I was appointed to the prestigious ABC Board of Governors, essentially as the Capital Cities representative, and Betty and I occasionally enjoyed lavish Governor's meetings held in exotic locales.

Being the manager of a famous media outlet brings with it a certain quasi-celebrity status, regardless of that person's proclivity for the limelight. After a couple of years, I began to experience such on the job in Buffalo and Betty was the first to zero in on it. She reminded me that the deeper I got involved in the station, civic affairs and community fundraising, the more my profile rose, and the more I seemed to revel in the attention. She was right, but I told myself I could handle it. I did not immediately recognize that my work, which, at the outset, involved her totally, was increasingly becoming solely my persona, and that it was negatively affecting her identity. More than once, she hinted, sometimes in jest, that she preferred to be known as Betty Beuth than Phil Beuth's wife. Gradually, she began to decline invitations to accompany me on what she called *"the rubber chicken circuit"* and I knew it had nothing to do with her COPD. I felt Betty's discomfort deeply, and pledged to her and to myself that my commitment to Buffalo and the station would be dialed back.

It was a reality check and the seeding of an important lesson for me. I was surely guilty of being single-minded at work and narrow-minded at home. We worked on that together and found that part of the answer lay 90 miles south of Buffalo on Lake Chautauqua. On a casual afternoon drive, we discovered the famous, remarkable, historic Chautauqua Institution. After a couple more visits, we purchased property on one of the lake's most beautiful settings, complete with a small, old wooden cottage. From the moment we entered the cottage, we knew it had to be demolished and that decision set a plan in motion that had a wonderfully positive effect upon all of us. I approached an Amish man named Enos Miller, as he was working on the porch of the Chautauqua Institution's hotel, and asked if he might be interested in tearing down our cottage. He certainly was interested, but also cautiously curious. That afternoon, as he brought his horse-drawn carriage over for a visit to our newly purchased land and the cottage, a memorable relationship was formed. I already knew that the Amish held a fundraiser each year for their school, and this gave me an idea. If Enos agreed to raze the cottage, he could keep whatever he was able to salvage. The cottage was well equipped, with a furnace, washer, dryer, many good windows, sinks, etc., the sale of which would likely exceed his entire school fundraising goal. Enos Miller was, and remains to this day, a smart, honest, reliable, Godly reverent man, whom I am proud to call my friend. His response to my request was several-fold. He asked why Yankees, referring not to baseball players, but to outsiders, think all Amish do is tear down. He said that if I provided $1,500 for the rental of a bulldozer, he would tear down the cottage at no charge, in exchange for the elements he could salvage. But there was more. Enos said that if he was going to dismantle the old structure, he also wanted the opportunity to bid on whatever we planned to build in its place. We shook hands. I did not tell him I had already received a bid from a Jamestown construction company for $420,000. We gave him the plans. A week later, Enos came back, and his response was unusual. He said that he had never undertaken such a large project, but since I had seen smaller projects of his, I should know he would do a good job. He also said he could not give me a bid, for two reasons. First if he underbid, he would be disappointing his crew of four master carpenters, because if he ran out of money, they would be obliged to finish without pay, and reputations would suffer. If, on the other hand, he overbid and charged more than he deserved, he and his workers and family could not abide the fact that they were taking even a penny more than the job warranted. Over a couple of bottles of root beer, we devised a plan, founded on mutual trust. The Amish operated a retail building supply store in the neighboring state of Pennsylvania and, according to Enos, they were *"understanding."* He could guarantee all building supplies we needed, including appliances, at just 5 percent over cost, and there would be no Pennsylvania sales tax. They would, however, charge $20 per shipment by truck to the site! He would put four master carpenters on the job over the winter at $8 an hour, no overtime no matter how long the workday. He then added apologetically, *"My rate is $10."* I could establish a credit with his bank from which he would pay his workers, backed by my American Express card. We talked about how nice it would be to combine labor and capital, and shook hands, sealing a remarkable paperless partnership. Not only did he build a beautiful home on time for me and my family, but it was built for under $200,000, less than half what I had been quoted by the Jamestown builder.

Over that six-month period in 1980, we became willing spectators and ardent participants in the lives of Enos and Nettie Miller. We celebrated Amish and other holidays with their large family and friends at least a dozen times. We were invited to join them for Thanksgiving dinner, an experience neither my family nor I will ever forget. We brought Frank and Virginia Woodbeck with us. Frank was running WKBW radio.

What was utterly astonishing to both us and to all those Amish youngsters was that Frank and Virginia were the first African Americans who had ever been in their home. Enos welcomed them warmly and felt it was evidence of the mutual trust we had established. After dinner, seeing half a dozen young girls in flowery, handmade dresses gather around a large black man for a bedtime reading session, was an emotional and heartwarming scene.

After we finished building our home, Enos and I collaborated on buying and remodeling a century-old structure called Marycrest into six condo units. It remains across from the library on the grounds of the institution. In every aspect, our collaboration was a memorable experience, shared with lovely, smart, honest people, devoted to their peace-loving culture. My family benefitted greatly from their friendship, which continues to this day.

Meanwhile back at the job, several forces were propelling the station to even more prominence. In 1979, we celebrated the opening of a brand new studio and office structure, which made headlines because the architect we chose had responded to the energy crisis with an extraordinary solution. Therein lies another story ...

In the late 1970s, the country was going through an energy shortage and conservation was popular, filling the evening's airwaves. When Dan Burke approved the funds to construct a new facility, he reminded me that it should be energy efficient.

That was about all he said about it, in pure Capcities style, but did add, *"On budget, of course!"* I had read about a wind project in Sandusky, Ohio. Curious, I called Sandusky officials, who put me in touch with the engineers doing the study. They were most enthusiastic about Buffalo wind, which would come off Lakes Ontario and Erie and they were surprised I did not know of a Buffalo-based energy expert and local college professor, named David Stieglitz. I wrote David's name down, intending to call. The next morning my secretary announced that a Mr. Stieglitz was in the lobby asking to see me. When he entered the office, I greeted him with: *"Hello David...so you got a call from the people over in Sandusky, and I am your new fish!"* David did not know what I was talking about, and had never heard from Sandusky. He confessed that he had passed our station every day and had finally, that day, gotten up the courage to come and make a pitch for the new station, about which he had read. Coincidence? Yes, I like coincidences...sort of a forecast of destiny. We spoke for hours; that is David did. I was fascinated with his concept for a self-sustaining city, capable of creating its own energy. Intrigued, I asked if he could fly to New York to meet Dan Burke. Two days later, we flew Mohawk Airlines to the city and were welcomed into Dan's office, for *"an hour before his lunch appointment."* David was nervous in those plush surroundings, previously the office of the Catholic Archdiocese, but he did not show it. What followed was a remarkable exchange between Dan and David, concentrating on the energy crisis and centered around David's theories on perpetual motion. Dan cancelled his lunch, and after some tuna on rye, we broke up at about 2:30 to catch the return flight home. As we all left the room, Dan lingered and whispered over my shoulder *"Don't let him get away."* That afternoon, on the return plane, we reviewed the points we had discussed regarding the construction, and, on a Mohawk napkin, I wrote an agreement covering terms and conditions. We both signed it. That was the only contract we ever had. The building was completed on time ... *and on budget!* David had designed and built an entirely new type of structure in Buffalo, with self-sustaining heating, using the thermals created by machines and people (traditionally exhausted to the outside), and storing it in two huge water tanks in the back of the studio. I labeled the tanks *"Gin"* and *"Vermouth."* They stored heat in the form of hot water, which was distributed around the building in a hot water system by simple electric pumps. Our energy bill was slashed by 30 percent! David prospered after that first break and has been recipient of many awards over the years. He also built our New Haven station a few years later. In a neat frame in David's Buffalo offices today, there hangs a Mohawk Airlines napkin scribbling the genesis of his company.

Buffalo was always a very special place for us, despite the fact that we lived there during some of its most difficult economic times. It had once been a busy shipping port, automobile and steel producing giant. Bethlehem Steel had at one time created entire worker communities along the banks of Lake Erie. But through the 1970s, the harsh economic realities became insurmountable and the plant finally shut down its last blast furnace in 1983. The city of Buffalo was forced to reinvent itself and for the past 30 years it had been doing exactly that, with varying degrees of success. It has developed a vastly different business landscape and is currently experiencing exciting growth in medical practice and research, downtown modernization, reclamation of rust belt properties, national sports franchise rebirths, and dozens of businesses spawned from the Internet. It is appropriately boastful of the nationally recognized Roswell Park Cancer Center and other prominent health facilities and higher education centers. Young people are now returning to a reborn Queen City!

In Buffalo, it was sacrilege for Buffalonians to be unfamiliar with the terms, *"Icing," "The Blue Line," or "The Hat Trick,"* since the Buffalo Sabres, with their French Connection of Martin, Robert, and Perreault, captured local hockey headlines for years.

Fortunately, I inherited a sort of a *Hat Trick, French Connection* of my own!! And while they did not always capture the headlines, they sure reported thousands of their own for decades as the most popular news, weather and sports trio, perhaps in the history of TV reporting in this country. Irv Weinstein, Tom Jolls, and Rick Azar are historic broadcast icons and their record for dominating a market as a team will likely never be duplicated. Over their many years of service they have won every sort of award offered in the business.
Irv Weinstein deserves a chapter (or a movie) of his own, in addition to the tons of copy already devoted to his career. He

will be a legend in Buffalo as long as people talk about TV news. Over tumultuous decades in the anchor chair, which Irv would characterize as more fun than frenzy, he sent hoards of unsuccessful competitors back home to their puzzled consultants. We once tried counting the many carefully quaffed competitors who came to Buffalo to depose Irv from his kingpin anchor position. We stopped counting at 32. Always number one on the *wit parade*, Irv was an astute writer, often titillating audiences with headlines that grabbed viewers with alliteration like *"Buffalo Blaze Busters Battle Bonfire — tonight at 11!"* *"Buffalo Blaze Busters in Beastly Battle at the Big Top — Tonight at 11!"* *"Pistol Packing Punks Prosecuted — Tonight at 11!"* And there was this one, which I doubt made it to air. A controversy about whether gays could be admitted into the Fire Department prompted this Irv suggestion: *"Homos on Hoses? — Tonight at 11!"*

He loved working for Capcities. Beyond the profit sharing and stock purchases, he genuinely cared for our leadership. He was thrilled every time Dan or Tom stopped by, or when they sent him notes about his numbers. Irv considered himself the News Director, regardless of who held that official title. School is still out on who learned the most from whom? And turmoil or no, all had to admit that Irv knew his stuff. People who did hold that title over the years included talented news executives like Joe Barnes, Bill Applegate, Steve Ridge and a man who went on to a long career at Capcities, Alan Nesbitt.

Maintaining growth of an already successful operation can be a challenging, thought-provoking process. However, with a new building, a budget that allowed investments in programs, promotion and people, and a competitive staff, we always managed to out-sell, out-program, and out-promote the competition. They were tough, but not as consistently tough as we were. Having Capital Cities as your parent, as any of my partners will agree, gave you an immediate advantage. We also had a rare executive talent who came to us because we were Capital Cities. His name was Mike Davis and he was a specialist in the promotion of stations and their news personalities, using extremely creative sales approaches in commercials with real entertainment value. Other stations used their own airtime to self promote, but Mike's promos were overwhelmingly superior. Again, we were making viewers love us, as they recognized the difference between our station and the competition. Mike just added another weapon to our already strong arsenal.

I had a friend named Dino Dinovitz, a super guy, who, while trying to teach me tennis, also managed the NBC competitor. One day after tennis, he congratulated me on hiring the local manager of a Burger King named Don Polec, who was rapidly proving himself the hottest feature reporter in the market. Dino had heard I hired him the day after I first met him, and he asked how I could do that, without budget approval. The hiring story is worth telling because it goes straight to Capcities core doctrine. There was a Burger King in the neighborhood, about which I would occasionally hear rumors of its unconventional manager. Irv first told me about this fellow, named Don Polec, so I asked Don to come in for a visit. Don arrived on time early one morning and sat not next to my desk, but at the far end of a long office. Seeing he was quiet and shy, I encouraged him to join me, which he did. During our brief interview, he explained that he had a talent for seeing things a bit differently and he expanded on that explanation, describing my desk as not simply an assemblage of maple wood, screws and glue, but as the source and repository of great personal experiences. He said his friends had always told him he should be on TV and he confessed this had been a lifelong goal. I asked him what his salary range was and he grimaced, replying *"About $8,000."* After telling him that he might likely run out of ideas after a week or two, he told me he did not think so. I then asked him to imagine that he was a feature reporter and to bring me five ideas for show segments by the next day. Twenty-four hours later, we were sitting opposite my repository of memories, as he handed me a piece of paper; single spaced typing on both sides, declaring, *"Here are your 55 ideas!"* I scanned them quickly, but was sold halfway down the first page. I then told him our reporters started at $14,700, and when I learned he could start that day, we walked directly into the newsroom, where News Director Joe Barnes put him to work. Don Polec fit in perfectly, and we soon had another award-winning addition to an already outstanding news team. Don became very popular as he applied singularly unique vision and creativity to any story he tackled; from highway congestion, to computer dating, the circus, stunt flying, et all. In short order, Don began to win just about every local and state award the industry offered. His impact was immediate, boosting our numbers substantially for years until the inevitable occurred and he moved on to greater things. It was quite natural that he move to Philadelphia, where he blossomed still further on our station there. His reel, definitely one of a kind, is still appreciated to this day.

... Back to my good friend and competitor, Dino. He said he had figured out how I was able to pull off the hiring of Don Polec so deftly and he put it this way: *"Taft, my parent company in Cincinnati, tells me, the manager, what I am going to do. The difference,"* he said, *"is you tell New York what you are going to do."* And that is pure Capcities.

We had a couple of experiences with celebrities who visited Buffalo and two stand out. Burt Reynolds and Goldie Hawn were starring in a movie called "Best Friends" requiring their presence in our fair city for six weeks. Burt was staying next door to our new station and I wrote him a note inviting him to appear on our talk show and to appear at the Children's hospital fundraiser. He responded with a call asking for a favor. The Academy Awards were approaching and this year they were saluting his good friend, Maria Tallchief. Since he could not be there, he asked if he could come to the station and make a videotape presentation to send in his place. We agreed and the tape was made. I repeated my request and Burt said he would try to make the show, but thought it would be proper for him and Goldie to first make a visit to the well-known intensive pediatric care unit at the hospital. They insisted on no press and I accompanied them personally to insure that was respected. Goldie began to cry the instant she saw the first child. We spent a couple of hours on the tour, which included many autographs, but no journalists. After the tour, the three of us took a limo and dropped Goldie, still sobbing, off at her hotel. Next stop was my car at the station parking lot. Burt and I agreed it was a good night and as he was thanking me, I said, *"Thank you too, Burt, but I would also like your autograph."* He looked a bit surprised as I added, *"On a check for the hospital."* He laughed and shook my hand, adding something having to do with my birthright! On the day of the show I got a call. *"Send me an escort, Phil. I will meet you at the back door."* He arrived; bantered with our event host Ted Knight, answered phones, and seemed to enjoy himself. And when he left, I found his autograph — *on a check for $45,000.* Our paths crossed again years later in a more serious situation. Stay tuned ...

Sammy Davis Jr. was in town making a speech to the organization of Christians and Jews and he appeared on our morning show to promote the event. As I spoke to him, he also asked for a favor. He wanted to tape a TV spot promoting the organization in general. When we were about to cut the tape, our producer asked if he needed a teleprompter and reminded Mr. Davis that 30 seconds would work perfectly. The response was *"Watch me ... I do this often."* The red light went on, and precisely at the 30-second mark he was finished, unaided. *Right on the money — one take!* We then went to my office for coffee, which we served to guests in a Channel 7 mug. We had a lively chat about Buffalo as his stretch limo awaited in the parking lot. We finished, and he was gone, leaving an indelible impression on all of us. Ten minutes later the limo reappeared outside my window. His driver was at my secretary's desk. *"Could Mr. Davis please have the Channel 7 mug?"* We were surprised and proud – *and all had a story to tell at dinner that night.*

Our years in Buffalo were among the most memorable and I visit there often to this day. Among my friends and acquaintances over time has been a man named Mike Billoni, a teddy bear sort of fellow who can update you on just about anything Buffalo-related in 20 minutes, and loves doing it! We share an experience we both like to recall. It has to do, of all things, with a simple softball game that had an indelible impact, especially upon me.

One evening in 1984, our *"Channel 7 Prime Timers"* softball team was playing Mayor Jimmy Griffin's crew of police and firemen for a Variety Club fundraiser for Children's Hospital. The match took place in the old War Memorial stadium, which had recently been given a facelift for Robert Redford's film, "The Natural."

The fundraiser was a big local event attracting about 150 spectators who filled the front rows. Mike, as the public address announcer, greeted and welcomed the crowd, which included a line of children in wheelchairs strung along the first base seats, accompanied by their parents.

The game progressed without too much excitement, with each team scoring six runs heading into the seventh and final inning. In an earlier inning, I had hit a ball over the second baseman's outstretched glove, for a standard base hit, but the right fielder, aware of my difficulty running to first base, fielded the ball and threw me out. That was a legit move, but prompted boos and catcalls from the Variety club fans, who presumably thought it unfair. The game was tied when we (as the home team), came to bat in seventh and final inning, with just this last chance to clinch the win. My turn at bat came with the potential winning run already on second base and two outs. Stepping up to the plate, I watched the same right fielder who'd thrown me out, move closer and closer with each pitch I took. He was crouched and ready to steal a hit from me again.

Finally, I shifted my feet toward first base and, with all the strength I could muster from my 150-pound frame, belted the ball clear over his head! The next thing I heard was Mike over the PA. *"The boss wins the game, the boss wins the game!"* There were hugs and high fives all over, but as they quieted down, a woman approached me, asking, *"Mr. Beuth, would you come over to see my son, please?"* The game-winning hit that every baseball player dreams about pales compared to what happened next.

I bent down and greeted a 9-year-old boy wearing a baseball cap to cover and hide his bald head. He asked me, *"Do you*

228

think I could ever do that?" I remembered another little boy decades earlier, facing challenges, who held those same aspirations, and assured him he could as I buried my head on his shoulder, holding him close to get hold of my emotions. I have difficulty controlling them as I retell this story. While the game was won, I learned again that putting things in proper perspective is what really matters; a reality I have carried ever since that memorable night at the old stadium.

Little did I know, New York was getting ready to announce something that would change my career beyond all expectations. And on the home front, Betty and I were to face difficulties and sadness unlike any we had ever confronted.

CHAPTER TWENTY-ONE

Tuesday's Child

Each child, born with a purpose:
'Tuesday's Child — Full of Grace'

Attributed to A.E. Bray
"Traditions of Devonshire," 1838

How does a father write about his blessed family's loss of a son? What were the events and circumstances in the life of this talented, exceptional young man, unconditionally loved by his parents and siblings that conspired to end his life? How could the second of three sons all born within 18 months of each other, and of the same gene pool, differ so in a multiplicity of ways?

For families, there are no perfect answers. Those questions might possibly be addressed by a recitation of his life, embellished by the accomplishments he enjoyed, but plagued by the parallel depression he endured. Based on parental and sibling collective experiences, cherished and otherwise, and Barry's unique independent spirit, the tale is told here about a remarkably sensitive soul, living in an inequitable world to which he could never concede or adapt.

Barry Michael Beuth was one of three picture-perfect, blonde, crew cut boys Betty and I proudly pushed on strollers through Albany malls in the late 1950s. We were even a featured photo op while leading the Union College Alumni Reunion parade in '59. As their personalities began to emerge at ages 5, 6, and 7, obvious differences between Barry and his two brothers became more and more apparent. All three were bright, curious and well behaved, but Barry differed. He quietly preferred to study or read (*anything in print*), rather than play outdoors. In Little League, he reluctantly played the outfield, as balls hit to him were rarely pursued. As he progressed in school, Barry became obsessed with learning. His academic performance all his life was consistently phenomenal, and may have qualified him as a prodigy. From his first report card, all the way through to being named valedictorian for the University of California at Berkeley graduation ceremony, he rarely scored less than a perfect score on any course he chose. All three boys made us proud parents, but Barry had the most disciplined approach to education. He was a very young student of foreign languages, becoming fluent in six. His older brother would tell about Barry's intention to finish a book while on vacation. Phil asked what the book was about. Barry's response was that it was *"a French novel ... written in Russian!"* He also taught himself how to play the organ, by ear and by note, convincing a Huntington restaurant owner to hire him at 15, to play during Sunday brunches. He was a handsome teen, well proportioned physically and quite masculine in appearance. Despite that, however, his choice of classic literature and music, his sensitive private nature, his remarkable ability to read people, his disdain for sports, and an occasional hint here and there, made us all suspicious about his gender preference.

He gave us pause, and I must confess, temporary comfort, when in Fresno, he began to date a girl we will call Jennifer. After a short while, he confessed that when he picked up Jennifer, much to her mother's relief about her date with a boy, it was a double-edged sham. They left Jennifer's house together and returned her at 11 or so. During those hours Jennifer met her girlfriend and Barry joined his male friend! Barry enjoyed that little mischief, but deceit did not fit him one iota. So, it was no great surprise to us, when, at 16, he told us he was gay. Our response, having prepared ourselves, was an immediate commitment of unconditional love and support.

At 17, he refused to attend his senior year of high school in Fresno, claiming that he could teach the courses better himself. He borrowed our second car and drove to Stanford and Berkeley, seeking admission without graduating from high school, and was admitted to both! He chose Berkeley, certainly influenced by Haight Ashbury and San Francisco, believing it was the right time and place in history for his destiny. There, his personality, behavior, politics, and worldview began to harden and mature rapidly, entrenched and reinforced by a rejection of society he recognized years earlier as bigoted and discriminatory. By this time, his natural, independent thinking had moved into high gear and he joined the gay rights movement. His idols included Joan Baez, Janis

Joplin, Larry Kramer, Harvey Milk and Maria Callas. To him, politicians were frauds and government was apathetic and insensitive to the needs of the powerless. He recoiled at any signs of racial or ethnic prejudice. If one's language included references to *"colored people,"* his immediate response was *"What color?"*

He became an outspoken critic of intolerance. Soon he was caught up in the country's sexual revolution where citizens of all persuasions were acting with abandon about sex, and where a window of hope opened for gays that equal rights might be on the horizon. (*The change he took to the streets to demand would be another 30 years in the making*). Berkeley was the right incubator for those views. Sexual freedom was rampant and gays were no exception, struggling to be free of prejudice and attempting to establish a recognized lifestyle amidst a straight American culture. His world came to include drugs, alcohol, and excessive sex. Along with this sexual revolution came a most unwelcome national health crisis, called the *"gay disease,"* or GRID, Gay Related Immune Disorder. Parents everywhere prayed for an early cure. Barry learned all he could about the disease, assured us that he would not become infected and promised that he would not become addicted to drugs or alcohol. He was unable to fulfill either of those promises. As hundreds, then thousands began dying, national prominence grew, and the word AIDS was finally spoken by the country's leaders. Barry was deeply caught up in the battle against AIDS. Betty and I were very worried as we became aware that he was faltering on his promise concerning drugs. On one occasion, he was arrested on Santa Monica beach and spent the night in jail.

We attended his college graduation, proud of his being selected valedictorian. However, when his turn to speak came and he did not appear at the podium, we left the ceremony only to find him sitting outside his dorm, blonde hair down to his shoulders, smiling and happily stoned. He apologized for not being able to make it and casually asked if we were dining that night at the Cliffs! After his college graduation when phone calls went regularly unreturned, we worried still more. Despite our hopes and prayers that a cure was imminent, our fears continued, unrelieved. Most of these events took place during my assignments in Fresno and Buffalo. Sporadically, I would visit San Francisco on business, and often could not reach him at home as he was inclined to stay with friends. Twice I walked the streets of Castro, peeking into gay bars, looking for Barry, only to run into other desperate fathers doing the same. I was never successful. The problem was too big, and out of control. Too many men were dying, without the kind of medical attention such an epidemic warranted. Betty and I felt quite helpless, still hoping for a cure. Unfortunately Barry grew distant from his mother. He called her smoking addiction *"a death wish."* This only exacerbated his own anguish and depression.

He was hired by Wang Laboratories who made use of his foreign language skills to interpret and write business agreements. That lasted a year or so until Barry advised us *"they fired me when they learned I was gay."* That added to his frustrations, anger and depression, redoubling his hatred of society. My daughter, Jane followed Barry's continued battles, sometimes up close; at other times by phone. She knew the extent to which Barry struggled and believes that the shock and terror of the epidemic was so overwhelming that Barry had become heart-broken and bereft. He was part of a minority oppressed culture in an intolerant time and got swept up in trying to hide it from those of us who loved him, as his friends continued to die in droves.

Fortunately, some good news came along amidst this constant uncertainty and apprehension. Barry met a lovely man from Chile named Pablo and their relationship became permanent. Pablo was immediately admired, welcomed and beloved by the family. The two of them traveled often, whenever Pablo could get off work from a restaurant, that would have fired him on the spot had they known he too was infected. Pablo had a calming effect upon Barry and we welcomed the respite and continuity, which lasted seven or eight years.

Another factor ironically contributed to Barry's distance from us and the resulting disrupted communication. Early in my career, I had given Capital Cities stock to each child, presumably to be used for college funds. It started as a distribution of a hundred or two hundred shares each and ended up, because of growth and stock splits, to take on far more value than was likely required at the time. This was a bonanza for Barry once he feared that he was, in fact, HIV-positive. He began selling the stock to support unannounced travel worldwide and to pay hospital bills, often for others. We would get midnight calls from Barry in far-flung places like Paris, where friends and partners had gone seeking cures. On one such trip, Barry traveled to Moscow where he was arrested in Red Square because he spoke Russian so well they did not believe he was an American. The late Congressman Jack Kemp, a family friend, had him released the next morning. The worst periods of this tale started one Sunday afternoon, when Jane, and Betty and I were playing a card game at our weekend home in Lake Chautauqua, south of Buffalo. The phone rang and Betty picked it up and walked away into the library. After a very long time, she returned in tears. Jane asked, *"Which one?"* The answer, hardly audible, was *"Pablo."*

We all helped Barry handle the details of Pablo's passing, and sent his mother a letter, written in Spanish, advising her and offering condolences. I can only imagine the depth of her sorrow, but I also know that Pablo could not have been loved by his own family any more than he was loved by ours. It was indeed sad, and sad to see Pablo had cut off the relationship with his family. This was poignant for Betty and me, because not for one moment was there any denial of love for Barry, contrary to the parental views of many of his friends. Our adult friends also never wavered from treating him with the same affection given our other children. For many, he was a favorite.

Pablo's death was devastating to Barry, as he began to contemplate his own. He fell more heavily into drugs, fighting the depression he had disguised so often in the past. His body began to rebel as symptoms of AIDS surfaced and his immune system started to concede defeat.

We continued to get calls in the middle of the night as he told us of the terrible body sweats he suffered, and of his occasional, short hospital visits. Betty and I visited San Francisco often, sometimes separately, other times together. Barry moved into Fox Towers, an apartment complex, from which he seldom emerged. He invited me to join him one day for a hospital visit to meet several of his friends. It was an unforgettably painful experience. We entered room after room as he introduced his friends Charles, Andy, Victor, and others, all in the last terrifying, ravaging stages of AIDS. They were all covered with telltale splotches of brown, birthmark-like lesions called Kaposi sarcoma, or k.s. as they called it. Some raised a head, nodding hello; others tried, but could not smile. Still others just lifted a finger or a hand. All knew they were condemned. It was an indelible experience for me, and I could only imagine the depth of sadness and depression these men, and when included, their parents endured.

As the months went by, there were minimal changes to Barry's appearance belying his actual condition and giving us some false hope. Having studied the disease and its prescribed medical treatments, Barry knew what to expect. He rejected most of the standard medications, questioning their effectiveness. Too many of his friends on those prescribed meds were dying. Our conversations by phone repeatedly covered the ravaging effects of AIDS and Barry's frustration about its pervasiveness throughout San Francisco, where no hope existed for attention and relief. As his condition continued to devastate him, his phone calls spoke about alternatives, including suicide. We tried to find answers that just were not there, escalating our helplessness. He finally decided to engage mental and physical assistance, conforming to what he told us was popular practice. He conferred with a group of medical students and hospital interns who routinely set up residential services and arranged for his bedroom to be equipped with a hospital bed, medical measuring devices, abundant linens and hospice-type care.

When the call came telling us that the end was near, Bob and I went out to be with him. Betty decided she could not handle it, so she and Jane stayed East; phone within reach. Barry spent much time sleeping while we were there, but we did have some memorable, precious moments while he was awake. The interns were in each day, efficiently and quietly attending to their functions, including the changing of bed linens, diet control, medications, and replacing the bundled supply of towels soaked from overnight sweating, which was profuse. Barry was surprisingly cogent when awake. He told us that he had hallucinated about his brother, Bob, as a large, purple-eared rabbit, and chided me, claiming that as a father I was too fair, treating all three brothers equally. Though he added, *"I really did not have to attend the Boy Scout Convention."*

He mentioned a few times that there was a paper bag in the fridge marked DO NOT TOUCH UNTIL … It contained a bottle of Wente Bros wine, to which we were all partial at the time; a celebratory drink. His breathing was quite heavy, audible throughout the small apartment.

On the third day of our visit, while one of the attendants was talking to us through an open door to the hallway, his hand went up, saying, *"Listen"* … All was quiet, very quiet. As we moved just a few feet toward the bedroom, an attendant at bedside looked up at the solemn group. In a whisper, he said, *"I am sorry, but he is gone."* As Bob and I embraced, assuring each other he was surely in a better place, I gazed into the distant living room and saw Dustin Hoffman accepting the Oscar for "Rain Man." The sound was off, but the vignette served as a strange sad counterpoint to what Bob and I were going through — one that was indelibly captured in my mind.

Things happened rapidly then, as though rehearsed. A phone call was made, and a routine ensued, prompted by the common frequency of such events. Within a half hour, two men from the morgue arrived, as though they had been on a neighborhood watch patrol. An attendant signed a paper or two, strictly routine. Bob and I released Barry's hands as the men transferred him into a black bag, zipped it up, and gurneyed our beautiful son and brother away …

Phil arrived about a half hour later, having driven up from Los Angeles. We talked for a while on the phone with Jane and

Betty; then raised a quiet glass, celebrating Barry's life. Bob later combined Pablo and Barry's ashes and the family members each took it upon themselves over the next few years to spread them to many parts of the world the two had visited. That included Polihale Beach in Hawaii, the Louvre in Paris, an olive grove in Tuscany, and the Grand Canal in Venice. My friend Roger King provided the family with a captain and his yacht for a ceremony off the Los Angeles shore. I recalled Barry's favorite song, "California Dreamer" while the sun stared warmly at us, just as Barry might have done, before it sank into the peaceful water.

Barry might have liked all of that, but again, we could never assume anything from his beautiful, unpredictable, limitless mind!

Against the Nunnery, (Top) Frank Smith, Tom Murphy, Harry Goldman, (Second Row) Dan Burke, Bob King, Joe Doughtery, John Sias

Early Notables Aaron Daniels, Jim Arcara, Warren Potash, John Shuff

1 The Beuth Family, 1964; 2 Lowell
Thomas and pupil; 3 Manning the WRGB
switchboard; 4 Greetings from Roger King;
5 Marching Band at Bermuda client party;
6 GMA's Charlie, Joan and Spencer;
7 Chautauqua home built by Amish;
8 My partner Jack Reilly; 9 Murphy / Beuth
40 plus year partners

Reunion Album: 1 (L-R) Bob Apfel, Dave Davis, Ken Plotnick, Bob Feldman;
2 Kathy Monahan; **3** Jim Arcara; **4** Bill Campbell; **5** Norm Schrutt; **6** Al Herskowitz;
7 Alan Nesbitt; **8** (L-R) Ron Doerfler, Bea Miller, Jon Miller; **9** Andy Jackson;
10 Jeanne Carusso-Theismann; **11** Art Moore; **12** Mark Howard; **13** Bill James;
14 (L-R) Steve Weisswaser, Charlie Keller; Aaron Daniels; **15** (L-R) Irv Weinstein,
Tom Murphy; **16** (L-R) Allen Bomes, Judith Curcio, Mike Helfand, Susan Santore,
Mark Hasson; **17** Eric Schoenfeld; **18** Stan Roman; **19** Tim Fleischer;
20 Mary Galda Sliwa

Reunion Album: 1 Sandy Josephson; **2** Frank Woodbeck; **3** Joe Condon; **4** Walter Liss;
5 Adrienne Cleere; **6** Jim Quello; **7** (L-R) Karen Freeman, Phil McGovern;
8 Vern and Millie Ore; **9** Joey Reynolds; **10** Wes Turner; **11** Jim Goldberg; **12** Steve Ridge;
13 Nick Lawler; **14** Dave Loweth; **15** Hal Youngblood; **16** Liz Dribben, Dudley Few;
17 Dick Rakovan; **18** Phil Meek, John Sias; **19** Tom Fenno; **20** Holland Cooke;
21 Bob Leeder; **22** Rick Azar; **23** David Branch **24** Hal Deutsch

Dick Rakovan

Hey Phil,

On my way to an interview with Joe Dougherty for the Providence GM job, I stopped for a while at Saint Patrick's Cathedral. I was there for about five minutes when I felt a tug on my jacket. It was Joe, doing the same thing. As he left he said, "You're going to make this interview a tough one!"

And ... In the mid-1960s I was invited to join a meeting with Tom and others. In the room were Dan Burke, Gerry Dickler, and Bill Casey. The subject was a possible acquisition, I do not remember which. I listened intently and kept my mouth shut. At the end of the meeting, Tom asked me to stick around for a minute. He then gently said that he did not ask me to a meeting to remain silent ... that he and the others wanted my opinion, and that I provided the view of a younger person because the others were a bit older than I was.

Dick Rakovan

Sales Executive, WKBW-AM Buffalo
Sales Manager Midwest, WPAT-AM/FM NYC
Sales Manager, WPAT-AM/FM NYC
Sales Manager, WJR-AM Detroit
General Manager, WPRO-AM/FM Providence

☙ ❖ ❧

Alan Nesbitt

Hey Phil,
Chiseled into our heads every year at our management meeting was Murphy's reminder that we could make honest mistakes, or miss our budgets, but if we put the company, or ourselves, in disrepute, there was no second chance at Capital Cities. Those words were the bible. Do the right thing was our personal road map. We were taught to avoid the quick-fix solution and when faced with a tough decision, favor the best long-term interest of the station, person or community.

Competition may sometimes outsmart us, but they will never outwork us. They may outman us, but we have better pay, better benefits and better opportunities for upward mobility. Capcities leadership may have high expectations, but the company's focus on autonomy also meant that you won't be blaming headquarters for your problems. You make your own decisions, and you have to live with them.

Larry Pollock, my boss for a long time, used to say that the politics of Capcities was the absence of politics itself. There were no favorites, nor a protected class, and it did not matter where you came from. If you were smart and determined enough to work hard, be a team player, be honest with yourself and others, you would thrive. Those who reached upper management knew the company code, taught repeatedly by their local manager. Some were better than others at immersion in this rarefied culture and the ability to impart it to the troops. But there was no denying that money talked to everyone. As individual profit sharing accounts began to grow and when employees began to buy, at discount, ever rising shares through the stock purchase plans, just about everybody was whistling Murphy's song ... all the way to the bank.

Alan Nesbitt

Reporter, WKBW-TV Buffalo

Asst News Director, WKBW-TV Buffalo

News Director, WPVI-TV Philadelphia

President, WTVD-TV Raleigh/Durham

President, WPVI-TV Philadelphia

President, KABC Los Angeles

Senior VP, ABC-owned TV stations

Irv Weinstein

My dear Phil,

Mavens of Wall Street know about the unparalleled success of Capcities. What they may not know is how the legendary company did it. As a long termer at their Buffalo station and one whose earlier employment history included working for people who ran the gamut from incompetent to clinically deranged, I knew smart when I saw it. Capital Cities' Tom Murphy, Dan Burke, and Joe Dougherty, lovingly referred to as "the Irish mafia," had a unique (at least to me) philosophy: All broadcast markets are different, and a blizzard of memos from corporate headquarters is a gross waste of paper. Hire talented and highly motivated people and let them do what they do best. Ratings and profits will follow. And so they did. There was very little of that "them and us" attitude so prevalent in most corporate-owned businesses. On those occasions when Tom, Dan, or Joe visited our station, they displayed friendliness, curiosity, and genuine interest in what everyone was doing. Broadcasting can be a tense business, so there were ample opportunities for bosses and staff to share a good laugh.

I recall, fondly, one such occasion. It was during a lunch break from a news directors meeting in New York City. Joe Dougherty joined several of us at a kosher style deli. It happened that on that day, the celebrations of St. Patrick's Day and Passover converged. Between bites of hot pastrami, Joe nonchalantly reaches into his pocket and placed a green skullcap on his head! That was vintage Capital Cities.

Irv Weinstein

News Anchor/News Director, WKBW-TV

Marc Edwards

Dear Phil,

One of my unique memories of Capital Cities? Well, forgive me if money is at the core of this memory, but, after all, those many years were not exactly spent as a hobby! Even though I was always a hard core loyalist to Capcities, on occasion I did give thought to calls from other broadcast companies. There were temptations, but the offers never made sense. Why? How about leadership? Murphy, Burke, Dougherty, and the others were like family to me. I loved them, and felt that love returned. But, too, it was the MONEY; and how it was delivered. No one could leave during a fourth quarter, giving up their share of the Profit Sharing Plan! No way! Leaving in the first quarter could screw up the exercise of options. There was also the Employee Stock Purchase Plan. Later in the year there could be a Shadow Stock award. That was a beauty! Now, we are back to year's end and Profit Sharing!

In the years before I became management, I was on the air talent and often showed the ego that can go with that work. Some of that ego was still functioning as I thought about the loyalty that kept me at Capital Cities for 40-plus years. Those financial incentives were deliberately spaced to make it costly for ME to give 'em up and leave. THEY did love me!

Marc Edwards (Arnold Freedman)

Promotion Director, WTEN-TV Albany

Promotion Director, WKBW-TV Buffalo

Sales Executive, WKBW-TV Buffalo

Regional Sales Manager, WKBW-TV Buffalo

Sales Manager, WTNH-TV New Haven

President, KFSN-TV Fresno

Aaron Daniels

Dear Phil,

Capital Cities changed my life. It gave me a sense of value, purpose and love for my fellow employees, (something I never had before CC). I also was taught how to manage others by such great role models as Murph, Burke, Dougherty and Arcara. And I will never forget after one of the Aaronak stage performances at our annual meeting. I gave the following answer, "Norm Schrutt, Norm Schrutt, Norm Schrutt". Then I followed with the question, "Why won't Capcities hire Jews anymore?" Tom came up to me after and said he did not like my Jewish reference to Norm. I answered "Since I am Jewish, I felt I could pick on him." Tom's remark, so pure, was, "I did not know you were Jewish." This after 23 years with the company ... those things did not matter to Tom, Dan or Joe. They promoted by ability and painted everyone with the same brush!

Aaron Daniels

Sales Executive, WPAT NYC

Manager, Fairchild Group NYC

Sales Manager, WPAT NYC

GM, WPRO-AM/FM Providence

President, ABC Radio NYC

৯ ❖ ৶

Steve Ridge

Hi Phil,

I always wondered why Capital Cities was often imitated, never duplicated. In my 30 years since, I've never seen another company capture their magic. Much of their culture went not only unwritten, but unspoken, as well. One had to absorb, even marinate in it over time. At first, the autonomy afforded management was a rush. Over time, however, the freedom to act began to weigh heavily, as a full appreciation of the true responsibility of carrying the Capcities mantle began to sink in.

I vividly recall traveling to New York City with you, as our GM, to present our capital expenditure requests to Tom and Dan. We were careful to rate items conservatively on a scale of essential, near and long-term investments. At the conclusion, Tom asked me why a night vision camera lens for surveillance by the highly rated investigative unit at the station was not "essential." I told him it was very expensive. He reminded me that my job was to protect and grow a successful brand. We walked out of the room with more money than requested and a good lesson in the philosophy of a great company.

Steve Ridge

News Director, WKBW-TV Buffalo

President, Media Strategy Group

Frank Magid Associates Inc.

Norm Schrutt

Hey Phil,
Around 1970, the GM's job in Providence opened up when Potash was transferred to Dallas. I pitched the job along with Rakovan. I really wanted the job and was told that Joe Dougherty was having a hard time choosing between us. I had a silver coin made with my name engraved on both sides.

I sent it to Joe with a note that said, "If it comes to the flip of a coin, please use this coin." I did not get the job, but about three years later, the GM job at WKBW became open and I went to NYC to pitch Joe again. When I walked into his office, he reached into his desk drawer, pulled out the coin, flipped it to me and said, "You waited this long, the job is yours." I knew right then I would NEVER work for another broadcasting company.

Norm Schrutt

Sales Executive, Local Sales Manager, General Sales Manager, WKBW-AM Buffalo

VP General Manager, WKBW-AM

VP General Manager, KZLA Los Angeles

President, WKHX-AM/FM Atlanta

President Owned Radio Stations, Capcities/ABC

Charles Keller

Dear Phil,

I was recently telling a friend how Capital Cities differed from Westinghouse when both companies had TV stations in Philadelphia. The difference was our commitment to letting our managers manage. Run the station like you own it and, by the way, here is some stock to make you an actual "owner" like those at headquarters. Westinghouse had layers of management above the station manager who dictated program decisions. They never came close to us. Ours was an enlightened, no interference approach, and we all prospered from it.

When Capcities bought WPVI-TV, my production unit was involved in a major project involving the Catholic Church's quadrennial Eucharistic Congress, a worldwide event in Philadelphia. It was a big budget item and I was facing a new company with a reputation for being lean and mean! My concerns were relieved in my first meeting with Joe Dougherty when I got the go ahead, not only to produce the final Mass and ceremonies, but to make the broadcast available to all stations free of charge. 200 stations carried the telecast!

Later our production unit concentrated on news documentaries and original, dramatic after school specials. Incidentally, profits from those programs were used to support continuance of those charitable activities. This "give back" commitment, directing the impact of our media operations to enrich and inform viewers, listeners and readers has always made me proud to be part to this unique and outstanding company.

Charles Keller

VP Production, WPVI Philadelphia

VP After School Specials, Capcities Philadelphia

VP Corporate Initiatives, CC/ABC New York

Dale Duncan

Hey Phil,

Tom Murphy called me at the paper in Wilkes-Barre late one afternoon with a shocking order. He told me we had to shut down our already brewing plans to add a Sunday edition because Warren Buffett had said it was a bad idea. This, after I'd gone to the trouble of explaining our plans to Buffett several weeks earlier expressly because he'd had a bad experience adding a Sunday edition in Buffalo. In that case, Buffett's competitor sued. It took many months and millions of dollars in legal fees before Buffett won court approval to compete on Sunday with The Buffalo Courier Express. Phil Meek, my boss as President of Capital Cities publishing, then made a gutsy call and convinced Murphy to listen to an appeal of his decision. A preliminary meeting at Teterboro was designed to have all reconsider, but Tom Murphy was firm. Meek then, with unprecedented persistence, convinced Murphy to accept another meeting "to review your decision." We convened at headquarters, explaining again that the investment was crucial to the success of our property: that the advertisers were supportive and that to back out now would be tantamount to giving up the market. We told him we could compete successfully — and legally — suggesting that he sell the paper to us if he was unwilling to proceed. It was remarkable how both Ron Doerfler, CFO, and Steve Weiswasser, chief counsel, supported our plan and urged Murphy to proceed. Amazingly, Murphy reversed himself. He concluded that launching the Sunday edition, despite the concerns of his largest shareholder, was the right thing to do for the paper. The message, sent to all operators, was loud and clear. While the chairman listens to everyone, he is likely to favor the men and women in the trenches. It was the bedrock of his philosophy of decentralization. And with this decision, there could never be a doubt.

Dale Duncan

President And Publisher, The Times Leader

Wilkes-Barre, Pennsylvania, 1986-1995

John Shuff

Dear Phil,

In December of 1965, Margaret Mary and I awoke to 5 feet of snow outside our rental home in Buffalo. I had never seen anything like it. Men came to the door asking to shovel this nightmare away and sleds abounded in the streets as we looked out in disbelief. Just another winter day on the Niagara Frontier, paralyzing the city! My dad, who had traveled the area, warned me about Mother Nature's behavior in Buffalo, but I never heeded his words. I became a believer that day. We moved to Buffalo when I became Business Manager of WKBW-AM and WKBW-TV, a big change from Cincinnati. But with this big change came bigger opportunities. I had learned about this small but growing company with a reputation for being aggressive and tough. The station manager, an effusive and congenial Bob King, met my plane in a swirling wind and freezing temperature, while I wondered why I had ever considered this new job. Buffalo became a lesson in the Capcities style and sense of collaboration. From King down to his department heads like Larry Pollock, Dick Shepard, Bob Niles, Red Koch and Don Kline; everyone worked together to make the station the market leader in sales and programming. No politics, no nonsense, just a devotion to being the best. Cost control was gospel, and the underlying factor in the company's magnificent performance. I stayed 18 months in Buffalo before being transferred to New York City and a series of new responsibilities, eventually working in literally all divisions of the company. As a very fortunate young man, I was exposed to various operations and personalities, especially those financial disciplines inculcated in all us. I can still hear Dan Burke in his famous budget sessions, "You can't control revenue, but you can control costs," or "Your budget is your promise to our shareholders." I can still see the numbers being flashed on the screen while attendees cheered the successes of their peers. Men and women worked together, played together, and helped one another. But the orchestra leader was Tom Murphy, Chairman. The tall, bald, blue-eyed master of the slide rule always made it a point at our company meetings, to repeat, "I can accept mistakes, but do not ever lie to me or anyone else in the company. There is no second chance here." Murph was proud of the small corporate staff and the autonomy he gave to his managers. If you needed help, it was there. But the bottom line was the budget and that was the manager's responsibility. Young people today seldom get the opportunity I was afforded with this fledgling broadcast company founded by Frank Smith in the mid-1950s. The exposure to men like Murphy, Burke, Dougherty, King, Sias, Beuth, Pollock, Doerfler, Fairchild, etc, just does not happen every day. Capital Cities was all about people with different talents from various backgrounds playing by the rules. They blended together to forge one of the most outstanding, financially successful media companies in history. When that golden ring came around on the carousel on a freezing day in Buffalo, I was fortunate enough to grab it. Capital Cities represented a culture whose values will remain as long as there are those remaining to tell the story.

John Shuff

Business Manager, WKBW-AM/TV Buffalo

Comptroller, Fairchild Group NYC

Assistant to President, Capcities NYC

VP Operations, Oakland Press

Publisher, Belleville News Democrat

VP/CFO, Capital Cities Communications NYC

President, JES Publications

After 2-for-1 stock splits in '66, '69 & '78, each share purchased in '57 had now become 8 shares

Price of stock - October 30, 1979

$42.50 per share

So, the actual value of an original $5.75 stock share
now equaled 8 x $42.50
or $340

CHAPTER TWENTY-TWO

Climbing the Mountain

The call came into the house about noon on Sunday, March 24, 1985. It was Dan Burke. Not particularly unusual. We at Capcities took pride in our "always on" work ethic. But the tone of Dan's voice was as intriguing as the brevity of his message. *"Philly,"* he said *"Come on down to 51st Street by 9 o'clock tomorrow ... We got something cooking"* ... and that was it! The lack of specifics certainly aroused my curiosity.

The next day, when I arrived at corporate headquarters in Manhattan, the halls were abuzz with the electrifying news: Capcities was merging with ABC! But hold the phone. That was just the tip of the story. We weren't exactly merging with the far larger company; we were buying ABC ... *a whale of a difference.* Once alone with Dan, he confided something he would repeat to the larger group later that day, *"this may be the best or the worst decision in the history of the company."* He also said Tom wanted me to sit in on the Board meeting as I had been the company's first employee. I was flattered and proud. Gathering the Capcities senior team, he outlined the deal in classic Burke style. He was eloquent, bold and forthright, seeming to embrace his role on a larger stage, while expressing apprehension as to how the move would impact the company and our personal lives. During the Q&A, he paused, struggled a bit and then, midsentence abruptly left the room for several minutes, overcome by his emotions. He later confessed he had been training for this moment all his life.

By the time our Board ratified the purchase, a contingent of senior ABC execs had arrived — mostly by limousine — and were gathered in Lowell's impressive office overlooking 51st Street. After pleasantries and handshaking, all departed to conclude the deal at ABC's corporate headquarters across from the Hilton Hotel on 6th Avenue. And, in an oddly prescient vignette worthy of Damon Runyon and perfectly evocative of our respective corporate cultures, the ABC executives piled back into their limousines for the return trip, while we, the executives of Capcities, elected to walk the six blocks. How prophetic, I mused!

The ABC lobby was awash with a sea of cameras and reporters, including, much to my surprise, our own Don Postles, a newsman from my home station in Buffalo. I had to chuckle as Tom Murphy carved a path straight through the mass of reporters to warmly greet our Buffalo reporter. This caused consternation among the other newsmen who weren't sure who either gentlemen was, but were clamoring nonetheless, petrified of not "getting" the story. I was again reminded of the humanity of our company and humbled by our Chairman who took such a genuine personal interest in all his employees. As I observed the scene, I was equally proud of Don's instincts and initiative. He had tried reaching me that morning and when he learned I'd made a lightning trip to the city, he got a broker friend on the horn and discovered *"something was up."* So, Don had buttonholed his photographer Mickey Osterreicher and the two hopped on a commuter so they could be on the scene holding their own amongst a throng of more seasoned journalists.

Wow! What an exciting day! So many questions from so many quarters! Who is this Capital Cities? Which one is Murphy? Who's Dan Burke? How did they pull it off? Someone held up and hollered the New York Post headline heralding us from that moment on as *"The minnow that swallowed the whale."*

Ruth Bassett Fitzgerald installed a second telephone line in Tom Murphy's office, which served as our de facto Public Relations department. Murphy's classic quip when asked about prime time show production was, *"You won't see me reading any scripts!"* The frenzy was at fever pitch as an over-zealous press pool played catch-up, digesting the enormity of the event and posing innumerable follow up questions: *"What was Warren Buffett's role?" "Which ABC stations would be sold?" "... Same for Capital Cities?" "How will the change affect prime time?" "Do these Capcities guys even know how to produce programming?" "Who will stay on as ABC management?" "And what about the ABC news division?"* In typical merger acquisition speak, most of the questions were answered generally and vaguely. The responses to questions relating to Warren Buffett's role were precise and complete. He was a major investor, who pledged his stock to Capcities. And WKBW-TV in Buffalo — where I was General Manager —

would be sold because of Warren's ownership of Buffalo's newspaper, The Buffalo News.

That evening ABC's trusted news anchor, Peter Jennings, announced the sale of his parent company to upstart broadcast group Capital Cities Communications. And on that day, in any case, "World News Tonight" was not simply reporting the news; they *were* the news!

When I returned to Buffalo at the end of a long day, the mood was anything but jubilant. The Buffalo News had run the article explaining how Buffett's ownership of the paper would mean a forced sale of the station. I was greeted by a staff of shell-shocked employees, worried about their destinies. Lacking any concrete information, all I could do was reassure them they could count on the company to carefully pick the right owner. Since I'd been singled out for a ringside seat to the merger, I privately knew my likely destiny, but preferred a *"wait and see"* public posture. Sure enough, Tom told me that while the new buyers — whoever they might be — would certainly ask me to stay; he wanted to extend his and Dan's personal invitation to remain with the company. Together, he said we would all *"climb the mountain."* And though I was tight-lipped about my future plans, all who knew me suspected I would never leave Capcities. They were right.

The new buyers were identified rather quickly; A substantial investor group called Queen City Broadcasting headed by the imposing, successful, attractive businessman and son of

Jamaican immigrants, J. Bruce Llewellyn. Llewellyn, who had built a supermarket powerhouse called Fedco Foods Corporation in the Harlem district of New York City, took advantage of a reduced purchase price for WKBW-TV designed to encourage minority ownership in broadcasting. Rolled into the succession plan fashioned by Murphy was the assurance that I would remain *"on loan,"* albeit with intermittent trips to NY, for a period of three months to help the new owners acclimate to Buffalo and their new business. And despite some nonsense newspaper headlines stating Llewellyn had made me *"an offer I could not refuse,"* I never led them to believe I would remain in Buffalo.

It became a busy time for me, shuttling back and forth between our headquarters in New York and the station in Buffalo. I enjoyed both ends and met some very nice people at the new owner group, who, as predicted, pressured me to stay and join their team. Their lead counsel, a smart, sensitive, humorous man named Burt Rubin, was my favorite. Despite how much Burt and I enjoyed each other's company, Burt never questioned my decision as he knew full well the degree to which I was committed to Tom and Dan. Burt and his wife, Sue remain our friends to this day. Queen City Broadcasting kept the station for about seven years and, as far as I can determine, considered it a good investment. Their last General Manager, Paul Cassidy, left the station in good shape.

Meanwhile, I was given a medley of ad hoc assignments on my weekly visits to the city. Tom asked me to review recent expenses reports at the network and to spend time with Warren Buffett, who was trying to get a handle on what had come along with the purchase price. I parked myself in a small room at headquarters where I plowed through piles of invoices, making notes of items that seemed excessive, though often without any baselines or comparables. I never knew where my notes ended up after they left my desk but they appeared to provoke a fair amount of heated discussion in the executive cafeteria.

I remember particularly that daytime costs seemed outrageous and that travel expenses merited additional scrutiny. A couple of ABC execs shared rumors that expense reports might have been shredded, but plenty of evidence of excessive spending popped up nonetheless: Flowers for "Good Morning America" cost $12,000 a week, over $600,000 a year!! When Warren got wind of that, he joked to me that he could do it for $50,000. I countered with $37,500! I came across an invoice for more than $20,000 for an 8-by-10 photo of Omar Sharif. $20,000 for a photo!? It had been part of a print ad campaign, authorized by Dick Connelly, a seasoned ABC veteran (whom I respected highly), to promote the movie, "Harem." When I asked for some background, I got a taste of a larger problem. According to Dick, Sharif had complained to the head of the network about the lack of publicity for the film. So an edict came down from on high to remedy the situation and *"get it done fast."* Apparently cost was not the principal issue. At first I thought these spikes were outliers and anomalies, but the more I delved — and later when I took over the reins at GMA — I learned that these excesses were anything but anomalistic. No Capcities-type cost controls in place, for sure! Oh boy, this was going to be interesting as the tight expense discipline that had always been a hallmark of Capcities business practices was about to be applied to a sprawling unruly network. I speculated that my peer partners at Capcities would have a field day reducing those expenses! Sure enough, I would soon be doing just that across the boards of the company on a larger stage.

CHAPTER TWENTY-THREE

Good Morning America

The three months of hand holding in the Queen City were apparently helpful to the new station owners. Though I was anxious to get to where the action was in New York, the way-lay period also eased my family's adjustment to the new assignment, especially as Jane was in a Buffalo private school.

Betty was not entirely happy about the ABC deal, though she greatly admired Tom and Dan. She had been through these executive moves on many occasions and always remained steadfastly and unselfishly supportive of my career. When I queried Tom about my potential duties at the network, he asked what I wanted to do. We talked about programming in LA, but that could never compete with the lure of my "home state" of New York. I told Tom I would like something measurable and challenging. This provoked some head scratching and pointed toward an underperforming asset in the Capcities/ABC basket. Our morning franchise, "Good Morning America," was being killed by NBC's mighty TODAY. Tackling that assignment was naturally appealing, as I viewed it much like a new station challenge, but with its own two-hour national programming block! And Dan, practicing his uncanny laser ability to anticipate, analyze and alleviate potential impediments, made a suggestion. Since Jane had a couple of years left at her private school in Buffalo, the company would provide its leased jet each week so I could make the commute on whatever schedule I saw fit. Typical of Capcities! That sealed the deal. And while those comfortable weekly trips to Buffalo or Chautauqua sometimes came in handy, I quickly found that grabbing a cab to LaGuardia and hopping the one-hour flight was simpler than trekking up to Westchester or over to Jersey to rendezvous with our cushy private plane. And as an *"old school"* Capcitizen, I had no problem flying commercial.

In March of 1985, the undisputed leader of morning television was the venerable TODAY, which had ruled early morning audiences ever since Dave Garroway and J. Fred Muggs, his chimpanzee companion, established the franchise in 1952! Their lead was more than one million households when Capcities inherited GMA. I had heard the old adage that turning around early morning audiences was harder than getting an ocean liner to make a pinwheel turn, but I was undeterred. I chose to view it as another station that simply needed new audiences.

Optimism counts for a lot, but the mountain was steep and the summit seemed lost in the clouds! I walked into GMA, an observer, smart enough to know that I could not immediately be of any meaningful assistance. I met a management team that demonstrated great operational chops and also had a remarkable grasp of the current events shaping the world all around them. Two talented women, Phyllis McGrady and Amy

276

Hirsh supervised a 110-person ensemble of writers, editors, photographers, on-air talent, promoters, and producers, all with a *"go live!"* deadline each weekday morning at 7 a.m. This Buffalo maverick was impressed!

Morning television is its own special animal, a mixture of news, culture, public interest and entertainment. One classic account of a typically diverse GMA morning schedule came courtesy of the sweet and humorous Joel Siegel, who described it as follows:

> *"If it's 6:30 a.m., and sitting in the far corner, reading a morning paper is the dignified, composed, Secretary of State Henry Kissinger, while across the room, his fingers in the dip, with sweat, makeup and hairpiece slipping off his bald head, is the actor Burt Young, Stallone's brother-in-law in the next ROCKY. And if, inside the studio, our hosts work to prepare a compelling report on an ice cream festival in Boston, a Turkey shoot in Ashville, and a 95-year-old teacher from Peoria ... then this must be morning television and you are in the Green Room of 'Good Morning America!!'"*

Morning shows funnel an extraordinary volume of information, from the newsworthy to the inane, showcasing and differentiating one from the other for a widely diverse audience with widely divergent interests. Early morning programming staffs face fierce, continuous pressures. The competition is intense, accompanied by an adrenalin-fuelled frenetic 24/7 pace far beyond what most programs demand. Veterans of the early morning television business are honed experts because the exhausting pace sidelines the faint of heart and the relentless drive for excellence weeds out mediocrity. It is a tough grind creating two hours of live television each day, five days a week, every week, producing more original content than just about any other media outlet, anywhere. Ten hours of original programming is the equivalent of five feature films each week! And it's live! The shows are typically run out of the Big Apple. So Sinatra had it right when he famously crooned *"If you can make it there ..."*

I learned after just a few weeks in New York, that newspaper coverage of the media and, specifically the management changes at GMA, unlike our company's disciplined self-imposed standards, was surprisingly sloppy and largely reliant on gossip and telltale hearsay from agent plants. I was naïve in expecting even a reasonable adherence to truth. At first humored by the press' field day as events unspooled, I finally became impatient with the drumbeat about *"the hick from Buffalo, of all places, coming in to run GMA!"* This man, they claimed, *"would certainly not pay Hartman enough to keep him on the job."* And so on, with a string of nonsensical rubbish. Not once, did a reporter pick up the phone and call me before printing his or her story, nor had anyone researched my past or prior career. I shrugged it off as the cost of playing in the big leagues. In fact, the unsavory news reports just fueled my appetite to succeed. Only one journalist, who wrote under the byline Executive Producer for Newsday, did call months later to apologize for not properly researching what he had written. I never established a cozy relationship with the fifth estate, but after a while did develop a level of trust with Vern Gay of Newsday and Bill Carter of The Times; and I went to them on those rare occasions when I needed to get, or wished to supply, information. Looking back, dealing with the press was not high on my priority list; rather, it was a necessary inconvenience of the territory.

A far more delightful part of the landscape, however, was getting to know and work with our neighbors just down the block. They, along with a few old acquaintances, made my arrival all the more pleasant. Within weeks, the man who personified Big Apple show business called, inviting me to a Mets game. I spent the next three hours with Regis Philbin, a genuine New York icon. But the truth is we didn't have much quality time at the ballpark, as I had to share him with the entire population of the city of New York (and most of New Jersey!). His phenomenal personality attracted throngs of fans, all of whom came and greeted him so warmly you would have sworn they were lifelong friends. It was a thrilling experience and the first of many opportunities to share time with this talented, unique individual. Being at GMA also allowed me to renew my acquaintance with another favorite — Kathy Lee Johnson, who by this time, was married to Frank Gifford and the co-host of Regis' morning show. Kathy Lee, whom I had known earlier in her career as a well-known singer, would always cheerfully pitch in when I asked her to participate in one of our charity events. *"Sure, just send me a ticket!"* She remains one of my favorite people, and together with Regis, Michael Gelman, and a long time Capcities manager, Art Moore, they enjoyed great success with their morning show, housed just down the block from our studios at GMA. The opportunity to be on the same team with such talent, and others like Jungle Jack Hanna — one of the most naturally unpretentious and committed men I know — will be long cherished by me.

For the first six weeks or so, after noting that a weekly floral display at my apartment door suddenly stopped, I watched, I observed. I also talked to many staff members, impressed at how this complex matrix came together like clockwork each morning. Over time, as I got the lay of the land, a few problem areas, just a few, began to surface. The staff had a generally positive opinion toward host David Hartman, whom they thought highly of and liked personally. At the same time, there was a feeling that his demanding insistence on perfection bordered on arrogance. I was told repeatedly that producers were reluctant to submit ideas for fear of their being rejected. Since David had total control over content and complete veto power, these reports came back with increasing regularity. I waited until I was confident I could make a distinction between reasonable and frivolous criticism and then brought the issue to David's attention. I made it clear that changes in line of authority were necessary. Capital Cities did not buy the network to let their talent, no matter how creative they may be, run these programs as they pleased, was my theme. And I told him as diplomatically as I could, that certain unilateral policies had to change. David's response, always gentlemanly and free of rancor, was that he felt he was protecting the quality of content and that his authority had been endorsed by previous management. He went on to say that he felt more comfortable doing his own thing and preferred to work solo. He did not particularly like co-hosting pieces with Joan Lunden, especially when it came to news segments, where he found she lacked credibility. David's contract renewal was looming and I advised him that if we were to discuss continuing, he would have to accept a role that offered him right of review on matters, but not of veto. He would no longer control all content. I gave him a memo with 24 suggestions about how the program might be improved and asked for his opinion. His retort was that his agent would have something to say about that. I had been forewarned by various sources, based on their experiences, to avoid tangling with David's notoriously difficult agent, Felix Shagin. I got the same advice from my pal, Steve Weiswasser, one of our senior attorneys, and from my exceptional new boss, John Sias. I did not take those admonitions too seriously, preferring not to prejudge the man. My partners expected a pitched battle, nevertheless. Felix and I met for lunch, and over a couple of Bloody Marys, had a very productive exchange. He was completely professional, and pleasant. However, he communicated to me that David could only accept one suggestion from among the 24 I had submitted. I told Felix that I did not wish to throw a grenade into the matter and so we explored David's suggestion that it might be time to *"pass the baton."* Together we arranged a mutually acceptable separation settlement and it was all accomplished very cordially in a relatively short time. I appreciated David's positive attitude throughout it all, and remain a fan.

This cleared a path for Joan, whom I doubt would have stayed if David had renewed his contract. Unlike many at the network, I never had a doubt about Joan Lunden, whom I believed to be an unappreciated asset to the show. Roone Arledge, the President of News and a highly respected talent in ABC management, was not a fan of Joan Lunden, nor was our boss, John Sias. I discounted Roone's critique as he made no secret of his desire to move GMA from Entertainment into his News division. In fact, he tried over a couple of lunches during the next few years to convince me to accept the idea, without any success. Roone might have genuinely believed GMA would be better a better fit with news, but most of our peers just thought he wanted to enlarge his sphere of influence, which was already considerable. John Sias' dubious view of Joan was more of a concern to me but not a deal breaker, because at Capital Cities, *"in charge"* meant exactly that so ultimately the only opinion that counted was mine. Plus, over the preceding years I had been fortunate to make some outstanding hires, so my batting average was respectable and my instincts respected. As I began to assess the team, I decided the time was right for more talent changes at GMA. Luckily, the next three hires were home runs.

The show needed a new weather person, and several possibilities were proposed to us by agents. But I found a candidate on my own by watching the local news on Channel 7 in New York. I had always been entertained by Spencer Christian's weather reporting. Meteorologists all essentially have identical material and data to draw from in making their predictions. To me, besides having an attractive physical appearance, weather presenters need also to be entertainers, with large personalities. Spencer jumped across the screen. He was smart, funny, and welcoming. I called, met him for lunch and, over a turkey sandwich, offered him a job at a salary far less than he was presently making. But I meant it when I promised him more notoriety, success, and eventually more money than in his present situation. He agreed, and in a reasonable time, those promises were fulfilled. Spencer Christian and his delightful, friendly, creative personality became a very strong positive force at GMA, which was now continuing its major makeover.

After a few months, it was obvious that both our Executive Producers, Amy Hirsch and Phyllis McGrady, had other career plans. I suspect Phyllis had her sights trained on the news division even before we met. She went on to notable success there, much to my delight. Amy hung in with me for a while. I enjoyed working with her and occasionally beating her at gin rummy. She and her cover-girl good looks left us for Hollywood, where she later married actor Wayne Rogers. Just as I was getting ready to scour the country for an Executive Producer to replace Phyllis, a former GMA veteran staffer named John Goodman stopped by for a chat. He always seemed up on things, and I liked to be enlightened by his inside track knowledge. He told me I should look up Jack Reilly, currently Executive Producer for Entertainment Tonight in Los Angeles. Jack had done a previous stint at GMA and John believed he would be a good prospect. It turned out to be excellent advice! I called Jack on the coast, learning that his contract was about up and that he would be interested. He flew to New York and, within an hour over an oatmeal breakfast at the Essex House, I knew he was the right man for the job. Modest to a fault, Jack exuded decency, loyalty, and gentleness. He walked with a slight limp from an early bout with polio and as he put it, *"Together we have a full set of legs... to take us anywhere!"* And, boy did they!

I told Jack he would not be working *for* me, but rather *with* me, as a partner. I recognized that he had more experience and savvy for this assignment than I did and so offered him the kind of unbound autonomy I had always enjoyed. In fact we agreed that no matter what the decision, either could nix it without fear. Jack had been around the track, with many companies, business friends and accolades. However, he did not cotton to all the corporate red tape, so he appreciated that I could run interference for him. I saw in him a person who knew what he was doing, where we were going, and how to get there. In time, I felt, with Jack on the team, we would be on top in the ratings. The clouds on that summit began to part ever so slightly. I still cherish notes from him saying he never had a better experience than the one we had together. And the feeling was mutual, as we fit together splendidly, without a harsh word ever coming between us. Again, I was the lucky one. Our partnership sired several other talented men and women, and a team was born which old timers at GMA claim might have been the best ever fielded. It was certainly the least political, I believe.

Jack became the third happy traveler (along with Joan and Christian) on the path I considered my imaginary yellow brick road. When it came time to replace David, which had to be done carefully, there were many possibilities about whom we thought and talked. Several might have fit certain roles or appealed to certain audiences, but we were looking for a one-size-fits-all. The list included Frank Gifford, Joe Garagiola, Al Michaels and a personal favorite, Tim McCarver, but they all seemed too sports oriented. David Birney, the actor held our attention for a while, but couldn't pull off a news role. Same with the late John Denver, who tried to convince me that "*a good news only*" strategy — with no tragedy reporting — was a sure path to dominant morning ratings. John would be sorely disappointed by morning television these days. While a handful of other candidates passed through the halls of GMA, Jack and I began to zero in on a young man who worked for ABC News, based out of our Washington, D.C. bureau. Charlie Gibson had occasionally substituted for David and, within a short period of time, Jack and I almost simultaneously came to the realization that he was the everyman we were seeking. We both knew Charlie well enough to believe his sharp journalistic mind, quick wit and curiosity would fill the news role perfectly. But Charlie also had that nice guy carriage that would fit the show's entertainment side. He quickly became our natural choice. In the D.C. news division of ABC, Charlie had been short-listed for bigger and better political and journalistic assignments and I was afraid that when it got down to it, Charlie might not want to leave the news division. And when Charlie's candidature was leaked, we were not helped by Ted Koppel's friendly teasing: *"I wonder what recipes Charlie will feature when he takes the helm at GMA."* And there was another hitch. As Charlie worked for news, I felt obligated to talk to Roone before approaching Charlie. I put it off, wondering if I wanted to run the risk of Roone saying no; and finally went forward, or rather *around* Roone. Charlie and I met in the ABC cafeteria for coffee and a chat. Charlie teases me to this day for choosing that cheap venue instead of the Plaza Hotel. I told Charlie how much I wanted him, how GMA would increase his national exposure, how he would enjoy hours of screen time far in excess of that of his peers, and how he would be at the epicenter of everything happening in the world. Though it may have sounded like hyperbole, I was absolutely convinced it was all true. None of that was news to Charlie. He saw clearly what GMA would mean in terms of exposure, but he also saw what had just happened to David Hartman, so was reluctant to leave the security of the news division. I told him I fully understood and we agreed to talk over the weekend by phone. ...We did. I remember those calls very well. I considered them *"persuasion occasions,"* a wholesale *sell-a-thon*. Charlie had me confirm that all of his news benefits would carry over to the entertainment side. I assured him they would, knowing full well that with my executive stripes, I could make it happen even if it did not go through automatically. He was cautious and careful making this decision and I kept up the pressure, confident this was absolutely the right move for him. Finally, on that weekend afternoon, I used everything in my war chest, including some closing ammunition I held as an officer of the company. As far as I knew, no one at ABC News held options on Capital Cities stock shares, whereas most Capital Cities executives and a few of our own news people did. I played that option card and by the time we hung up, Charlie was not only the new co-host of GMA, he also held valuable rights to buy future shares of company stock at current prices. That afternoon we had each made a smart decision. I felt particularly good, not only with the outcome, but because again the Capcities system had worked! There had been no memos, no meetings, no discussions, no request for approval, just independent judgment by an executive who had the trust of his superiors and the best interests the company at heart. Charlie later claimed that those Capital Cities shares assured the financial security of his family for generations. That may be true, but the real winners that day were our viewers. And then there were four: *Spencer, Jack, Joan and Charlie, ready, locked and loaded. Off the see the wizard!*

During the process of finding Spencer, Jack and Charlie, I squeezed in a courtesy visit to Brandon Stoddard in Los Angeles, the man who ran ABC Entertainment and who, theoretically, would have been my new boss. However,

Brandon chose to take a pass on ABC Daytime and "Good Morning America," leaving them to New York's choices of ABC's exceptional Dennis Swanson and me. That was ok as far as I was concerned, since as an affiliate station manager and a member of the ABC Board of Governors for the past several years, Brandon had impressed me as bright and talented in our group sessions. At our meeting, he greeted me cordially as we talked about family and jobs. He said he was delighted I would relieve him of GMA responsibilities so he could concentrate fully on prime time. He then led me to a table upon which was a large hard cover book about 3-foot square. As he paged through it with me, he described it as a shooting bible for the epic ABC miniseries, Herman Wouk's "The Winds of War." It was fascinating and I wished I could spend hours with it, but we settled in on a page describing a scene where hundreds of warriors on horseback thundered through a mountain pass somewhere in Europe. I do not know if that scene made final cut, but when my eyes wandered to the bottom right corner and I read an estimated cost of $7 million, I could see why it might not. Surprised, I commented *"Wow! Wouldn't that scene cost a lot less shot in Montana?"* His response, respectfully, was, *"I suppose so, but we would lose my director, Dan Curtis."* As we spoke further, Brandon made an observation that remained with me. He said, *"The difference between you Capcities guys and us is you guys live rich and work poor, and we work rich and live poor!"* I am not sure he was right about his living poor, but I would bet he believed what he said about us.

Food for thought ... but I had a morning show to run. Still badly trailing TODAY, we needed to either pluck some of their viewers, or attract entirely new ones to morning television. The former option seemed more sensible, but in either case we had to build a better product and provide television that was meaningful enough to grow our audience base and motivate our staff. We formulated a set of goals and identified the problems. The questions were rather basic. Which markets and audiences preferred NBC, and why? Which ABC stations were strong enough to grow? Who were the most receptive and motivated ABC General Managers? We quickly identified 20 markets where our show was either second in the ratings or in first place and strong enough to attract new viewers; and we began working in concentrated fashion on those pre-qualified affiliate stations. At the same time, we had to produce a more interesting, more appealing, more inviting show. And I promised our affiliate General Managers, many of them personally, that we would do just that. Luckily, I had a number of friends at those target markets, who had known me as a station manager before I became a network guy. They all knew me and knew I fully understood the network/affiliate relationship and its long-term mutual benefit. Convincing them of the dollar value of even one additional rating point or two for their morning block was an easy sell. A number of joint promotions were initiated, which continued for a year or more. We started doing live cut-ins from different cities, or bringing affiliate weather persons to New York to work with Spencer. Soon we were broadcasting entire shows from different cities, bringing a bit of show biz glitter to their local markets. We helped stations insert individually crafted promotional ads into our high audience broadcasts like "Oprah" and we reached out and solidified relationships with some of our brand new affiliates. Cooperating with affiliates was not a particularly new idea, but concentrating in such focused manner on the dollar value of every extra rating point was novel. No one had done this in such granular fashion. And that began to turn the trick, not overnight and sometimes with varying degrees of success. GMA audiences grew quietly and steadily in the first year to year and a half in the target markets. In fact, at an ABC affiliate conference in LA, special recognition was made by several station managers applauding our new, more profitable, more interesting, and better-promoted "Good Morning America."

By the end of 1987, we could see an audience trend developing in our favor among some key demographics. This improvement, station by station, market by market, was happening because the show itself was an evolving, exciting and fresh television experience, even to us! Charlie and Joan were clicking as partners who genuinely liked each other, and the family we had put together was feeding our viewers interesting, entertaining and newsworthy television to fill and excite their mornings. Of course, our competition remained tough so growth was slow, but it was steady. And gradually, little by little, the fruits of our labor and the realization of my dream began to lay tiny specks of gold along our yellow brick road!

Our program content was as varied as the times. Changes in lifestyles, the economy, medicine, technology, and education, along with Third World and Middle East conflicts, fed us countless opportunities to provide our audience with information they could understand and appreciate. We relied on ABC News for hard news, but also provided liberal helpings of people-oriented content. Producers carefully matched stories with predetermined audience interests and demographics, scheduling segments and promotions carefully. Our everyday broadcasts were purposely regimented and predictable. The theories and applications that had worked for me in programming and on air promotion for years were gradually integrated into a daily rewrite of the GMA rundown. Certain new features dealing with finance, science, and family issues were written, produced, scheduled and promoted, often airing in the same half hour each week. Michael Guillen would tell viewers how things like cellphones or ATM machines worked at the same time each Thursday, and others like Dr. Tim Johnson, Arthur Miller, Julia Childs, Nancy Snyderman, Steve Fox, and our dear Joel Seigel, and Tyler Mathisen, whose unique talent made finance compatible with the morning rush, would air their pieces with regularity, doling out meaningful, valuable, information about the important issues of the day. We were blessed with talent. Field producers like Rudy Bednar, Howie Masters, Jeff Jason, Fred Dorn and others complemented our studio segments with reports from all over the country. The team played well together. Line producers like Rickey Gaffney, Patrick Tague, Jerry Liddell, Roni Selig, Steve Lewis, Kevin McGee and others like Randy

Barone, David Sloan, Bill Clarke, Bob McKinnon, V. Gantt, Patty Neger, Jessica Stark, and Joe Tucker were not only key to keeping this perpetual 24/7 machine purring, but were part of another aspect I considered essential. I firmly believed in openly sharing information with staff as a way to bond them to Capital Cities/ABC. I kept them current regarding ratings, rates, sales, profit sharing, and all our company activities, reminding them over and over that they were part of a great company. They continued to do excellent work, despite my constant — perhaps ad nauseam — harping on costs, urging thrift, not at the expense of quality, but to avoid the waste of stockholders' money. My upbringing at Capital Cities made cost control a perfectly natural adjunct to my management style, sometimes to the point of single-mindedness. It just made sense to me. I continued to sell a simple principle. We all prosper when the company's earnings grow and then rain down in the form of profit sharing. Some of our personnel immediately recognized the attractive monetary rewards linked to cost controls, while others who were less attentive, considered them a nuisance. That is, until new information about earnings increased the price of their stock and the value of their profit sharing. That snapped them to attention.

I had some good ammunition to build my case for controlling costs. An instance of terrible waste on a field production had come to light just after the takeover. It was a taped fashion segment featuring several models. The cost exceeded $20,000! It surely would have gone unnoticed had I not identified it. The post mortem went as follows, as accurately as it could be reconstructed: Someone concluded that a segment on fashion naturally required a special fashion-credentialed producer from Los Angeles, who was called in to New York for a few days, staying at a five-star hotel. On the day of the shoot, the models were each driven to the location from Manhattan in separate limos, each one of which waited for five hours! A couple of associate producers from New York also attended, enjoying a plush fully catered lunch. There were several additional perks and everyone, not surprisingly, had a great time! The segment, when it aired, was well received I was told, but its real value was not to our viewers, but to me. As most of the cost of that segment had not gone onto the screen, I used it as an example of unacceptable waste and the need to be cost conscious at all times.

In 1986, the production budget for GMA was $50 million a year, or approximately $1 million per week. The network had a personnel pool that was called the Unit Manager system. Unit Managers were assigned to individual projects or programs to assist or sometimes control production line items. I never understood the concept or benefit of the system, but went along with it as historic policy or protocol. It looked to me like an unnecessary layer of personnel and administration. Unit Managers reported to the Senior Vice President/Tape, Rod Rodomister, a long-term respected ABC veteran, who had no reporting line to persons like me. As part of the system, I was privileged to have talented Unit Managers assigned to various aspects of the show, but I would have preferred them as staff members under my direction. Since they influenced and sometimes controlled costs directly, I decided to offer one of my favorites, Dom Nuzzi, a chance to showcase his talents. Dom was popular, quiet, hardworking, and smart. Even though he technically worked for, reported to, and was paid by Rod, I considered him GMA staff. We reviewed our numbers regularly, and I told him I thought we could reduce our operating production budget by $15 million the following year. He would have the help of another of our best production people, Jessica Stark, who booked and managed techs wherever we originated video or live broadcasts. Since I had no control over his salary, I offered him a $5,000 bonus if we saved $15 million! I was confident we could do it and felt that $5,000 would be an appropriate and welcome bonus. I viewed the proposal as creative delegation. We shook on it and then I told Rod, his boss, who exploded over the phone. He said they did not give bonuses; that they would have to keep this secret from the other Unit Managers; and that the decision was just plain unacceptable. I told Rod I thought it would be a good test case for the other Unit Managers; that he ought to consider such incentives in his department, and that I fully intended to proceed. The difficulty came when we saved the $15 million and Rod refused to pay! That was late December. I kept reminding Rod, but he would not agree. Finally I told him that I was writing a personal check to Dom, and putting it on my expense report for Dan Burke to approve. That did it and Dom got his check. However, Rod intimated that he felt he had to give all his Unit Managers the same bonus! I recommended strongly against it. I doubt he pursued that idea because it went nowhere. Rod and Dan Burke probably had words about it, but Dan and I never discussed the matter. Shortly thereafter, Rod took his early retirement. I hope it was planned, but I felt badly about him, regardless. He was a good man, loyal and devoted to a policy that, though it might not have passed independent scrutiny, was gospel to him. Different strokes, different operating philosophies, different cultures. (Dom Nuzzi now holds an important executive position with Disney in Los Angeles.)

Another important addition to our talent roster came in the form of our Hollywood Reporter, Chantal. How she came to us provides an unusual anecdote. It was not uncommon for me to visit Los Angeles to attend a conference or a convention. On one such occasion, a friend arranged a meeting in the lobby of The Century Plaza Hotel, with one of my heroes, Muhammad Ali. While Ali was active and healthy, I saw him from time to time, often with his constant companion, photographer, Howard Bingham, who sometimes posed us together and always sent me the prints. Ali likely never did remember my name, but he called me his *"little friend from ABC."* He sent me one of his books, which I still treasure.

On that day, Howard was not with us. It was just Ali and me as we sat alone for a half hour chatting mostly about Howard Cosell while he sipped orange juice and I nursed a scotch and soda. It was a quiet afternoon, with few people in the hotel lobby. As we talked, I noticed an unusually dressed woman near the bar who kept looking over at the two of us.

I figured she was trying to get Ali's attention. Finally, she approached the table. Years later, she wrote me the following:

"I was supposed to meet you that afternoon, to talk about Bill Ritter, but we had set no particular time. So I arrived at the hotel to find you in a very intense but friendly conversation with Mr. Ali. Well, I adored him, but YOU were the man I wanted to talk to. I hung back for a while and thought, Damn ... they're going to talk forever, and you probably had an appointment with someone else following Ali, so I finally sailed over and said, 'Excuse me, sirs, I wanted to introduce myself.' Ali stood, graciously shook my hand, and asked my name. But I stopped him, and explained that while it was a great honor to meet him, I was actually there to see Mr. Beuth! Ali charmingly said it was the first time in a long time he'd gotten second billing! Ali roared, and so did you."

The woman was Judy Bowen, agent for Bill Ritter, later hired by GMA, and, as of this writing, remains the main news anchor for ABC's flagship, WABC-TV in New York. As Judy and I talked, I told her that while I thought Bill was great, we had no spot for him at the time. However, I was looking for a Hollywood reporter if she had any ideas. She said that the only such talent she might recommend was a woman who went by the single name, *"Chantal,"* and who was working for Channel 9 in Los Angeles. I picked up a matchbook, tore off the cover, and wrote Chantal, Ch 9 on it, sticking it in my shirt pocket.

Two weeks or so later, when the shirt came back from the laundry, I noticed this crumpled matchbook cover, still in the pocket, with the name still legible! That was fate, I fancied. I dialed Channel 9 and reached Chantal Westerman, who later told me she *"almost died"* when she learned I was calling from GMA! That week we flew her to New York for an interview. I should now introduce the reader to the late Sonya Selby Wright, a remarkable woman on the GMA staff. Sonya was an extremely well bred British lady of stature, who could be respectfully called the Mother Superior of the staff. She had a lot to say about what should or should not air on the show and was generally right on target. When we met, she was rather cold and distant. I assume she had concluded that, coming from Buffalo, I had certainly never read Vanity Fair or eaten at Le Cirque, was in way over my head, and impossibly under-qualified to head up GMA! But by the time we interviewed Chantal, we had established an uneasy mutual trust. It was a chilly winter evening when we all met for dinner at the Cafe des Artiste on West 67th Street. Sonya and I and were treated to a candid, startling description of Chantal's life. She began by confessing that if she was lucky enough to get this job, we should know beforehand that we might regret the decision because of some embarrassing information about her past that might come to light. She had overcome a drinking problem, had been in AA for a few years, had once posed topless for an art magazine as the "Sexiest Woman in Dallas" and had endured blackout periods in her life, the details of which her memory could not recall very clearly. As we heard the lurid details of Chantal's past spill out before us, Sonya, the sophisticated high priestess of class, must surely have thought I was out of my mind to even take the interview! However, the more Chantal talked and reassured us that the past was past and that she was now a responsible working professional, the more Sonya and I grew to like her and to see the potential star qualities in the startling figure sitting opposite us. We walked back along Central Park West, left her at the Mayflower Hotel, and hired her the next morning. Chantal added a delightful dose of charm and Hollywood chatter to the show for years, becoming the interviewer of choice for many celebrities. She never did embarrass us, by the way!

Chantal made many lasting and warm personal connections with Hollywood celebs and became one of our hardest workers. One of her fans — yes she had many — was Bette Davis, who followed her career to the point of calling me from time to time to put in a good word for Chantal. I had met Ms. Davis for a smoke-filled lunch at the invitation of Jimmy Griffin, a major domo at William Morris, but I never imagined she would remember me. One day, years later, at a production meeting on the island of St Croix, a hotel clerk interrupted the group, announcing that an important caller was on hold for Mr. Beuth. To the astonishment of all, he also announced, *"It is Betty Davis from Hollywood!"* Ms. D had tracked me down to suggest that since Chantal was so important to GMA, I should consider adding more staff to her production crew so she would not have to work so hard! *"Sorry to bother you Philip, but I had to tell you,"* she concluded. Such was the power of Chantal.

One of Chantal's favorite celebrities was Burt Reynolds, whom she interviewed on several occasions. One day Jack Reilly asked me into his office to watch a Chantal/Reynolds taped segment that concerned him as it was so terrible. It only took an instant to see what Jack meant. Burt wore a purple suit, which might have been ok, but he looked sickly, tired, gaunt, and weak. Jack said he did not want to run it and asked what I thought. It was an easy call to agree because something was obviously wrong with Reynolds. Later that day Jack returned, telling me that Burt's people had called with an unusual request. They agreed it was terrible and that under normal circumstances they would ask it to be pulled, but they wanted the piece to air specifically to force Burt to face some unpleasant facts and take the long overdue decision to enter rehab. They believed that once he saw the clip, he would realize the gravity of his condition, and seek help. We talked it over and decided to run the clip, *in Burt's best interests*. Later in one of his books, he acknowledged that our airing of that segment might have helped rescue him from utter self-destruction.

Morning TV "situations" like the Reynolds one arose quite often, and they make good show biz anecdotes. Many stories deal with the network competition for celebrity appearances and involve the celebrity bookers, the toughest soldiers in the morning TV wars. They battle to get the hottest, biggest stars for their network. Which show gets the next big star? Is it the highest rated? Do celebs have favorite interviewers? (That is a definite yes). I recall a humorous, bordering on ridiculous anecdote. The networks were being offered Sylvester Stallone, who was promoting the latest of his many Rocky movies. His people were trying to bargain with the morning shows. What would GMA or TODAY offer? Nothing more than our audience was the predictable answer. They asked GMA for a round trip for two on the Concorde, and probably asked the same of TODAY; same negative answer from each of us. After a day or two, just as we were ready to walk away, an unusual ask came in. Stallone, his rep claimed, had a specific request. He wanted a white stretch limo, a dozen tuna fish sandwiches, a dozen bottles of water, and an empty Green Room. Jack said, *"What the hell, we already have the stretch and the sandwiches are easy. That we can do."* I asked him if Sly had an entourage with him and no one knew. Since it was a post tape scheduled at 10:30 a.m. the next day, clearing the Green Room was also easy. On the taping day, my curiosity peaked. So I went down to the Green Room about 10 a.m., and there, as ordered, were the sandwiches and bottled water. Also in the room, reading the paper, was playwright Neil Simon. We chatted briefly and he told me he had a post tape at 11 a.m., and hoped he was not in the way, noting the sandwiches. I explained who we expected and added that the sandwich thing was a mystery. Simon got up and said something like, *"Thanks for tipping me off. I'm gonna' walk around for an hour. I don't need to be here for that party."* He left, and I waited. At about 10:20 a.m., Stallone came in from the white limo, alone, ran right past the Green Room to the studio, did the interview, and was gone in a flash, never even looking in. It made me wonder if Stallone's reps were pulling our leg or whether Stallone even had knowledge of the details of the Green Room request. In any case, the crew was grateful and all lunched on tuna sandwiches that day. A year later Stallone did a spot for us in Hollywood on an AIDS show we were putting together, with no zany Green Room requests. I never asked him about the 12 tuna sandwiches.

For the first few years, ABC News participated actively in GMA, but at a price. When we asked for a Sam Donaldson report from Washington, for example, we got it. However, for each segment, the news department assessed GMA a seemingly arbitrary fee. Since there was no specific rate card, the practice caused Dom Nuzzi and his counterpart in news to waste hours in weekly negotiations over which ABC pocket got which fees. I then decided on an unconventional maneuver. On my next regular meeting with Murph, I told him that I wanted to give half of GMA's profits to News in return for unrestricted access to their people and facilities. Murph's reaction was thoughtful, saying, *"Philly, you are the only one around here with enough stripes to get away with that ... and Roone ought to love it."* I responded *"We'll put a footnote on all the financials to be sure we all see the GMA contribution."* And it was done without fanfare or corporate memos, allowing ABC News to announce within short order that they were, at last, profitable. That gave Roone some satisfaction, especially as their competition, NBC News, had been profiting for years from the success of TODAY, whose profits accrued to the news division.

In late 1987, a woman named Briggita Hedenstead, representing the country of Sweden, made a cold call to my office. I believe we were her second call, having been turned down by TODAY. She asked us to consider doing a week of broadcasts from Sweden, which was about to celebrate an important date in their history the following year. Jack and I listened to her presentation, describing the attractions her country could offer to our production. We were intrigued by the possibility, but also concerned about staying on budget, an area where we were doing well. I explained my reservations to Brigitta, telling her that our costs might explode by more than $500,000. Brigitta responded with some welcome information. She had a budget from the Swedish tourism department that she might be able to allocate to offset our costs. I checked with our attorneys and confirmed what I had suspected. As a division of ABC Entertainment (not News), I could accept production assistance as long as we did not charge or receive direct payment for programs. Such assistance had to be noted carefully in the show's credits. We had done it on our American cities shows, thanking affiliates for their technical support. We could accept assistance from any source as long as it was appropriately and legally noted on the air. That ushered in a new, unanticipated, but most welcome and enduring advantage over TODAY, which, due to its news identity, was bound to stricter expense controls than we were. For instance, our camera crews could operate cameras leased by the Swedish tourist group, thus vastly reducing our production costs. We used this legitimate advantage repeatedly, taking GMA all over the world ... and

302

then solidly into first place in the ratings war! We began devoting each June and some November weeks to overseas broadcasts, which enabled our viewers to get a vicarious peek at a variety of lifestyles worldwide. Our experiences in those countries could fill a separate book: Sweden, Holland, The United Kingdom, Hong Kong, Australia and other foreign land broadcasts treated viewers to incomparable visual landscapes and lifestyle portraits of people and places most Americans would never experience in a million years. The reaction from our viewers exceeded our most ambitious hopes, boosting our morning ratings to new highs. We were assisted by many outside organizations, tourist bureaus, and travel experts everywhere. Continental Airlines personnel greeted us like family and the Los Angeles PR firm Murphy O'Brien, led by Karen Murphy, arranged attractive gratis hotel space worldwide on a par far beyond that which our meager budget could have afforded. Although more than 20 years have elapsed since GMA visited all those interesting foreign countries, dozens of memorable events stay with those of us who produced the broadcasts, prompting stories to be repeatedly told and retold.

Some, like this one, stand out. To prepare for our very first international production, Jack Reilly and I were invited for a weeklong scout to Sweden, courtesy of the Swedish Tourist Bureau, the Swedish government and SAS Air. Upon arriving in Stockholm one late spring morning, we were greeted by Brigitta, her interpreter, a publicity man, a helicopter and pilot. Over the next three days, we were flown to dozens of fascinating locales all over Sweden, including overnight stays at mountain and seaside resort hotels. We were supplied with clothes to wear, head to toe, and did not see our regular luggage until three days later at our Stockholm hotel.

That tour included a visit to Lapland, where we lunched with a local Sami family. The father sat at the head of a table, able to reach down to the floor and lift the cover for access to their in-ground cooler. He brought up a piece of meat that was passed by hand to each of us, along with a knife for cutting off a portion. Laplanders identify their herds of reindeer by clipping off different patterns from their ears. Hanging these sewn-together earpieces from a fireplace signifies economic status. The deer are moved in a caravan up to the mountaintops each summer. We arrived on the day of such a move. They proudly showed us their new system of transport, which took less time than the traditional weeklong trek. We watched as helicopters lifted the animals to the top of the mountain chain, one by one in sling harnesses, completing the whole process in a day or two.

Our helicopter pilot was exceptionally skilled, but had a tendency to show off his prowess by mixing a few thrills into his regular duties. We white-knuckled it through the pilot's antics, while a distressed and embarrassed Brigitta scolded him in Swedish to no avail. He once put the copter into a straight up ascent and suddenly cut the motor, letting us drift down in free fall for a few seconds before restarting the motor. The result was more harrowing than the most death-defying roller coaster drop. As Jack and I were seated in the bubble upfront, his popularity with us was tentative at best! On another trip, he took us to a stand of 200-foot high pine trees in the center of which was an opening all the way to the ground just wide enough to accommodate the width of the blades. He positioned the copter over the center, descended straight down to the ground, and then up at full power. Then he challenged Brigitta to the breaking point by proceeding to top off one of the trees with the rotor blades! Brigitta threatened to fire him on the spot if he tried a prank like that again, causing him to modify his behavior ... for a little while. But, it was all in good fun.

We went up mountains above the Arctic Circle, with a half-dozen stops along the way, arriving atop the summit of the tallest mountain for a midnight glass of champagne ... *in broad daylight!!* That day and evening included white water rafting, ice breaking in a huge lake, lunch in a year round gigantic tent outfitted like a hunting lodge, and a memorable, once in lifetime stop for a sauna in a very tiny lakeside village. The helicopter put down at the edge of a large lake, where a small house sat on the adjacent lot. Brigitta, who was a tall statuesque woman of about 40, left the party of males who had all been invited to *"take sauna."* Jack and I watched as the interpreter, pilot, and the other men disrobed, showered, and proceeded into the large wooden heated room. Jack followed and then I was last in the shower. All of a sudden, someone was behind me. To my shock and her amusement, it was Brigitta, stark naked, leading me to the sauna where the rest of the crew chuckled at our initiation into this commonly practiced ritual! What surprised Jack and me further was that after a short while Brigitta got up, bounced her way out, and sprinted to the lake for a dip in the freezing water! A memorable visit, complete with *au naturel* Swedish hospitality!

When it aired on GMA, the week we spent in Sweden was a colossal success. Our coverage was excellent and the content varied and interesting. Stories from all over that beautiful country drew huge audiences and, better yet, brought us thousands of brand new morning viewers. Deciding to do more international getaways was a no-brainer. We chose Holland for our next venture, and immediately ran into some flak from Amsterdam's welcoming committee; a contingent of gentlemen who looked straight out of central casting and whose jovial, red-cheeked faces hinted at enthusiastic consumption of their favorite beverage — *Dutch beer!* As soon as we were able to persuade them we were not there to exploit the well-known Dutch legality of prostitution and marijuana, things settled down and we enjoyed our time with this tourist committee. In fact, we held a town hall type meeting to reassure them we were not in the cheap exploitation game, assuring them we were more interested in their windmills, tulips and canals than in their red-light district and pot bars. I gave a 10 minute talk to a gathering of about 40 businessmen, telling them what our show had done to boost Sweden's tourism and promising that our program would concentrate on positive Dutch lifestyles and customs. When they asked how many new tourist dollars came to Sweden, I gave a ballpark number, qualifying it cautiously. When pressed, I called on our Unit Manager, Joe Tucker, to amplify from the sidelines. He did a fine job, quoting some numbers and satisfying the crowd. The meeting ended across the street at the Heineken beer hall. In a conversation with one of their leaders, an interesting dialogue took place. *"Mr. Beuth,"* I was asked, *"What college taught you salesmanship?"* *"I studied English at a small college in New York,"* I replied. *"Well you did something no Dutch businessman would ever do,"* he added. *"What was that, sir?"* I asked. *"You asked a subordinate to answer a question for you in public. No Dutch businessman would ever do that. He would rather make something up!"* At that, we all raised another mug, and the committee endorsement was assured. Again, we had a ratings hit on our hands, and sure enough brought tulips, windmills, museums, dikes, fascinating people profiles and beautiful landscapes to our screens ... *and to a host of new viewers across the U.S.*

By the time we got around to broadcasting live from Great Britain and Ireland in 1990, we had overtaken TODAY in the ratings because we had a show that worked and a staff that was excited about making good television. Like a well-oiled machine, our everyday shows were expertly produced and complemented by more remote broadcasts over the next several years. These travels, cementing our leadership position, took the program to Puerto Rico, The Virgin Islands, Australia, Hong Kong and other countries, continuously providing our viewers with visual treats and cultural profiles they would never see at home, but now came to expect from their TV sets.

We set audience records with an extensive tour of Alaska, assisted by another unusually talented man who made a cold call on us, inviting us north. His name is John Litten. John, whom one could legitimately call "Mr. Alaska," is still the best guide to this land of personal opportunity and nature's wonder. Friend and associate of Governors, adviser to air and cruise lines, John calls Sitka his home and was an invaluable aid to our crew in Alaska. He made connections for us from Anchorage to Fairbanks, Juneau to Skagway, Sitka to Ketchikan and on to Denali, teasing our cameramen and women with spectacular sights to send back to mainland viewers, provoking volumes of thank you fan mail. His associate, Ray Majeski, a man of Polish extraction, who referred to himself as Alaska's "Original Fishing Pole," was a gracious host, port commander, motorcycle cop, fishing guide, salmon expert, and consummate storyteller. Ray was willing to bet that he could satisfy a fisherman's limit within 10 minutes. He did it with me, when we fished for king salmon. I caught a monster on my first cast and he reminded me that the limit was one per day!! At the end of each travel week, we allowed our viewers to purchase a video of the week's highlights for $25. We sold thousands of those GMA travel videos, but more from Alaska than from anywhere else, even more than from Australia and New Zealand, where the crew and our talent, Joan and Charlie, bungee-jumped from a bridge without my prior knowledge!

When it seemed that we had tapped out the obvious foreign countries to visit, Jack came up with a variation on the genre. He arranged tours via motor coach, taking the staff and crew around our own great country, visiting a dozen regions like the Great Midwest, New England, The Great Northwest Pacific Coast, and so on, to the delight of our continually growing audiences. My staff's recurring commentary was *"And we get paid to do this?"*

Working as smartly and as diligently as we could, with constant tinkering to our increasingly well-oiled operation and a lucky break or two, it had taken us almost four years of chasing Bryant Gumble's well-run show before we caught and overtook it. We then held the lead in morning audience viewership for the next five years. (When I left GMA in late 1994, and was given a memorable retirement party, I was pleased that emcee Tom Murphy reminded all we were still number one!)

GMA represented the most fun I've had throughout my career and brought far more profits to the company than any of my other 16 assignments over more than 40 years. I kept pretty good tabs on the dollar contributions, and during the process of this writing, asked one of our best finance people, David Loewith, to research some GMA financials. He reminded me that when we started in 1986, the entire ABC Entertainment division, prime time included, had a pre-tax profit of $43 million and that by 1992, GMA alone showed a more than $50 million profit on sales revenues of $80 million. And the following year, 1993, revenue climbed to $87 million, and profit grew to $54 million. And those numbers grew each year as a solid staff built an exciting and ambitious programming triumph for our ever-expanding audiences.

CHAPTER TWENTY-FOUR

Fun & Games Capcities Style

But hold the phone! This retelling of events and personalities is running ahead of itself. Accurate chronology insists on some catching up regarding a fun and important task that fell into my multi-tasking basket nearly a decade earlier. I always welcomed the occasional *out-of-left-field* call from Murph or Dan, who considered me their *"go to"* guy for the odd, ad hoc, ancillary assignment. And those extracurricular missions happened with fair regularity over the years. Chief among them was the annual company meeting held every January. I had been tapped to help put them together starting at our earliest days back in Albany. Every year, regardless of the job I held at the time, I welcomed a chance to help all the participants from our varied and growing divisions, present their reports to the company and enjoy an all important week-end of congenial fellowship. Then, when Tom made the Annenberg deal, we inherited a huge bonus, and I welcomed a partner in crime onto my one-man annual company meeting team. The Triangle purchase brought a man who not only became one of our most valuable and popular Capcities partners, but who was also proved a magnificent addition to the steering committee organizing our annual meetings and parties. Charlie Keller, head of a WPVI-TV production unit, continued his work on major public service programs, but caught the eye of Dan Burke, who threw him into my multi-tasking mix to my everlasting pleasure. Over the years, Charlie demonstrated character beyond reproach, humility that bordered on the saintly, and a moral compass that made him the widely considered conscience of our company. Partnering with Charlie over the years was one of the highlights of my career. Those memorable company meetings we organized were held in Nassau, Scottsdale, and various Florida locations, including the Far Horizons Resort on Longboat Key off Sarasota where we settled in for years ... until Murph came in from the beach one uncharacteristically chilly January morning to say, *"Philly, can we go someplace warm next year??"* Charlie did some sleuthing, and starting the following year, we began a very long relationship at our new end-of-January home, The Biltmore in Phoenix, Arizona. For years, at Super Bowl time, we met for the purpose of putting our results up for all to see. Dan ran the meetings with a mix of business savvy and creativity. Each of our operating units presented their numbers, which were, on par, generally superlative, though they included occasional blemishes that the presenter would go to great lengths to talk around instead of graphically expose. But everything was there in open display through theatre-like illustrations. It was truly inspiring, throughout these sessions, to see the remarkable results and high profit margins, one after another, coming from our various divisions. In addition, the meeting included dinners with entertainment, high stakes poker games, and various, mostly harmless, sometimes hilarious high jinks. Burke challenged Charlie and me to produce each meeting based on a different theme, like "Churchill" (successful!), "Jefferson" (a flop!), "Bite The Bullet," "Nothing is as it Seems," "Wheel of Fortune" (the actual set of the game show placed onto a golf course!). The evening shows generally included good-natured horsing around by our staffers and guests. One of the biggest hams and best sports was none other than Warren Buffett, who attended the events with glee and consistent regularity. Warren, a closet performer, loved to sing on stage — one time dressed as Babe Ruth, swinging a lefty bat and warbling lyrics I had written:

"I'm a big hitter, so they say,
When I'm in play, get out of my way.
I swing, I hit, I make a mighty splash,
And if we win the pennant, Burke gets back his cash."
(Dan had just bought the Portland Sea Dogs baseball team.)

Another of our favorite hams, Aaron Daniels, dressed like Johnny Carson's soothsayer, CARNAK, was introduced as AARONAK by me, playing Ed McMahon. I would give him an answer, like, "RUIN ARLEDGE" and Aaron would display an envelope, questioning, *"What will bad numbers do to ABC News?"* Comic material ranged from the sublime to the ridiculous, with none of us exempt from the mostly kind-hearted roasting and satiric fun poking. We had some wonderful times at those company meetings, as we worked hard not only to present our revenues and profit margins, but also to share an unforgettable, cherished experience of corporate brotherhood.

ABC Entertainment, headed by Brandon Stoddard, gave us lots to cheer about at the company gatherings, not only with hit series like "NYPD Blue," "Roseanne," and "Home Improvement," but with landmark mini-series like "Roots," "Winds of War," and "War and Remembrance." For a company like Capital Cites, it was high cotton, indeed, and exciting to have climbed to the mountaintop with such talented partners, reaching first place in daytime as well as prime. Those audience victories were crucial to the company's bottom-line. Revenues and cash flow hit record heights and the stock climbed steadily. Wall Street reflected the fact that the debt from the ABC purchase had been paid down within the first five years! We celebrated for years using the promotional theme, *Still the One"* as a refrain and anchor for all our program presentations.

At the same time, with perhaps less fanfare, the company was prospering in ways that were not as clearly delineated as our bottom line. Abiding by a firm practice of *"doing well and doing good,"* a number of Corporate Initiatives were implemented by Dan Burke, whose creative mind produced numerous projects aimed at introducing our employees to public service. The company endorsed and enhanced an ABC Literacy endeavor, led effectively by former network president Jim Duffy, and succeeded by Charlie Keller. It also established a drug prevention and rehab program, an advanced management-training unit for women, and numerous additional after-work volunteer activities for employees involving the general public. Most of these programs were Burke originals, and many were duplicated later by other companies. Since Charlie Keller was responsible for the success of many of these initiatives, I asked him to give me some of his recollections in writing. Here are his words:

Dear Phil,

Thanks for asking. First, it should be noted that Dan insisted all profits from our community programs and after school specials go directly back to the organizations featured in those shows.

His ideas were remarkable. The Advanced Management Training for Women (at Smith College) attracted 20 women employees each year. Similarly, the JV management meetings, for up and comers, was very popular. Burke brought his senior execs to participate in these sessions and insisted they get prominent attention, beyond my report on Corporate Initiatives at our meeting each year.

One of our favorite memories relates to the riotous video you produced, Phil, of Murphy visiting Herman Wouk's house, (Wouk played by our attorney, Roger Wollenberg) to get Wouk to soften his commercial restrictions on 'Winds of War.' 'Herman Wouk,' wearing a prayer shawl and yarmulke, at one point says to Murphy, 'I understand you are a very religious man, although from one of the newer religions!' What a line. It brought down the house!

The next day, Burke opened the sessions with, "Yesterday, we all saw Herman Wouk make reference to Tom's religious commitment. I'm a member of that faith, and we have a prayer that asks forgiveness not only for what we have done, but for what we have not done!" At that point, Burke started to choke up and handed me the mic, saying, 'Here's Charlie!' So much was involved for him there. His personal faith, his commitment to "give back," his concern that we do even more to use the power of our media to benefit our viewers, listeners, and readers, all came out brilliantly. It was very moving.

Corporate Initiatives were just part of a philosophy that made Capital Cities such an extraordinary company. And most moving to me, Murph and Dan did not do these things for show. They did them out of a sophisticated conscience that they obeyed regardless of how successful and powerful the company became. Fortunately for all of us, we had a chance to demonstrate that a business can succeed while operating at the highest standards.

All the best,
Charlie

ও ⌘ ও

316

CHAPTER TWENTY-FIVE

The Wick Burns Both Ends

With affairs at the network going well, the attention of management turned to the potential represented by programming late night after Ted Koppel's "Nightline." The midnight program block had been dark on our network for several years, faced with the towering dominance of Johnny Carson's "The Tonight Show" on NBC. Before we took over the network, while Capital Cities owned three important ABC affiliates, we were never particularly anxious to take a late night programming feed from ABC. To us, it made better economic sense to program movies for two reasons: First, costs were minimal and movies were often pretty effective counter-programming to the Carson juggernaut. Furthermore, network compensation paled compared to the revenue local stations saw from inserting a ton of two-minute breaks into late night movies. But by 1990, John Sias began to take a hard renewed look at late night. He faced a mixed bag of station clearances. In fact, "Nightline" itself had continual clearance problems, so we didn't have that natural lead-in in certain markets. And many other important markets preferred their local status quo, making a new late night vehicle a tough sell. Still John was gung ho and hired a former CBS program executive named Michael Brockman to address the situation. Brockman chose popular Los Angeles radio personality, Rick

Dees, around whom he crafted a new show. And then, he and Rick spent months visiting markets looking for station commitments. The program premiered with a checkered station lineup and that difficult midnight timeslot, following "Nightline." For a while, despite anemic ratings, I thought the show, offering a fresh, creative personality, might take off. Unfortunately, with no visible signs of growth, the patience required by our network affiliates dried up and they began to abandon ship. Sias then dismissed Brockman and put in a call to you know who, asking me to add late night to my already heady slate of duties! Though I never asked, I could see the imprint of Murph behind the idea of calling on me.

GMA was in decent shape. Jack Reilly had left, seeking new challenges at CNBC, and was replaced by Bob Reichbloom, who helped us hold a respectable lead over TODAY. Even though audiences were never to be taken for granted, I felt the show was in pretty good hands. I also knew that if I took the West Coast assignment, I would have carte blanche autonomy to do whatever I thought would work. Though I loved a challenge, these two assignments were at opposite ends of the country (New York and Los Angeles) and opposite ends of the clock (7 a.m. and midnight)!! And reviving a show with a lackluster lead in and a less than 40 percent clearance, all the while up against Carson, seemed a bit like David facing Goliath, armed only with a pebble. Ever the company man, I turned the stone over in my hand several times and fitted it into my slingshot.

Using an unoccupied ABC office in LA, I started a bicoastal routine that went on for the next nine months. On arrival in LA, I met Marianne Henderson a program executive who became a valued partner, and proved my ace in the hole. She was quick-witted, intelligent, and devoted to the task, but more importantly, she knew the territory and helped me navigate the Byzantine political maze that is Hollywood. That was a new experience, having enjoyed the largely apolitical atmosphere of Capcities. I learned a lot in a short time. I relied on Marianne to keep things moving when I was not there, and to occasionally run interference with network procedure. She never did disappoint, and working with her was a pleasure.

My stint in LA gave me a treasure of memorable moments. One time I was sitting in the makeup room reading a paper when a man came in and sat next to me. When I looked up, it was the legendary star, Kirk Douglas, about to do a guest shot and looking very vigorous despite his age. This was prior to the dreadful stroke he suffered. After a pleasant exchange, he asked me, *"You are not a reporter are you?"* I responded, *"No, I am supposed to be in charge here."* At that, he got up, shook my hand, and then approached a mirror, where he began to curl his eyelashes! He headed off into the studio, but not before turning back and flashing that famous smile. What an impressive man!

But as I was hired to fix this ailing vehicle, I needed to focus on the problems at hand. I thought the Rick Dees program, much like his radio show, revolved too much around Rick personally. He was a one-man band and asked too much of himself. My Rick Dees intervention was initially positive as he seemed receptive to my notes and suggestions ... to a point. I tried various approaches to have him agree to add a foil or second banana to the show. Specifically I wanted to hire the comedian Sinbad, an upstanding, savvy, politically aware African American comic who could handle second chair duties and elevate Rick at the same time. Just as important, Sinbad's sense of humor was not as off-color as that of many of his peers, so I knew it would pass muster with the network. I could not make that sale to Rick and the show seemed in terminal lack of oxygen. I brought in a couple of talented executive producers, including Barry Kibrick, who later developed a PBS series, "Between the Lines," still airing on Public Television. Also, when I took a closer look at the financials, I noticed that the highly esteemed William Morris Agency was charging a production fee of $4,000 a show, $20,000 per week ... more than $1 million a year! My natural reaction was, *"Show me, please!"* I learned that during the first months there were indeed William Morris people on the set, making notes and overseeing the production. But that had all stopped, only to resume when I appeared on the scene. I liked the men who showed up and found them talented, but was also convinced there was little they could to do to rescue the show, and they knew it. I advised the agency that we would no longer honor the fee, citing the ratings decline and change of conditions. A few days later I got a call from Dan Burke in NY. He told me that the Morris agency president had called and complained about my behavior. Dan told them exactly what I expected, *"That they could not drive a wedge between us, and they would have to deal with you, Phil."* We stopped paying the $20,000 each week, but my gripe was not with the agency that I still hold in high regard.

We should have thrown in the towel right there, but John and I decided we owed it to ourselves to try to salvage the opportunity by finding another personality to headline the show. Rick was certainly a gifted performer, but Late Night opposite Carson was just not the right spot for him. Almost overnight, I was bombarded with interview requests from agents and actors. That was fine, but on a half-dozen occasions, those requests were accompanied by lavish gifts and personal, handwritten notes, as though they'd come from old friends. I was sent a Rolex watch by a producer I hardly knew, and a fine leather wallet and briefcase from others. We did not accept such generosity at Capcities. With thankful explanations, the gifts were returned. Marianne was surprised, but dutifully returned her gifts as well. One evening, I saw Tony Danza charging up the stairs to Spago's restrooms, and followed him. We had met briefly once before, and I had done him a favor by recommending his daughter for a job. I do not think he remembered me when I approached him in the men's room, but he took it in stride. I asked point blank if he had ever considered late night. We talked for a while and, within a few days, I had convinced him to give it a shot. He did the show, and demonstrated some promise. He was so grateful for the experience that he refused any compensation. So, I donated his fee to UNICEF in his name and gave him the tax deduction! He did a good job, but had other goals, which did not include being chained to a host seat five nights a week for a show that was a long shot at best. The closest we got to something potentially permanent was Brad Garrett, who was brought to me by my dear friend Stan Moger. Brad did a few weeks for us, but also had too much on his plate that seemed more attractive. (Years later, Brad had a fantastic run as Ray Romano's brother on "Everybody Loves Raymond.") I still think there are great things ahead for Brad.

Others came through my office. I had always loved Steve and Eydie, starting way back with their first appearances on the legendary "Steve Allen Show." When their agent called asking me to meet them, I was delighted. They wanted to do Late Night, and I curious to hear what they had in mind. We met, joked, took pictures, and had a delightful lunch a day later. But while they were stars in my head and heart, I couldn't see them holding down a show that would attract the affiliates we needed. My office was continually visited by hopeful actors, young and old, experienced and naive. My open door was filled with enthusiastic, charming artists; everyone from Carroll O'Connor to George Hamilton to Jerry Van Dyke and even to Burgess Meredith who, throughout the meeting, kept protesting, *"I will never do another penguin!"*

Along the way, I met many wonderful talents, who never ceased to surprise me. Since I conducted business with an open-door policy — sometime to the distress of Nicky Goldstein, my invaluable, over-protective assistant (who, in those days, was more often called my secretary) — I often booked appointments myself. Such was the case with a young, intelligent, and ambitious man named David Saltz, who showed up for an appointment I had put straight into my book. Looking every bit the rock music producer, David was tall, thin, with earrings, faded jeans and an unorthodox hairstyle. Ordinarily, this colorful character might have had trouble getting past my overzealous assistant, but he just breezed by, glibly telling Nicky *"Mr. Beuth asked me to come in ..."* David had called several weeks earlier, wanting to speak about rock and roll on TV, or rather, the absence thereof. I liked him immediately because, though his look was exotic, what he said made perfect sense. TV is always pleading for younger demographics, but seems to tirelessly program content that younger viewers would never watch! He made the convincing case that younger demos are fiercely loyal to rock stars. And he asked why we couldn't bring R & R to network television in a format similar to the former ABC "In Concert" program that had now been off the air for a decade. I was looking for something to program Friday or Saturday night, especially something that did not have to air live, but could be programmed, if the affiliates preferred, at a time of their choosing. As David reeled off the *"red hot"* rock bands he could get, each of which had *"tremendously loyal fan bases,"* I thought I was living on Mars. I had hardly heard of any of them. I told him that if I had to persuade affiliate managers, who were all closer to my age, to program this show, he'd have to provide me with some balance, like Cher, Manilow, or Bennett, for example. The very next day, David was back in

323

my office. He dialed my phone and handed it back. I found myself on the line ... *with Cher!!* And she was telling me what a genius David was, saying she would appear anywhere he asked, at no charge! That got my attention.

David introduced me to a number of stars in the music business, including worldwide icon, Paul McCartney. David arranged for me to have lunch with Paul McCartney and his family at their hotel. McCartney was the most naturally unaffected person one could hope to meet; someone who seemed to disguise his celebrity with casual ease. Our lunch was so pleasant that I pitched the idea of his becoming a spokesperson for our on-air promotional spots. He chuckled and smiled at me with bemused compassion. *"Ya Know, Phil,"* he spoke across the table, *"I could go out to 42nd Street and shout Boodweiser and get paid a million dollars! What you're talkin' about sounds like a lot of work."* He was so cool. On another occasion, David invited us to the preview of a McCartney film special at the Beacon Theatre on the West side and was careful to sit us right upfront. And just as the lights came down, David shuffled us to seats in the back, next to the man himself!

David and I made a deal for a weekly rock and roll show we called "In Concert '91," expecting to test it for the summer of 1991. I had some initial difficulty clearing it, but the new program eventually got sufficient clearances, attracted very respectable youth-oriented advertisers and ended up running for nine years!

Things did not look rosy for our Late Night campaign. Walter Liss, GM at WABC-TV in New York and one of our most influential and successful operators, preferred the extraordinary profits his late night movies produced and his vote carried weight with the other stations. That chorus, *"If you can make it here, you can make it anywhere"* also applies to the syndication business in reverse. If you can't clear New York you're kind of dead in the water. I kissed the idea of launching our own Late Night goodbye and folded my LA tent. I honestly felt that any further pursuit would represent a waste of energy, since neither our owned stations nor the larger group of affiliates really wanted a network feed. I finally returned to New York and my now beloved GMA, relieved the bicoastal routine had drawn to a close.

But I was proud of the success of "In Concert." We produced some 400 programs, including performances by virtually every rock group active in the 1990s. David went on to considerable success, bringing The Beatles to ABC, producing many half-time shows at Super Bowls and staging events at the Dolphins stadium in Miami. He remains one of the most savvy music mavens in the business.

CHAPTER TWENTY-SIX

DIFFA

All my day to day activities, including duties at GMA, occasional trips out to LA, regular visits home to Buffalo and a couple of volunteer positions in Manhattan kept me very busy. In the aftermath of my son's death from AIDS in 1990, I was struck by the informational void that existed, as the mainstream media largely ignored the subject of this horrific epidemic. President Reagan and candidates like Clinton rarely mentioned the word. AMFAR was emerging as the leading agency dealing with the issue and was gaining momentum in the press as more and more young gay men fell to the disease. The organization attracted many celebrities and was effective at raising money and awareness — two essential weapons in the battle. I felt a compelling need to do what I could to shed light on this national scourge. Barbara Walters, co-host of ABC's "20/20," had done a number of segments on the AIDS epidemic. So the next time I enjoyed some java at her notoriously well provisioned personal office coffee station, I asked if she happened to know of an AIDS organization — one perhaps equally worthy but less high profile than AMFAR — that might appreciate our network's support. She immediately asked her assistant to call one of the world's leading specialists in infectious diseases at a renowned New York hospital. Doctors of this caliber are often harder to get on the phone than Tom Cruise, so I expected the return call would take a day or two. To my astonishment the physician called back not three minutes later while Barbara and I were still chatting. This was Barbara Walters after all! And the doctor did have a suggestion. That is how I became associated with DIFFA, the Design Industries Foundation Fighting Aids. DIFFA had been founded by a handful of courageous forward-looking individuals who had lost family and friends to the "gay men's cancer" and were now dedicating themselves selflessly to the eradication of the disease. Unlike their better-financed fellow organization, AMFAR, DIFFA was struggling to raise funds to advance their good work. Shortly after I began working with DIFFA, I was introduced to a dynamic television producer named Joe Lovett. Joe was an "out" gay "20/20" producer who had spearheaded early AIDS coverage with Geraldo Rivera, Barbara, and Tom Jarriel.

Though it may not be customary to quote a lengthy testimonial in the middle of my own memoirs, what Joe wrote is so appropriate, I am compelled to share it. Here is Lovett's recollection in his own words:

> *One day I got a call from Barbara Walters. 'Joe,' she purred, 'Phil Beuth is President of GMA, and wants to get involved in an AIDS project where he can make a difference and I thought you might know of something. Would you meet with him?' Would I meet with the head of GMA? Well, yes, absolutely! At the time, I was making a film called 'Heart Strings,'*

about a musical traveling around the country. It was a parable about how people react to AIDS and it was produced by Atlanta-native David Sheppard and DIFFA. I hoped Phil would be interested enough in our cause to help me raise some much needed production funds. When I called Phil, he said 'Sure, Joe, come on over.' Phil was an incredibly warm and enthusiastic guy who immediately put me at ease. 'So what do you have?' he asked. I showed him a clip from 'Heart Strings,' consisting of interviews and musical numbers, and brazenly asked if he had any ideas on raising funds to complete the project. His reaction was immediate and positive. 'Well, you know,' he started, 'this is a nice idea, but if we do it for television, we should add some star power and get more publicity. Let's enhance the project with major celebrities who are active in the cause and put it on ABC one night next summer … in prime time!'

I was totally dumbfounded! I had to wonder if I had heard him correctly. Our beleaguered cause was struggling for public attention and, at that time, raising money for anything AIDS-related was next to impossible. No one would even talk about it. Few wanted to help. Most everyone wanted to ignore it. And here was one of ABC's top executives saying, 'Yes, let's do your idea, but make it much, much bigger. Let's get more publicity on this than you can imagine!'

What had just happened? I soon learned that Phil's son Barry had recently died of AIDS. So this powerful ABC executive had personal knowledge of what so many of us had been going through and he now wanted to wake up the nation and help bring an end to this ongoing horror. Working with Phil over the next three years was a pure delight. We produced a prime-time two-hour telecast each year called 'In a New Light; an AIDS outreach and entertainment special.' The shows wove together star performances and interviews with celebrities talking about how AIDS had affected them personally. Short vignettes told how different people, groups and the medical community were dealing with the AIDS epidemic. And, as if a prime-time ABC showcase were not enough, Phil arranged to have the network cover all production costs. Then, having joined the DIFFA Board, he further announced that the network would donate every dime of sponsor revenue derived from the broadcast back to DIFFA!

Phil also took on the personal task of lining up the celebrities, often enlisting Larry King to assist us in the process. The first show, July 11, 1992, was hosted by Linda Lavin, Robert Guillaume and Bruce Davidson. It starred dozens of celebrities who talked about losing friends, sons and brothers, interwoven with scenes from 'Heart Strings' urging that government and medical agencies increase their support for AIDS research and treatment. Celebrities included Elizabeth Taylor, Dustin

Hoffman, Carol Burnett, Shirley MacLaine, Kathy Bates, Lou Diamond Phillips, Joel Grey, Christopher Reeves, Clint Black, Gloria Estefan, Barry Manilow, Arthur Ashe, and many others. We shot in the ABC studios in LA and partnered with the CDC National AIDS hotline. Nothing like this had ever been shown on any network in a prime time special. Both ABC and the CDC received record audience responses. Many people, after seeing the show, finally understood firsthand how they might be at risk of contracting and transmitting the disease. The dissemination of concrete data in the specials we produced might well have saved millions of lives.

The second show was hosted by Arsenio Hall and Paula Abdul. Arsenio was eager to help as he credited Phil with discovering him on a cruise ship, inviting him to perform at a Capcities/ABC meeting and thus jump-starting his television career. The third show was hosted by Barbara Walters, whose impeccable credentials and professional reputation allowed us to present very candid, straightforward information on AIDS transmission, accompanied by explicit graphics and animation. I was shocked ABC let us do that on air in prime time!

As I look back at this over the years, that first fortuitous meeting with Phil may well have contributed to significant early breakthroughs in the history of the

AIDS struggle for attention. Phil retired from ABC after the first three shows and ABC News inherited the next two specials in 1995 and 1996, presenting valued updates on therapies, which helped change the course of the disease. We were not allowed to do a sixth season as I was told by Bob Iger, who took over the network after Capital Cities sold to Disney, that 'AIDS is over ...'

Now, all these years later, though there are still 50,000 new cases of AIDS each year in the U.S. alone, and while there is less and less media coverage about how to end transmission, we nevertheless have stalled the rate of infection. And a measure of credit, along with my personal gratitude, is due to Phil for his persistence in helping shine a light on this horrendous disease.

Faithfully,
Joe Lovett

That's a very flattering recounting of this adventure that I consider one of the most worthy achievements of my professional career. We did do some important work. But it was not clear sailing. Enlisting celebrities proved a much more difficult task than either Joe or I imagined. It was not difficult to get commitments once I was able to speak personally to the celebrities, but going the traditional route through agents and public relations people was a mine field. Agents and talent reps simply did not want their clients associated with that dreadful word, AIDS. For example, I was turned down by agents for Rosie O'Donnell and Lily Tomlin, each of whom I knew to be dedicated to the cause. When I was finally able to reach Rosie directly, her response was unequivocal: *"Give me the time and place and I will be there."* And when I did get through to Lily Tomlin at her home, she was surprised to learn someone had declined on her behalf. I think I shamed her into appearing. She was astonished, telling me no network person had ever taken the trouble to get to her personally. Same with Gloria Estefan, who accepted at a black tie dinner … Larry King gave us lots of plugs. The CDC reported that their phone lines were flooded with more than 98,000 calls due to our special before midnight, 16 times more than their previous high.

This book often speaks about the uniqueness of a company. Another significant aspect of this whole episode was pure Capital Cities. When I first brought the idea to Dan Burke, he thought for a minute and said, *"Go to it. Spend what you need, and while you are at it, give AIDS whatever advertising dollars we get!"* Ad revenues were slim indeed for our first show, but hit six figures for subsequent shows. As a result, David Sheppard, Executive Director of DIFFA, made many teary-eyed visits to the bank.

❧ ⌘ ☙

CHAPTER TWENTY-SEVEN

Segue

Those first years of "Good Morning America" had been tremendously exciting ones for me professionally. I enjoyed the bigger stage and felt good about rebuilding a national network show. Despite that excitement, my marriage was not going well. Those years were a difficult time for both of us, but especially for Betty, who was depressed about her health, and, at the same time, that of our son Barry, as well as my prolonged absences. There were no overt expressions of deep anger between us, and no financial problems or disregard for each other. But after a few years it was painfully clear that our 30-year bond was no longer strong enough to sustain us.

Betty surprised me by asking for a divorce and over the next several years as I worked on GMA, back and forth during summers at Lake Chautauqua and other times in Buffalo, I felt I was living two lives: putting on a sunny face with my colleagues at GMA, while hiding my family stress. I did confidentially share my situation with Dan Burke and, later, with Jack Reilly. Night after late night, Betty and I spoke by phone with Barry trying to manage the impossibly difficult personal pain we suffered. Our calls were sad, but loving, and continued month after month either between Betty and me or each of us until his sad demise. This naturally put an undue strain on Betty and on our marriage. I disguised my depression as well as I could, masking it at the job. I ask myself often what I could have done better, considering how well I had been blessed otherwise. Sadly, I have never found a satisfactory answer. However difficult it was for me, I knew it did not compare with the toll it was taking on the rest of the family for those couple of years. Finally, the marriage was over, but not our relationship, which carried a host of considerations and responsibilities important to both us. Those would endure for our entire lives.

As Betty's health declined, she was provided with the best medical help she needed and occasionally perked up and displayed some of her former wit and sense of humor. She had periods where there were signs of improvement and normalcy, but her condition was incurable, and lingered on for years. When the final visit to the hospital emergency ward happened, Betty could hardly breathe at all, making it necessary to intubate her to allow breathing through a machine. With Jane, Phil and me at her bedside, she handed me a note upon which was written, *"Let me go, please!"* The attending physicians concluded that Betty could no longer breathe on her own and would not survive extubation.

Their conclusions were correct. Later that week, she left us, carrying with her a piece of our hearts. She was a great lady indeed.

ᔍ ⌘ ᕒ

CHAPTER TWENTY-EIGHT

Doing Good, While ...

A former President of the Chautauqua Institution named Robert Hesse had moved from Buffalo to New York about the same time I did to take a position with UNICEF. I had been an unofficial adviser to Bob at Chautauqua, and he thought I would like to join him in his new role. Among the volunteers he inherited was Hugh Downs of ABC, a devoted advocate. Together they recruited me, and I was appointed to the rather prestigious Board of Directors. It was an important volunteer assignment. I took it on enthusiastically, zeroing in on raising funds to help address the catastrophic number of children dying from disease and malnutrition throughout Africa — estimated at 40,000 a day! I am proud of the work we did, although there were constant and legitimate concerns about the security and delivery of precious medicines and food that organizations like UNICEF provided. There was also the challenge of getting our much needed pregnancy prevention kits past well-intentioned religious officials. We saved children, only to learn that many of those who survived perpetuated the problem by becoming pregnant at an early age, having been denied birth control information by the church. Active in such programs were Julia and Harry Belafonte, Angela Lansbury, Audrey Hepburn, Roy Clarke, Jane Curtin, Andrew Young, Roy Disney, and many more dedicated, notable persons. But Belafonte stood apart. He served eagerly, above and beyond the call, and I cherish his friendship.

On one occasion, an unexpected event took place regarding the lovely actress Meg Ryan, who was at the time, a UNICEF ambassador. I was assigned to set up a welcoming line of celebrities for a large, 300-guest dinner party in the main dining parlor of the United Nations building on the East River. The dinner featured parents from all over the world, with their children dressed in traditional attire.

Meg Ryan agreed to head the welcoming line; and to be sure all would go smoothly, I arranged a lunch with her to go over the details. During lunch I reminded her that she should be in line before 6:30, after which time, she would join Hugh Downs at the head table for some remarks. About 40 children would be seated in a semi circle on the floor, facing the huge dais. At 6:15 everything and everyone was in place, except Meg Ryan, who did not show up until 7, after all were seated. When she arrived, she hurriedly explained she'd had trouble getting off the phone? Disappointed, I quietly ushered her to a seat next to Hugh, and shortly thereafter, she was at the microphone, where she proceeded to make a startling announcement. To the utter disbelief of the guests, she told the audience that over the years, especially when she was younger, she, like thousands of others, had collected money for worthy children using those familiar UNICEF containers. Then, she took on a mischievous conspiratorial tone, leaned forward and confessed that she had always kept the money instead of turning it over to UNICEF! An audible gasp came from the audience. Meg then said she was going to make a donation to cover the money she never turned in. More gasps. I was standing with two female reporters who were just as shocked as the rest of us, but also elated to be getting this scoop firsthand. I looked at them both and ran a finger across my mouth, implying that we needed to give this the silent treatment. It must have worked, because neither reporter wrote about it. I have thought about that incident over the years, and wonder what would happen if it had taken place in this day of ubiquitous recording devices. It would surely have been the rage of YouTube, Twitter and Instagram accounts around the world!

I thoroughly enjoyed my years with UNICEF, an organization whose task is impossible and endless. Progress comes, but slowly and roadblocks are everywhere. Hundreds of staff and volunteers dedicate their lives, addressing the hunger, illness, and despair of children and parents in life-threatening Third World settings. I was privileged to participate, getting a close-up view of man's inhumanity to man, but also a keen appreciation of the army of good people working tirelessly to fix a seemingly irreparable, tragic condition.

At about this same time, I began hearing from some good friends about Broadcast Pioneers, an organization started many years ago and dedicated to providing financial assistance to broadcasters who had fallen on hard times. I was invited to join by a number of long-time friends like Joe Reilly, who ran the highly esteemed New York State Broadcaster's Association, and a handful of others like Dennis Swanson, Dick Foreman, Stan Moger, Nick Verbitsky and Skip Finley, along with so many other committed individuals that I could not possibly recall them all here. Bottom line; I was invited and privileged to be part of a rebirth of the organization. I spent several years directly involved, working with people like Bill O'Shaughnessy, Deborah Norville, Jerry Lee, Scott Knight, Wade Hargrove, Gary Chapman, Erica Farber, Dave Barrett and so many others, to help Chairmen Ed McLaughlin and Phil Lombardo rebuild the organization to remarkable heights. Unfortunately, my limited mobility has hindered my active participation lately. The Broadcasters Foundation of America has made gifts totaling $1,100,000 to more than one thousand broadcasters in need. Lombardo's lengthy leadership has been a phenomenal industry achievement, and I am honored to still be a Board Member. Memories of the actions of the group fill me with pride, and the memory of one of its stalwarts, the late, irreplaceable Tony Malaria still brings me joy.

CHAPTER TWENTY-NINE

There's Something About Mary

Regardless of how busy I was in Manhattan, it was exactly what I anticipated and very much to my liking. I had my own show, now turned around. I was working for the best company in the business and my career was moving along nicely. Every aspect of the work was exciting, and its variety was stimulating. My finances were stable and growing. Happiness, on the other hand, was another matter. I was learning that there are multiple levels of happiness; and financial success does not guarantee automatic joy, or fulfillment. On the job, I did not allow my distress to show and leaving my office in the evening to have a cocktail was never was my style. I tried it, of course, but seldom. Back and forth from business in Manhattan to unrest in the family in Buffalo began to take its toll when I realized that I could not control several unwelcome elements, the most significant of which were a terminally ill son, a wife who had severe health problems, and a 30-year marriage that was in lingering jeopardy. 1985 to 1989 were difficult times, especially at night, when the telephone amplified all of our depression, coast to coast or back and forth to Buffalo.

The next important development regarding my future came about rather indirectly due to a perk enjoyed by a dozen or more senior executives in the company, including me. Those in the program were provided estate planning and financial advice from Chemical Bank. My contact was a man named Bill Worthington at Chemical in Manhattan, who was quite effective, arranging and monitoring tax shelter investments in Oregon and Puerto Rico. Unfortunately Bill passed away, and I eventually checked in at Chemical in Buffalo, where an Assistant Vice President named Mary Grace took over my account. I had met Mary previously at business functions, but did not know her well. We had lunch together, and soon realized we liked each other's company. Mary was a quiet, reserved lady, and very smart. She was popular, and had the discipline required of bankers. Our relationship began to grow and we dated on and off, with long periods of no contact, until we finally eloped to the Caribbean in 1991. That began my road back to normalcy, not just for me, but for my sons and daughter, who became impressed with Mary's personality and intelligence. She welcomed the chance to become "Gammy" to my grandchildren and stabilized my life with her care and attention at a critical time. In the later stages of our foreign broadcasts, I arranged for our business manager, Joe Tucker to include Mary on trips at my expense, and she fit in quite comfortably with our staff, several of whom maintain friendships with her today.

At this writing, after 17 years of retirement, it is hard to believe that we have been married 24 years. Again, I am a lucky guy.

❧ ⌘ ☙

CHAPTER THIRTY

Dusk Came Early

In the founding days of the company, someone of authority determined that the proper retirement age should be 65. It may have been Smitty or the Board, but whoever instigated this policy, it was not destined to be a popular one, or terribly sensible once longer life expectancies became the norm. If that policy had been altered or modified, it would have had a significant impact on our ranks and might have contributed to even more success for our company, as it would have extended the careers of a host of talented able-bodied individuals. The rule also denied many of our Capcities execs and employees valuable benefits, like profit sharing, which compounds nicely in later years. We should have had a flexibility modifier tied to actuarial tables, but we did not.

Murph had already passed the 65 threshold and left our ranks, but he did return later to assume the mantle of Chairman. The person who may have been most negatively affected by the mandatory retirement cut-off was probably the ever-pragmatic indispensable Dan Burke, who in 1994 was vibrant and sharp as ever ... not exactly retirement material. Burke went on to purchase a semi-pro baseball team, but the decision smacked of a man who still had plenty of game and felt the need to channel it onto another field. He told me that while he was committed to his purchase of The Portland Sea Dogs in Maine, he privately regretted leaving Capcities.

Things began to unravel rapidly as, one after another, our leading execs hit that 65 marker and fell to the side of the race. John Sias, who was by this time our CEO, was next. He left to join the San Francisco Chronicle Co., representing a huge loss for Capcities.

Now that Burke and Sias were gone, I was the lone old guard Capcities division head at the network. With Dan's wise watchful presence gone, so was the sense of camaraderie, teamwork and just plain fun, with which I had become so comfortable. I saw no immediate evidence that the fundamental principle of Capcities autonomy had changed, but to me, at least, the atmosphere seemed different, even threatened. I began to experience, for the very first time, an emptiness and pang of wistful longing for the company we had all formed and that I loved so much.

Bob Iger, a rising star over at ABC, took over for John Sias. I had had little occasion to work directly with Bob prior to his appointment, but, in an instant, I had inherited a new boss and I sensed we'd been bred in different cultures. Our first interaction followed a contact I'd made with Rush Limbaugh, thinking we might integrate him into ABC Late Night. Bob and I met with Rush, but quickly decided it made little sense for either party, especially after our flagship New York station, WABC-TV rejected the idea.

Then came the news that Letterman was available, though it was going to be tough to lure him to ABC as he wanted that all-important 11:30 slot opposite Leno, and we were not ready to throw "Nightline" to the wolves. Still, discussions with Letterman ensued and I, as President of Late Night, admit I was less than pleased when Iger brought in some heavy Hollywood types for the negotiations, bypassing my clear authority. My only consolation was that they got no further than I would have, as Dave was intransigent about the time slot. Letterman, as many who followed the high drama Late Night saga know, finally got what he wanted from CBS: a start opposite Leno, and ownership of the show following his.

Back at GMA, our activity levels remained in high gear as our hosts, guests, and personalities were clicking well. The welcome addition of Robin Roberts and Diane Sawyer helped us hold a consistent, though occasionally tenuous audience lead over TODAY and I started looking at other foreign countries to visit in 1995, like Mexico and Africa.

Then came a shocker. Bob Iger called me in to his office and following a flurry of compliments about my performance and energy, told me that he wanted his own team everywhere, proposing that I take an early retirement. I was 62. He suggested strongly that I be paid full salary for an additional three years, with an office and secretarial assistance. He said I would remain an officer of the company.

I called Murph, who acknowledged that it was painful, and regrettable, but added that it was part of our system. The boss is the boss, and I had been accorded and had enjoyed the same autonomy on my watch. When I talked to Dan, he was less gentlemanly. Angrily critical, he tore the decision apart with razor sharp vitriol. We reflected a bit about the great ride we had shared, agreeing that it was best for me to take the high road. *"Besides,"* he added *"you have time and money enough to do whatever you like."* That was true. However, the three years of full pay came with a less than silver lining because my historically substantial bonuses were not included. I could have challenged the settlement but it was still Capital Cities and that was not our style. Over the three-year period, that high road would cost me about $1.5 million in lost bonuses and profit sharing.

Still an Officer of ABC, it was decided that I should represent the company on the Board of a fresh flower company in which Capcities was invested. The irony that cut flowers on the set of GMA had been a source of interest and jest between Warren Buffett and I was not lost on me as I dutifully fulfilled this assignment.

Truthfully, while money always counted, what hurt most was the loss of one of the most enjoyable jobs in the business. My reaction to the early dismissal, quite naturally, was deep disappointment coupled with absolute disillusionment. The work, which had always been so much a part of me, was being snatched away; the fullness of it

346

replaced by emptiness. Add to that, I sensed that Capcities as an entity and fabled institution, was fading away, and that was sadly unfortunate!

A wonderfully crowded, occasionally emotional and hilarious farewell party was arranged by the GMA staff, attended by many who just could not understand why it was happening. I received a couple of dozen letters, and a like amount of calls from Capcities and ABC people who considered the decision plainly unjustified and unfair. I wrote a parting note to the staff, taking a positive tone, wishing everyone well. Burke loved it. Some suspected my fingers were crossed while typing it! They were not. I meant every word.

After a brief vacation, I began to concentrate on the flower company, only to discover that its management was so cowed by its talented headstrong owner that outside opinions were either unwelcome or just plain ignored. I gave it my best, but after a few months, asked to be replaced. I fielded a bunch of calls from folks trying to get some traction developing new shows, until a headhunter came along and recommended that I do some consulting. What followed was an 18-month association with a *Fortune* 500 company that shall be unnamed as per our confidentiality agreement. It was great fun and I dealt with some lovely people. I also agreed to assist a money management person named Rosemary Ligatti who had developed a financial concept that needed exposure and backing. My last presentation for that project took place at an office in Rochester on the infamous morning of Sept. 11, 2001. That fateful day threw things in perspective and seemed like the right time to drop the curtain on all this extracurricular activity.

CHAPTER THIRTY-ONE

Ever Wistful

Regardless of wealth, titles, ratings, accomplishments, compensation, or accolades, the most memorable recollections about my career have to do quite naturally with the colorful cast of characters I met through it all. To me people always mattered most, and I was blessed to know so many who were extraordinarily impressive, both within our company and without. The company, from top down, was filled with remarkable people who were dedicated to their jobs, but also to having some high-spirited fun along the way. And we did that well!

Two larger than life characters, in particular, stand out. Their personalities were starkly different. Both are gone, but they remain unforgettable. The first was the legendary broadcaster who holds the record for the longest running continuous broadcasts in history. Lowell Thomas had been on network radio for more than 25 years when I first met him in 1956 and he was negotiating a renewal with CBS when he died at 89 in 1981. His audience has been estimated in the billions of listeners worldwide, and he is credited with the birth of Cinerama, and the discovery of Lawrence of Arabia. An author of 56 books, he was a world traveler by his early twenties. His High Adventure series ran on TV for years. Tom Murphy called him a man *"who lived the life of five men."* His financial backing provided the birth of Capital Cities, giving me an incomparable experience of sharing time with him often over the years, producing a half-dozen film reports with him, and most importantly, hearing about some of his worldly escapades.

In early 1973, I shared a small private plane with him from The Bohemian Grove in California (known as the most exclusive men's club in America) to Fresno, California where he was to make a luncheon address. At about 7 a.m., over the din of a single engine airplane, he asked me, *"What is this all about today?"* I shouted my answer, *"Fresno is the largest agricultural county in the state, its school enrollment is up almost double in the past few years, and its neighboring county, Kings, just declined a proposal for a Disney-like park."* He listened as I went on and on, but took no notes. I was not sure he could hear me. When we landed we did a TV interview and then headed to the Hilton Hotel. He reminded me that it was a special day for CBS radio, an anniversary as I recall, and that, *"the world is waiting for me at 7:15 New York time."*

The standing room only crowd loved him as he walked through the luncheon tables without a mic, telling marvelous stories about Will Rogers, his childhood love of the Wright Brothers, Wiley Post, and, of course, Lawrence. After standing ovations and post talk conversations, we walked to the CBS radio affiliate for his broadcast. Lowell proceeded to the

Teletype machine, where his script had been sent. After tearing off several sheets of script, slashing occasional sentences with an editing marker, I saw him write at the top of page the letters, H.E. I learned what they stood for when, on cue, he began with his standard opening line, *"Hello Everybody!"* After thousands of broadcasts, he still took no chances. He then astonishingly repeated almost word for word all I had mentioned to him in the airplane that morning. *"Hello Everybody, I come to you today from Fresno, the leading agricultural county ... etc."* He spoke as my guest again in Buffalo in '78, and was an occasional guest at our home in Chautauqua. What a thrill it was to be with him.

The next most unforgettable person I ever knew was the most effective salesman I have ever encountered. We met shortly after my transfer to Fresno, when I was trying to reprogram the station and long before he was famous or ever expected to become an institution. His name was Roger King of King World syndication. His brother Michael and I enjoyed each other's company as he serviced our station with syndicated fare. Years earlier, their father Charles added "The Little Rascals" TV series to his radio syndication and traveled coast to coast, reviving that black and white film classic in America. He apparently passed on some selling skills to his sons. The brothers developed a kinship with the high spirited and creative Merv Griffin, resulting in some licensing coups that became extremely value enhanced when Roger convinced a highly coveted Chicago talk show host named Oprah that her destiny was not network television, but syndication.

That trifecta of "Wheel of Fortune" and "Jeopardy," topped off by "Oprah Winfrey," established the most valuable long-term cash machine in syndication history. It also became the most profitable partnership Capital Cities ever enjoyed with a syndicator. It is quite fair to say that for more than 10 years Oprah as a lead-in to our local news programs became the best audience guarantee in the business and our profits in early fringe time periods till 8 p.m. exploded with King World shows.

From the moment I met Roger, I knew he was a solid guy. A bit of a rascal himself, he could infect people with his energy, enthusiasm and ability to make one see things as big, as bright, and as positive as possible. And that is what he was ... big, bright and positive. I was lucky to be with him to witness some classic characteristic moments. For instance, I remember him calling the manager of the Sands late one night (even by Vegas standards) after the casino had closed because of a championship fight at another hotel and talking the manager into opening up the casino so he and our group could gamble. Two hours later, in the midst of frivolity, he realized he'd lost heavily at "Chemin de Fer" (a high rollers card game akin to Baccarat). It mattered little as long as everyone had a great time. His parties at his Bay Head, New Jersey home were so far over the top, he had to discontinue them because they were finally beyond control.

He was at his best with his prospects. He could remember facts and numbers for his shows in dozens of markets and his programs made many general managers extremely wealthy. He lived life fully, albeit carelessly, and was a real friend. I loved seeing him, although I cringed when we met as he would always put me in a headlock and kiss me on the cheek. What an imposing, unforgettable man.

Lowell Thomas and Roger King; I am rather sure they never met. But they left vivid memories for us and what Dr. Norman Vincent Peale said in Lowell's eulogy, may have applied to both, *"The world needs more such exciting and different characters."* Exciting and different, indeed!

To me, the real enjoyment and satisfaction came from meeting so many men and women, predominantly from our own ranks, but from the outside as well. As I start to recall my favorites in the company, I am incapable of ranking them because they all rise to the top, right up there with Smitty, Murph, Burke, Dougherty, King and Sias. When I say Keller, there is McGovern, say Potash, there is Daniels, Jason-Appleton, Reilly-Gibson-Christian, Nuzzi-Stark, Quello-James, Pollock-Nesbitt, Gaffney-Tague, Irv-Rick-Tom, Meek-Hale, Edelson-Doerfler, Loewith-Helfand, Brady-Newman, Schrutt-Fenno, and on and on, each reminding me of another whose friendship and partnership mattered.

ABC also abounded with talent and I enjoyed so many who functioned and appreciated the Capcities playbook. Fond memories are connected to folks like Dick Connelly, Larry Fried, Mike Mallardi, Buzz Mathesius, Julie Hoover, Ida

Astute, Dick Beesemyer, George Newi, Mark Mandala, Jim Duffy, Ann Gray, Jozie Emmerich, Jackie Smith and so many more including, of course the classy, ageless Herb Granath …

… And others like the incomparable self-deprecating presence of Warren Buffett. His cheerful dispensing of anecdotal wisdom was the best common sense business education any of us ever experienced. It was a singular and exclusive privilege that came with the Capcities brand. His down-home persona projects a strong dedication to integrity and truth; fundamentals he believes are essential to success in business.

I write this book, with 20 years of hindsight, to celebrate a company which prospered in the free enterprise system, concentrating on doing the right thing and doing it well, benefitting by the strong character of its leaders. It was an experience beyond compare, and very rewarding in every sense of the word. If anyone ever asks what I would rather have done with my life, I would simply say, *"Do it all over again, maybe a bit better, thank you very much!"*

Price of stock - December 30, 1994

$85.25 per share

Three prior 2/1 splits meant that every original share of Capcities
stock now equaled eight. A June 1994
10/1 stock split turned those eight shares into
80 shares. So, each share purchased
in 1957 for $5.75 now had a value
of $6,820!!

Stock valuation, after the sale of the company
to Disney in '95, experienced similarly
substantial gains in the
ensuing years …

POST (*manu*) SCRIPTA

by
K.C. Schulberg

I met Phil Beuth not long after moving to Naples in 2012, when I joined the Naples Press Club, where Phil serves on the Board. We fell in easily as we both have open, generous personalities and have each conducted our careers in the entertainment industry. Phil has a grand, infectious, mischievous charm that few can resist.

Several weeks later, I invited Phil to my house, where 12 pretty fair raconteurs gathered around my dining room table for a sit-down dinner, accompanied by liberal libation and banter. But we amateurs were sidelined as Phil and *La Duena* of all things cultural and charitable in this fair city, Myra Daniels (founder of the Philharmonic), began trading quips and stories before an audience of rapt invitees.

Phil and his lovely wife, Mary, have, since, been frequent guests at our home and I have been a reliable invite to functions at their gracious home in Collier's Reserve. Over the course of a burgeoning friendship, spiced with Phil's always colorful remembrances, I got wind of his desire to put his career and back story to print. I strongly encouraged him to pursue this endeavor as I was convinced the rise of a young man from humble beginnings to the highest ranks of executive leadership, combined with the unique qualities of the singular company he joined — Capital Cities — could resonate with a far larger audience than simply his friends and family.

And so began our weekly "Tuesdays with Morrie" sessions in the den of Phil's house, during the course of which, I heard a vast number of the anecdotes contained in this book. I also learned just how engaged Phil is in community service. He is a Senior Board Member of the Guadalupe Center, which attempts to change lives and break the cycle of poverty for disadvantaged youth through education. He is an adviser to the Board of the Gulfshore Playhouse and sits on the Board of the Naples Press Club, where he revived a dormant Student Scholarship Program. He was voted Citizen of the year in Buffalo, by the Buffalo News back in 1986 and still regularly travels back to the Queen City. His largesse toward his beloved alma mater, Union College, is attested by the building that sits on its campus, sporting his name. Through the Beuth Foundation, he's awarded grants to more than 200 worthy nonprofit charities over the past 20 years. So, when Phil talks about being imbued with the Capcities doctrine of *"Doing well and doing good,"* he is not just spouting platitudes.

Not mentioned in the book is the fact that every two years, since 1997, Phil has single-handedly organized the Capital Cities alumni reunions. To this day, he is viewed as the company's "glue." And, somehow, despite a regimen that would wind a man 30-years younger, he and Mary also found time to build a small resort in the Caribbean.

The process of shaping Phil's story and seeing it gradually take shape has been an unmitigated delight; and it has bonded us as collaborators and as friends. In fact, I'm privileged to say that I now have an insight into Phil's life that few, outside his family and closest friends, have shared. Now corrupted by this knowledge, I can honestly say that I love Phil Beuth.

And I just about have him at the tipping point of commencing work on the book's sequel — *covering the next four decades of his life and career.*